ON THE
MOST ANCIENT WISDOM
OF THE ITALIANS

GIAMBATTISTA VICO

ON THE
MOST ANCIENT WISDOM
OF THE ITALIANS

UNEARTHED FROM THE ORIGINS

OF THE LATIN LANGUAGE

Including the Disputation with the

Giornale de' letterati d'Italia

TRANSLATED WITH AN

INTRODUCTION AND NOTES BY

L. M. PALMER

CORNELL UNIVERSITY PRESS

ITHACA AND LONDON

First published 1988 by Cornell University Press.

International Standard Book Number (cloth) 0-8014-1280-3
International Standard Book Number (paper) 0-8014-9511-3
Library of Congress Catalog Card Number 87-47865
Printed in the United States of America
Librarians: Library of Congress cataloging information appears on the last page of the book.

The paper in this book is acid-free and meets the guidelines for permanence and durability of the Committee on Production Guidelines for Book Longevity of the Council on Library Resources.

To Max Harold Fisch

CONTENTS

PREFACE

Since Robert Flint introduced the thought of Giambattista Vico to the English-speaking world in 1884, the *De Antiquissima Italorum Sapientia* has been in a peculiar position. It has been widely mentioned by Anglo-American philosophers but, unlike Vico's *Study Method of Our Time* and the *New Science*, little known in its entirety. Because the *De Antiquissima* contains Vico's fullest statement of the *verum-factum* principle, there are many references to the work, but the absence of an English translation until now may explain the lack of full-length monographs devoted to its significance in the development of Vico's philosophy.

De Antiquissima was first printed in Naples in 1710 at Felice Mosca's press. On the title page appeared: "DE ANTIQUISSIMA ITALORUM SAPIENTIA EX LINGUAE LATINAE ORIGINIBUS ERUENDA, libri tres, Johannis Baptistae a Vico neapolitani, regii eloquentiae professoris." The edition also includes the subtitles LIBER PRIMUS METAPHYSICUS, LIBER SECUNDUS PHYSICUS, and LIBER TERTIUS MORALIS, as well as the dedication "Ad nobilissimum Virum Paullum Matthiam Doriam Prudentissimum Philosophum scriptus." Thus, there were to be three books of a projected system of philosophy. The book on metaphysics—with an appendix on logic—was to be followed by a second volume on physics and a third on moral philosophy. For reasons that are still unclear, the whole system was never completed. In 1713, from notes for the second book, Vico assembled a monograph titled *De Aequilibrio Corporis Animantis*. It was eventually published in the Neapolitan periodical *Scelta miscellanea*, but not until fifty years after Vico's death.

No issues of the *Scelta* in which it was printed are known to exist, and the work is now lost. The third book seems never to have reached the draft stage.

As soon as the first volume on metaphysics was published, it received two long and careful reviews in the prestigious *Giornale de' letterati*. Vico responded to these in 1711 and 1712 with two equally long replies, which he had published on their own: "Risposta del Signore Giambattista di Vico nella quale si sciolgono tre gravi opposizioni fatte da dotto signore contro il primo libro *De Antiquissima Italorum Sapientia*, ovvero della metafisica degli antichissimi filosofi Italiani tratta da' latini parlari (in Napoli MDCCXI, nella stamperia di Felice Mosca)"; and "Risposta di Giambattista di Vico all' articolo X del tomo VIII del *Giornale de' letterati* d'Italia (in Napoli MDCCXII, nella stamperia di Felice Mosca)."

After these polemic exchanges the *De Antiquissima* remained virtually unknown for over a hundred years, although during Vico's lifetime it was widely read in Neapolitan academic circles. It may even have been given to Isaac Newton and William Burnet by A. C. Shaftesbury. At the beginning of the nineteenth century an anonymous writer, perhaps Vincenzo Monti, translated it into Italian (Milan: Felice Mosca, 1816). In 1829 Pierre Simone Ballanche published the first reprint of the volume in his *Essais de palingenesie sociale* (vol. 12; Paris: Jules Didot l'ainé, 1829). Six years later Jules Michelet translated the volume into French and published it in abridged form in the second volume of his *Oeuvres choisies de Vico* (2 vols.; Paris: Hachet, 1835).

During Italy's long struggle for independence the majority of Vico's works were edited by the archivists Giuseppe Ferrari (Milan, 1835–37; 2d ed. in 6 vols., 1852–54) and Francesco Saverio Pomodoro (8 vols.; Naples: Morano, 1858–69). With these and with the classical edition of Fausto Nicolini and Giovanni Gentile (Bari: Laterza, 1914; vol. 1, 2d ed., 1968), the *De Antiquissima* finally reached a wide audience.

During the twentieth century several Italian translations have appeared. Noteworthy are those of Fausto Nicolini (Milan: Ricciardi, 1953), Paolo Rossi (Milan: Rizzoli, 1959), and Paolo Cristofolini with an introduction and notes by Nicola Badaloni (Florence: Sansoni, 1971). In 1972 the *Bollettino del Centro di Studi Vichiani* announced a new edition of the complete works of Vico; for this the *De Antiquissima* will be edited and newly translated by Vincenzo Plagella, with particular attention to punctuation and terminology.

In addition to the abridged French translation of Jules Michelet, there is also a Spanish translation by Jacinto Cuccaro (Buenos Aires: Instituto de Filosofia, 1939) with the title *Sabaduria primitiva de los italianos desentrañada de los origenes de la lengua latina*. A German translation by Stephan Otto and Helmut Viechtbauer with an introduction by Otto uses the simple title *Liber Metaphysicus* (Munich: Wilhelm Fink Verlag, 1979). Recently Leon Pompa has translated Chapters One–Three and Six–Eight in his *Vico: Selected Writings* (Cambridge: Cambridge University Press, 1982).

In preparing this volume I have used the above-noted edition of Giovanni Gentile and Fausto Nicolini, *Opere di Giambattista Vico*, vol. 1. For several difficult passages I have compared my rendition with the standard Italian translation of Fausto Nicolini and that of Paolo Cristofolini, as well as with Otto's German version and Leon Pompa's English.

I thank the American Philosophical Society for a travel grant that enabled me to spend the summer of 1980 in Italy to do research on the history of the *De Antiquissima* at the Scuola Normale of Pisa. Many Vichian friends and scholars have read various versions of this volume and have given me generous and valuable criticism. I am particularly grateful to David Lachterman of the Philosophy Department of Pennsylvania State University; to the director of the Institute for Vico Studies, Giorgio Tagliacozzo; and to Donald P. Verene of the Philosophy Department of Emory University. Paul Durbin of the Philosophy Department of the University of Delaware helped me in the final revision of the volume's introduction. Mary Imperatore of the Philosophy Department coped with the vagaries of my handwriting through numerous retypings; without her skill and patience this volume would never have reached a readable form.

Finally, I express my warmest gratitude and enormous indebtedness to my colleagues, friends, and former teachers Max H. Fisch, Professor Emeritus of Philosophy at the University of Illinois; and H. S. Harris of the Philosophy Department of York University. Although I am solely responsible for the final version of this volume, I owe to them much more that I can possibly acknowledge.

LUCIA M. PALMER

Newark, Delaware

ON THE
MOST ANCIENT WISDOM
OF THE ITALIANS

INTRODUCTION

Elio Gianturco translated Giambattista Vico's *De Nostri Temporis Studiorum Ratione* into English in 1965.[1] He began the introduction to that volume by pointing out the extent to which modern times in general, and the 1960s in particular, have been affected by the Cartesian paradigm of mathematical intellectualism and science worship. Gianturco claimed that a reexamination of Vico's views on the unity of the sciences and on human wisdom—so brilliantly defended in 1708—would prove a healthy antidote to modernism.

Although our modern culture has become increasingly technological, modernism has since lost the grip it held on our philosophical sensitivity twenty years ago. The "mirror of nature" characteristic of Cartesianism seems to have become less and less transparent.[2] The paradigm of Descartes's foundationalism has shifted, and the clarity and distinctness of his *Cogito* is slowly being replaced by a new paradigm. For better or worse, our "normal science" is being overtaken by a vague, and still directionless, philosophical and scientific historicism.

In this context, it is worth turning once again to the thought of Vico, to appreciate how he, among other thinkers of the past, has contributed to the shifting of our paradigm. Perhaps we can find in

[1]G. B. Vico, *On the Study Methods of Our Time*, trans. Elio Gianturco (New York: Bobbs-Merrill/Library of Liberal Arts, 1965).

[2]The allusions are to Richard Rorty, *Philosophy and the Mirror of Nature* (Princeton, N.J.: Princeton University Press, 1979).

his polemic against Descartes not just edification, but some elements of a new humanism.

Vico's *De Antiquissima Italorum Sapientia* was published in 1710, a year after the *De Nostri Temporis Studiorum Ratione*. Unlike that work, whose import is primarily pedagogical, the *De Antiquissima* is philosophically and historically significant. Philosophically, it offers a criticism of Descartes's phenomenalism comparable, in many ways, to that found in the works of C. S. Peirce and John Dewey. Unlike other treatises of the early Enlightenment, it transforms the paradigm of the knower as contemplator of unchanging ideas and processor of mental sensations into that of the knower as maker of truth.

In the history of thought the *De Antiquissima* is significant because it marks the transition in Vico's intellectual development from the professor of rhetoric to the philosopher of historical knowledge. Hence, for those interested in the *New Science*, the *De Antiquissima* displays Vico's intellectual position before he turned to examine the foundations of legal thought in the *Il diritto universale*.[3]

It is commonplace among historians of philosophy to describe the seventeenth century and the beginning of the eighteenth century as a period of great metaphysical systems. These systems were devised in part to provide philosophical justifications for the new sciences of Kepler and Galileo and in part to offset the wave of skepticism that followed the various revolutions in religion, the humanities, and the natural sciences. As has often been remarked, the birth of the modern age was characterized by a deep feeling of disorientation, pessimism, and a sense of a loss of values. These sentiments are supported by the works of Cornelio Agrippa, Francisco Sanchez, and Michel de Montaigne. As early as 1527 Agrippa, in reviewing all fields of knowledge, had proclaimed the uncertainty and vanity of human wisdom. His *Declamatio de Incertitudine et Vanitate Scientiarum et Artium* was reprinted and debated until the middle of the eighteenth century.[4] This skepticism echoes in Sanchez's claim that nothing is known, just as it

---

[3]Vico uses this title to indicate the following works: *De Universi Juris Uno Principio et Fine Uno Liber unus*, including the *De Opera Proloquium* (1720) and the *De Constantia Jurisprudentis Liber Alter* (1721). *Notae in Duos Libros: De Uno Universi Juris Principio et Fine Uno*, and *De Constantia Jurisprudentis* (1722).

[4]Eugenio Garin, "Vico and the Heritage of Renaissance Thought," in *Vico: Past and Present*, ed. Giorgio Tagliacozzo (Atlantic Highlands, N.J.: Humanities Press, 1981) 1:99–116.

does in Montaigne's despairing question of whether we lack certain knowledge because we lack true being.[5] It is against this general background that one should evaluate Francis Bacon's *De Dignitate et Augmentis Scientiarum* (1623), René Descartes's quest for certainty in the *Discours de la méthode* (1637), and Vico's new system of metaphysics in the *De Antiquissima Italorum Sapientia* (1710).

When Descartes, a brilliant mathematician, arrived in Paris in 1628, he was already on his way to the discovery of a principle "so certain and so assured that all the most extravagant suppositions brought forward by the skeptics were incapable of shaking it."[6] His often recounted meeting with Cardinal Berulle, as well as the Chandoux episode,[7] may have been instrumental in the development of his new philosophy. We are told by Adrienne Baillet that shortly before Descartes composed the *Rules for the Guidance of the Mind* he met at the home of the papal nuncio, Cardinal Bagni, to discuss with other avant-garde thinkers the advantage of scholastic philosophy.[8] In that company, which included Marin Mersenne, Descartes heard a talk by the learned Dr. Chandoux, who praised probability as the standard of truth and condemned scholastic philosophy. Descartes replied to the successful speech with a series of counterarguments. First, he agreed with Chandoux's antischolasticism; second, he showed how probability generates and increases skepticism. For if probability is taken as the standard of truth, any false proposition may be considered true and any incontestable truth proven by probable arguments to be false. Having shown the shortcomings of taking probability as the standard of truth, Descartes launched his attack against skepticism. He believed that a new philosophical system was needed; only within his new system would modern science be possible without endangering human dignity.

The Rules for the Guidance of the Mind was composed at the end of 1628. Nine years later, Descartes replied to Montaigne's skeptical

[5]Descartes, *Philosophical Writings: A Selection*, trans. and ed. Elizabeth Anscombe and Peter Thomas Geach, with an introduction by Alexander Koyré (London: Nelson, 1966), p. ix.

[6]Descartes, *Discours de la méthode*, in *Oeuvres de Descartes*, ed. Charles Adam and Paul Tannery, 12 vols. (Paris: L. Cerf, 1897–1910), 6:32.

[7]Richard H. Popkin, *The History of Scepticism from Erasmus to Descartes* (New York: Harper, 1964), pp. 177–80. See also J. F. Scott, *The Scientific Work of René Descartes* (London: Taylor and Francis, 1952), p. 7.

[8]Adrienne Baillet, *La vie de M. Descartes* (Paris, 1691), pp. 72–74.

essays with the *Discourse on Method* or his *Itinerarium Mentis in Veritatem*. By the time of Galileo's death in 1642, the second edition of the *Meditationes de Prima Philosophia in Qua Dei Existentia et Animae Immortalitatis Demonstratur* had been published in Amsterdam. The European learned world was consumed with a Cartesian fever. It seemed to the supporters of the new system that with the existence of God as the creator and sustainer of the universe securely demonstrated, with matter defined as pure extension, and with mind characterized as pure thought, all scientific difficulties and all moral problems had been solved.

No sooner had Descartes's work gone to press, however, than a flood of objections and counterobjections began. From Paris the Jesuits, led by Pierre Bourdin, attacked Descartes's method. They claimed, scornfully, that such a method could never generate certainty, that "it takes away our previous instruments, but it does not bring any to occupy their place."[9] From "the father of the skeptics," Pierre Daniel Huet, came the cry that Descartes was a Socinian, a Libertine, and a heretic.[10] From Mersenne and Pierre Gassendi came a criticism of the very criterion of truth which Descartes had considered "the only intellectual fortress capable of withstanding the assault of the skeptic." "Tell me," asked Gassendi, "what else can we infer to be true as being clearly and distinctly perceived, except that that which appears to anyone, does appear so?"[11] Even the most Cartesian of the Cartesians—Antoine Arnauld—repeated the same charge: from Descartes's *Cogito* nothing but the empty certainty of one's beliefs can be derived.[12]

In England, Descartes's metaphysics, physics, and geometry slowly but steadily became a focus of concern for Thomas Hobbes, the Cambridge Platonists, and the empirical scientists. Mathematical

[9]Pierre Bourdin, as cited in Descartes, "The Seventh Set of Objections," in *The Philosophical Works of Descartes*, trans. E. Haldane and G.R.T. Ross (New York: Dover, 1953), 2:318–19; in *Oeuvres*, 7:528–29.

[10]Pierre-Daniel Huet, *Censura Philosophiae Cartesianae* (Paris: Apud D. Horthemels, 1689).

[11]Letter from P. Gassendi to M. Descartes, in *Philosophical Works*, 2:151.

[12]"The Fourth Set of Objections," in *Philosophical Works*, 2:79–95. Arnauld's objections are particularly relevant for Vico's criticism of Descartes. Compare "Vico III Inaugural Dissertation," p. 35 (G. B. Vico, *Le orazioni inaugurali*, ed. G. Gentile and F. Nicolini [Bari: Laterza, 1968]) with Arnauld's objections to Descartes's criteria of clarity and distinctness (*Philosophical Works*, 2:94).

properties seemed to them too inconsequential to sustain the weight of the physical universe. John Locke attacked Descartes's theory of *res extensa* because it limits the power of God and it endangers His spirituality. He suggested that a way to solve Descartes's problem was to restrict the term *extension* to matter and apply the term *expansion* to space in general, "with or without solid matter possessing it." Only space is expanded; body is extended. Thus God is linked with space, not with matter.[13]

Writing to Nicholas Malebranche in 1679, Leibniz gave a clear summary of Descartes's achievement: "He has given us only some beautiful beginnings, without getting to the bottom of things. It seems to me that he is still far from true analysis and the general art of discovery. For I am convinced that his mechanics is full of errors, that his physics goes too fast and that his metaphysics is all these things together. . . . In my opinion," Leibniz continues, "I believe that you [Malebranche] have gone only half way and that still other consequences can be drawn than those which you have made."[14] What Leibniz wanted Malebranche to add to his philosophical position was a radical change of Descartes's conception of matter and a system of metaphysics grounded on the notions of force and power, that is, on the infinitely small and the imperceptible. In a final blow, in his critical notes (1692) on the *Principia Philosophiae*, Leibniz attacked Descartes's conception of the nature of body and his laws of motion.[15]

By the beginning of the eighteenth century the skepticism that Descartes had hoped to eradicate from the domain of knowledge pervaded the new physics. Once again a reexamination of the foundations and process of knowledge, of scientific methodology, and of the distinctions between branches of learning came to be the subject of philosophical controversy. The seventeenth century had bequeathed to the Enlightenment the problem of the validity of human

[13]John W. Yolton, *Thinking Matter: Materialism in Eighteenth-Century Britain* (Minneapolis: University of Minnesota Press, 1983), pp. 64–89. Locke's concept of space is analogous to that which Vico develops in Chapter Four of the *De Antiquissima*. Thus there is another element to add to the similarities between Locke and Vico argued by Gustavo Costa in his "Vico e Locke," *Giornale critico della filosofia italiana* 1, no. 49 (1970):344–62.

[14]G. W. Leibniz, *Philosophical Papers and Letters: A Selection*, trans. and ed. with an introduction by Leroy E. Loemker, 2d ed. (Dordrecht: Reidel, 1970). "Letter to Nicholas Malebranche" (1679), pp. 209–12.

[15]Ibid., pp. 391–412.

knowledge. Now, at the beginning of the new century, Pierre Bayle produced his great *Summa Sceptica*, and in his *Historical and Critical Dictionary* (covering everything from "Aaron" to "Zuylichem") he did a complete exposé of the philosophical dreams of his contemporaries.

In 1710, Berkeley published his *Treatise Concerning the Principles of Human Knowledge*, in which he investigates "the chief causes of error and difficulty in the sciences, with the grounds of skepticism, atheism, and religion." In the same year Leibniz published his *Theodicy* and Vico the *De Antiquissima Italorum Sapientia*. With this volume, Vico claimed to offer a metaphysics within the limits of human reason that would be consonant with the new experimental physics because it was grounded on the epistemic principle that people can know only what they make. Based on a critique of knowledge, it was a metaphysics that would curb both the pride of the dogmatists and the foolishness of the skeptics.

Fifteen years later, in 1725, Vico produced the first edition of his *New Science*. Here he brought the *verum-factum* principle (people know only what they make) to its fulfillment: the only indubitable science is the science of human institutions. He restated this position in the second edition of the *New Science* in 1733 and again in the final version of 1744[16]—the same year George Berkeley published his *Siris*. In *Siris* Berkeley reinforced the Platonic foundations of his idealism; Vico had the more ambitious aim of doing for the world of nations what Newton had done for the world of nature. He consciously opposed his new science on the course of human institutions to the "new science of Galileo on the course of heavenly bodies." Unconsciously, he fulfilled the wish that Kant would express forty years later: "We shall leave to nature," Kant stated in 1784, "to produce the man capable of composing 'the clue to history.'" Kant claimed that nature produced Kepler, who in an unexpected way subjected the

---

[16]The third *New Science* was published in July 1744, six months after Vico's death. The passage alluded to here is the often quoted paragraph 331, in which Vico replies to Cartesian skepticism by asserting the indubitability of the science of human institutions. In an earlier edition of the *New Science* (1725) the same claim is made in language that calls to mind Kant's famous passage in the *Critique of Pure Reason*, in which he makes the transition from the analytic to the dialectic. See G. B. Vico, *The First New Science*, p. 40, and *The Third New Science*, p. 331, in Leon Pompa, *Vico: Selected Writings* (Cambridge: Cambridge University Press, 1982), pp. 99, 198.

eccentric path of the planets to definite laws, and Newton, who explained these laws by a universal natural cause; but Kant left for the future the task of discovering laws of human institutions.[17]

This in brief is the intellectual environment within which the *De Antiquissima* should be understood. When Vico wrote it he was forty-two years old. At a time when several philosophers traveled "abroad"—either to read "the book of the world" or to escape from political and religious persecutions—Vico was born, lived, and died in Naples (1668–1744). Even when he went to Vatolla for nine years to tutor the nephews of Monsignor Geronimo Rocca, bishop of Ischia, he returned frequently to Naples, where he participated in the lively debate of that city's Cartesian and anti-Cartesian academies and intellectual circles.

Though the age in which he was born might appropriately be called "the age of splendour and wit,"[18] it was also the age of the great academies, in which the new experimentalism mixed unself-consciously with Renaissance ermeticism, mysticism, and magic.[19] The Academy of the Cimento in Rome, which survived for only ten years, continued the work of Galileo in mechanics and mathematics. The Academy of the Investigators, where studies in medicine, law, and mathematics flourished, was founded in Naples by the mathematician Tommaso Cornelio (1614–86) and the physician Leonardo da Capua (1617–93) and survived into the middle of the eighteenth century. Not only did Vico live under the shadow of the Investigators,[20] but some of his speculations in medicine and mathematics are incomprehensible if one ignores the direct influence of the Investigators on him.

[17]Kant, *Idea of a Universal History from a Cosmopolitan Point of View*, trans. Lewis White Beck (Indianapolis: Bobbs-Merrill, 1963), p. 12.

[18]The phrase is from M. Mooney's description of the Italian Baroque period in which Vico was born. M. Mooney, *Vico in the Tradition of Rhetoric* (Princeton, N.J.: Princeton University Press, 1985), p. 60.

[19]For the influence of iatrochemistry and spagiric medicine on the new mechanics, see N. Badaloni, *Introduzione a Vico* (Milan: Feltrinelli, 1961). See also *Reason, Experiment and Mysticism in the Scientific Revolution*, ed. M. L. Righini Bonelli and William R. Shea (New York: Science History Publication, 1975).

[20]M. H. Fisch, "The Academy of the Investigators," in *Science, Medicine, and History: Essays in Honor of Charles Singer*, ed. E. A. Underwood (London: Oxford University Press, 1953), p. 552.

Vico's Naples was the "freest" city in central Europe.[21] It had been the seat of the Academy of Pontano, and thus was more receptive to the "new philosophy" of Epicurus, Lucretius, Gassendi, and Descartes than any other center of cultural life in Italy. Yet that freedom did not help either Pietro Giannone or two of Vico's intimate friends. Giacinto De Cristoforo and Nicola Galizia (both promoters of the *De Antiquissima*) were persecuted as heretics by the Inquisition for espousing the teachings of Epicurus and Lucretius. It is not unlikely that the myth of isolation which Vico so carefully crafted in his autobiography is a device he used to escape suspicion.[22] It is also possible that some of the remarks on Christian dogma that he makes in the *De Antiquissima* are a function of his deep fear of being forbidden to write and publish. Unlike Descartes, Locke, and Berkeley, who could enjoy the leisure of scholarly meditations, Vico did much of his thinking in the classroom and in the "midst of the conversation of his friends and the cries of his children."[23]

Vico's education did not follow the rigorous curriculum Descartes enjoyed at La Flèche. Although, like Descartes, he was educated by the Jesuits, his training was mainly that of a Renaissance humanist. He was well versed in the logic of Peter of Spain, in the philosophy of Duns Scotus, and in the metaphysics of Francisco Suarez. His prodigious erudition, mostly acquired in the rich library of the Rocca family, encompassed the poetry, literature, and law of the classical and Renaissance writers. Plato and Tacitus were his first philosophers; he read Bacon three years before he wrote the *De Antiquissima* and Grotius around 1713.

As a professor of rhetoric at the University of Naples, during the years 1699–1708 Vico delivered seven inaugural addresses. Of the seven only the last one, *De Nostri Temporis Studiorum Ratione*, was

---

[21]The words are from L. A. Muratori as quoted in B. Croce, *History of the Kingdom of Naples*, trans. Frances Frenaye (Chicago: University of Chicago Press, 1970), p. 159. But compare a very different evaluation of the intellectual life in Naples at about the same time given by George Berkeley in a letter to Alexander Pope, in *The Works of George Berkeley*, ed. A. A. Luce and T. E. Jessop (London: Nelson, 1964), 8:107–8.

[22]For a detailed analysis of this hypothesis, see G. Costa, "Vico e il Settecento," *Forum Italicum* 10 (1976):10–30.

[23]G. B. Vico, *The Autobiography*, trans. M. H. Fisch and T. G. Bergin (Ithaca: Cornell University Press/Great Seal Books, 1963), p. 163.

published during his lifetime. The other six remained in manuscript form until the middle of the nineteenth century.[24]

These speeches, given to young students about to embark on an academic career, mark the beginning of Vico's philosophical speculations. They are the first examples we have of Vico's social ideas, of his theory on the encyclopedia of knowledge, and most of all of his attitude toward Descartes and Cartesianism. In disorganized and fragmented fashion, they adumbrate themes he will develop fully in the De Antiquissima, the De Uno, and the New Science.

Speaking of these addresses in 1725, Vico says that although it should be evident to anyone reading them that he "was agitating in his mind a theme both new and grand, to unite in one principle all knowledge human and divine," in fact, the addresses "fell too far short of it."[25] Vico was happy he had not published them, and unfortunately some of his best critics have taken this last remark too literally.[26]

In the first three of these speeches, Vico develops a series of arguments that run through all of his works. It combines in a compelling way elements of the rhetorical tradition of Cicero and of Renaissance Platonism. Γνωθι σεατόν is the most important motivation for bringing to completion the cycle of all human sciences. But the knowledge of oneself reveals the creative and constructive power of the mind. So that, Vico claims, "Tandem Deus naturae artifex: Animus artium fas sit dicere, Deus" (God alone is the maker of nature: the human mind, may I be allowed to say, is the god of the arts). The creative power of the mind is particularly evident in the force of the imagination which makes human nature Godlike. It is imagination that creates (finxit) "maiorum, minorumque gentium Deos" (the gods of the greater and lesser gentes). There is no criticism of Descartes in this first approach

[24]Recently the first six inaugural lectures were translated into Italian by G. Visconti as part of a project of the Centro di Studi Vichiani in which a new edition of all of Vico's work will be published. See G. B. Vico, Le orazioni inaugurali, I–VI, in Opere di G. B. Vico, vol. 1 (Bologna: Il Mulino, 1982).

[25]Vico, The Autobiography, p. 146.

[26]B. Croce pays no attention to these early speeches and begins his study of Vico with the De Antiquissima (B. Croce, La filosofia di G. B. Vico [Bari: Laterza, 1911; 4th ed., 1947]), whereas for reasons that cannot be explained fully in this context, G. Gentile considers the orations the first stage of Vico's philosophy (G. Gentile, Studi Vichianai, 2d ed. [Florence: Le Monnier, 1927]).

to a philosophy of mind. Indeed Vico explicitly endorses Descartes's causal proof for the existence of God in the third meditation and uses it as evidence of the power of the human mind. He does so because, as he says, only a mind endowed with infinite creativity can demonstrate the existence of God through a chain of deductive arguments.

The tone begins to change when we turn to the second and third speeches. After a phenomenological sketch (in the second speech) of the foolish person who refused to understand the pragmatic intentionality of self-knowledge, he addresses himself in the third to what may be called intellectual bad faith. *Mala fraus* means disregarding evidence, certainties, indisputable facts. Far from showing sympathy toward Descartes, as many Vichian scholars have argued,[27] in this third speech Vico for the first time rejects Descartes's application of the geometrical method to physics. Admittedly, the criticism is embedded within a rejection of all forms of intellectual pretension. Contemporary philosophers who disregard historical evidence are in bad faith. Also in bad faith are the Aristotelians who refuse to look into the telescope, or the philologists who boast that they know all the roads in Rome. Finally, Descartes, who in defiance of Malebranche and Leibniz pretends to have demonstrated the laws of motion a priori, is in bad faith.

The theme of the creativity of the human mind in sense, imagination, and discursive thinking is developed fully in the last inaugural dissertation of 1708. In the *De Nostri Temporis Studiorum Ratione*, Vico argues that the method of teaching "criticism," or the logic of Arnauld and Descartes, before the logic of invention and induction, or the ancient art of topics, stifles the natural growth and creativity of the human mind. In the same way, the teaching of Descartes's analytic over Euclidean linear geometry destroys the natural ability to form images and freely create chains of arguments. The simple remark in the second speech that Descartes stubbornly refutes empirical evidence in favor of the application of geometry to physics becomes in his last speech a full-blown argument against the mathematical method of Descartes. Still this criticism is presented in a half-moral way. Descartes claims to demonstrate a priori the structure of the physical world; in so doing, Vico argues, Descartes misunderstands the mean-

---

[27]Fisch, in Vico, *The Autobiography*, p. 37. See also Peter Burke, *Vico* (Oxford: Oxford University Press, 1985), p. 17.

ing of demonstration. Mathematics is a demonstrative science because, through *ingenium*, we create its elements. Hence the mathematical method applies to geometry but not to physics. For if one
were to demonstrate elements in the physical world, one would have
to make them. Thus Descartes's method is not only inadequate but
also deceitful, because "it causes to pass as true" what is only probable. Both these themes are at the foundation of the *De Antiquissima*.
The view of the natural creativity of the human mind, together with
the primacy of topics over criticism, yields the philosophy of mind in
the final chapters of this work, and the argument that mathematics is
demonstrative because it is a product of human design represents its
epistemic foundations.

The *De Antiquissima* is Vico's first uncommissioned work. It is written neither to persuade young students of the utility of a university
career nor to please papal nuncios. Its audience is the learned circles
of Paolo Mattia Doria, Agostino Ariani, Giacinto di Cristoforo, and
Nicola Galizia. Each of these men belonged to what has been called
the new generation of Italian Cartesians.[28] Di Cristoforo and Galizia
were lawyers as well as mathematicians; early in the century Ariani
had published a controversial work in geometry which considered
the relation of geometry to physics and the role of hypothesis in
mathematics.[29] During this period Doria was still a convinced Cartesian. He had just written a treatise on physics and was about to
publish a work on political theory. Like Vico, Doria was in search of a
principle on which to found the science of humankind and that of
nature. Unlike Vico, Doria was convinced that Descartes's metaphysics could be used successfully for the unity of human and divine
science.

The broader audience to which this work speaks is the European
audience of Leibniz, Spinoza, Malebranche, and the followers of John
Locke. All were involved in the search for a new method and a new
art of criticism with which to solve the inconsistencies of the Cartesian system.

[28]See Federico Amodeo, *Vita matematica napoletana: Studio storico* (Naples: Giannini,
1905). See also Nicola Badaloni, "Vico prima della *Scienza nuova*," *Rivista di filosofia* 59
(1968):127–48.
[29]See Agostino Ariani, *Intorno all' utilità della geometria* (1701), in Maria Donzelli,
Natura e humanitas nel giovane Vico (Naples: Istituto Italiano per gli Studi Storici, 1970),
pp. 164–88.

Commenting on the broad scope of the *De Antiquissima*, Antonio Corsano remarks that Vico shows the same attitude toward Descartes as did Pascal, Leibniz, and Spinoza, but he was writing some thirty years later.[30] There is some truth to this remark, for Vico's "attitude" toward Descartes is similar to that of Pascal, but his anti-Cartesianism in the *De Antiquissima* is of a different type from that of Malebranche and Spinoza, to which Corsano compares it. First, Vico, unlike Malebranche and Spinoza, does not substitute one type of mentalism for another in his criticism of Descartes. Second, the consequences Vico drew from his reactions to Descartes were more far-reaching than those of his contemporaries and predecessors. As Garin suggests, Vico understood better than most of his European contemporaries the inconsistencies of the Cartesian system and he set himself to find an alternative.[31] The internal difficulties within the Cartesian system had been evident among his followers, as the objections and counterobjections to the meditations I mentioned earlier testify. Descartes argues that clarity and distinctness are the criteria and rule of knowledge. But Descartes is never clear as to what guarantees the correspondence between clear and distinct ideas and what guarantees their correspondence in the physical domain of nature. As several contemporary scholars have remarked, Descartes attempts to find a guarantee for the truth of an idea in the idea itself and its relationship with other ideas, and yet to mean by truth a kind of correspondence to an external reality. The problem can be avoided either by abandoning the criteria of clarity and distinctness or by rejecting dualism of metaphysics and physics. Spinoza, Leibniz, and Malebranche in different ways took the second route; Locke, Berkeley, and Hume took the first. Vico did both, without being either an empiricist or a rationalist.

In Chapters One through Three of the *De Antiquissima* Vico draws the implications of his own epistemological principle and rejects Des-

---

[30]Antonio Corsano, *G. B. Vico* (Bari: Laterza, 1956), pp. 85–86.

[31]Eugenio Garin, "Cartesio e l'Italia," *Giornale critico della filosofia italiana* 4 (1950):385–405. The most interesting challenge to Vico's criticism of Descartes's system is that of Yvon Belaval. In his "Vico and Anti-Cartesianism," Belaval argues that although Vico was successful in pointing out some of Descartes's weak points, his reading of the Cartesian texts was inaccurate and most likely the product of secondhand information. Yvon Belaval, "Vico and Anti-Cartesianism," in *Giambattista Vico: An International Symposium*, ed. Giorgio Tagliacozzo and Hayden White (Baltimore: Johns Hopkins University Press, 1969), pp. 77–91.

cartes's criteria of clarity and distinctness. In the fourth chapter he bridges the dualism of God and extended matter by using the hypothesis of metaphysical points, constructed *more geometrico*. In the last chapters, by using the hypothesis of a unifying principle of life, he avoids the dualism of *res cogitans* and *res extensa* and develops a theory of mind at variance with that of Spinoza and Malebranche.

Vico's constructive theory of knowledge is different from that of traditional empiricists. His ontology or theory of reality is not a form of reductionism, because he remains a Neoplatonist. Yet his Neoplatonism does not prevent him from demonstrating the possibilities of the experimental method in the natural sciences. The reviewers of the *De Antiquissima* were correct in several of their complaints: that this book of metaphysics is only a sketch, an outline in which many theories are mentioned but not argued; that "its learned author crowds speculations without number into every page, even into every line";[32] and that Vico mixes inconsistent propositions "since some come from the Peripatetics, some from the Moderns, and yet others from somewhere in between."[33] In fact, in less than a hundred pages Vico develops a constructive theory of truth and knowledge, a metaphysics of matter and motion, and a philosophy of mind in which *ingenium* and not reason is the "proper" faculty of knowledge. In addition, Vico uses elements from his yet unpublished *Lectures on Rhetoric* and establishes the foundations for a new logic of scientific discovery. Each one of these elements is fully developed in the *New Science;* what is more, the *New Science* begins where the *De Antiquissima* ends, and the last words of this work echo the themes found in the inaugural orations.

Before I discuss the work's overall structure, it is necessary to consider two general issues regarding external and internal hermeneutics. As I mentioned in the Preface, there are no monographs devoted exclusively to the *De Antiquissima*. But there have been many interpretations of the place this work occupies in Vico's intellectual development. It would not be an exaggeration to claim that much of Vichian scholarship has been a discussion of Vico's theory of knowledge and, hence, indirectly a footnote to the *De Antiquissima*.

[32]See below, p. 117.
[33]See below, p. 144.

Some scholars have regarded it as central to Vico's historical and intellectual development, a precursor of the *New Science*. Others go a step further and call *De Antiquissima* a logical necessity without which the *New Science* remains incomprehensible. Others disagree with both views, insisting that the *De Antiquissima* is meaningless and of little value, an anomaly in Vico's works.

The anomaly thesis was first propounded in 1867 by a student of Benedetto Croce.[34] Carlo Cantoni argues forcefully that the *De Antiquissima* is philosophically inconsistent with and methodologically contradictory to everything Vico went on to establish in his mature work. In addition, Cantoni claims, Vico himself openly repudiated this work, thus making the study of it useless. Recently this thesis has been restated by Michael Mooney[35] and indirectly by Perez Zagorin.[36] Zagorin argues that the central theme of the work, the *verum-factum* principle, is irrelevant to the understanding of Vico's *New Science*; it can stand or fall as a science of history on its own without the epistemic support of the *verum-factum* principle. Therefore, in Vico's thought, the *De Antiquissima* is a useless appendage.

Mooney, on the other hand, interprets Vico exclusively within the rhetorical tradition of Italian humanism. Furthermore, he considers humanism conceptually at variance with the scientific experimentalism of the Renaissance, so he divorces Vico's philosophical works from those on rhetoric and pays much more attention to Vico's *Lectures on Rhetoric*, the *Inaugural Dissertations*, and the *De Nostri* as necessary stages toward the creation of the *New Science*.

At the other end of the spectrum are arguments recently developed by S. Otto and Helmut Viechtbauer.[37] Otto grounds his interpretation of logical necessity on "the transcendental argument for the pos-

---

[34]Carlo Cantoni, *G. B. Vico* (Turin: Civelli, 1867).

[35]Mooney calls the *De Antiquissima* "a hodgepodge of fascinating and fanciful ideas drawn from a score or more sources and served up as a finished metaphysics." Mooney, *Vico in the Tradition of Rhetoric*, p. 192. Nevertheless he offers useful insights in many controversial sections of the *De Antiquissima*. See, e.g., his arguments in favor of the historical derivation of Vico's *verum-factum* principle from the rhetorical tradition of the Italian Renaissance (pp. 100–135).

[36]Perez Zagorin, "Vico's Theory of Knowledge: A Critique," *Philosophical Quarterly* 34 (1984):15–30.

[37]See *Liber metaphysicus. Risposte*, trans. S. Otto and H. Viechtbauer, with an introduction by S. Otto (Munich: Wilhelm Fink Verlag, 1979); and Helmut Viechtbauer, *Transzendentale Einsicht und Theorie der Geschichte. Überlegungen zu G. Vico's "Liber Metaphysicus"* (Munich: Wilhelm Fink Verlag, 1977).

sibility of historical knowledge." He considers the *New Science* incomprehensible without the *De Antiquissima*, in which Vico develops analogous arguments for the possibility of geometry.

Recently Nicola Badaloni has restated his earlier interpretation and joins Otto in arguing if not for logical necessity, then for the historical continuity in the *New Science* of the categories of the *De Antiquissima*.[38] Although his interpretation is different from that of Otto, he agrees with him that without the *De Antiquissima* the *New Science* would be without foundation.

In the center of this debate are the historical interpretations of Croce,[39] Giovanni Gentile,[40] and F. Nicolini.[41] In different ways, each argues that the *De Antiquissima* represents a stage in Vico's philosophy, which is reelaborated and transformed in the *New Science*. The historical thesis is carefully defended by Max Fisch,[42] who sees the *De Antiquissima* as a stage of nominalism in Vico's thought which gives way to the realism of the *New Science*. As is often the case with debates of this type—and Vico scholarship is notorious for them—the either-or position is easy to refute simply because one of Vico's characteristics as a philosopher is to escape any either-or classification.

There is some evidence in the *New Science* that Vico rejected the *De Antiquissima*.[43] But as late as 1733, ten years before his death, in a long letter to Munzio Gaeta,[44] Vico describes the *De Antiquissima* in minute detail, and the tone of that letter is not that of a philosopher who wishes to forget an aberration written just to show how well he is acquainted with philosophical debates.

The transcendental interpretation so ably defended by Otto and the German school is tantalizing and reopens in a novel way the Kantian interpretation initiated by Jacobi two hundred years ago. To be fully appreciated, however, the transcendental interpretation requires a

---

[38]Nicola Badaloni, *Introduzione a Vico* (Bari: Laterza, 1984). This recent work is slightly different from Badaloni's *Introduzione a G. B. Vico* (Milan: Feltrinelli, 1967).

[39]Croce, *La filosofia di Giambattista Vico*.

[40]Gentile, *Studi Vichiani*.

[41]Fausto Nicolini, *Saggi Vichiani* (Naples: Giannini, 1955).

[42]Max H. Fisch, "Vico and Pragmatism," in *Giambattista Vico: An International Symposium*, pp. 401–24.

[43]*Prima scienza nuova*, Book III, Chapter XXII, in *Opere di G. B. Vico*, ed. Fausto Nicolini and G. Gentile (vol. 1) and B. Croce (vol. 5 [Bari: Laterza, 1931; 2d ed., 1968]).

[44]Gian Battista Vico, *L'autobiografia, il carteggio e le poesie varie*, ed. B. Croce and F. Nicolini (Bari: Laterza, 1929), Letter LXXVIII, pp. 263–66.

rereading of Vico's works in accordance with recent developments in contemporary hermeneutics. The historical thesis is plausible, but it leaves problematic the issue of the extent to which the epistemological principle of the *De Antiquissima* is at the foundation of the *New Science*.[45] Badaloni's recent interpretation seems by far the most convincing. It breaks new ground for understanding the complex scientific environment of the *De Antiquissima*, and it attempts to show the continuity in Vico's thought between the natural and human sciences. In this context, however, it is more fruitful to consider the open texture of Vico's epistemological principle and to assess the *De Antiquissima* not only as a stage toward Vico's *New Science* but also on its own, as a model of an eighteenth-century philosophical treatise.

This brings us to the other difficulty anyone approaching the text is bound to encounter. Almost all philosophical treatises written during this period mirror the epistemological concerns of the age in their titles. Hence, Vico's title, *De Antiquissima Italorum Sapientia ex Linguae Latinae Originibus Eruenda*, may seem peculiar and eccentric. It is certainly at odds with the transparency of George Berkeley's *The Principles of Human Knowledge* (1710); or the simplicity of Benedict Spinoza's *Ethica Ordine Geometrico Demonstrata* (1677); or Nicholas Malebranche's *Le recherche de la vérité* (1675); or even G. W. Leibniz's *La monadologie* (1720), though this last is not quite so transparent. Vico's claim that the philosophical theories he presents are to be found in the thought of an ancient civilization seems unusual and inconsistent with some of the fundamental insights of his mature work. For the main thesis of the *New Science* is that the primitive mind is poetic and not philosophical. In addition, by attributing his own philosophy to past thinkers Vico himself falls into the trap of the *boria dei dotti*, namely, the mistake of which he was later, in his *New Science*, to accuse many eminent thinkers. Only vain scholars, he argues there, "want whatever they themselves know to be as old as the world." Hence, the majority of Vichian scholars have ignored Vico's philological and historical method and concentrated solely on the philosophical theories of the *De Antiquissima*. Nevertheless, Vico's investigation into a primordial wisdom is not only characteristic of his whole approach to philoso-

---

[45]One of the best solutions to this much debated issue is that of Leon Pompa in his *Vico: A Study of the "New Science"* (Cambridge: Cambridge University Press, 1975).

phy, but also represents his own peculiar way of presenting a method of investigation at variance with that of the Cartesians.

In his autobiography Vico says that the idea of unearthing principles of knowledge and wisdom from ancient Latin terms came to him while reading Francis Bacon's *On the Wisdom of the Ancients*. He adds that the method he uses, that of Plato's *Cratylus*, is different from the one followed by contemporary grammarians. He deliberately set his historical-philological method up against the introspective method of Descartes. The *primum verum* is not to be found by inspecting the content of one's consciousness, "sitting in front of the fireplace and garbed in a dressing gown." The philological-historical method is a method of discovery. In the case of the *De Antiquissima*, this method yields the first truth, which becomes the proper foundation of all human sciences.

Although some of the philological findings that Vico adduces in support of his theories are fanciful, others are signposts around which the philosophical system of the *De Antiquissima* can be organized. At the epistemic level there is the thesis that *verum* and *factum* are identical in meaning, as are *causa* and *negotium;* at the metaphysical level the same can be said for *punctum* and *momentum;* at the psychological level there are the derivation and analogy of *ingenium* and *natura* and the distinction of *animus* and *anima;* as a conclusion Vico offers the thesis that *fatum* and *factum, casus* and *causa,* are identical in meaning.

The *Verum-Factum* and Descartes's Rule and Criteria of Clarity and Distinctness

De Antiquissima opens abruptly with the central epistemic thesis that *verum* is identical in meaning with *factum*. The principle is presented as the result of philological and historical investigation. The ancient wise men of Italy, Vico states, maintained that the true is identical with that which is made and done. At the outset Vico offers no other argument in support of his principle but its philological origin. The reviewers of the *De Antiquissima* challenged Vico with a series of questions which have been repeated ever since. Namely,

"On what grounds does he conclude that in the Latin tongue *factum* and *verum* mean the same thing?" After presenting the principle, Vico suggests a substitution of the Ciceronian *reciprocantur* (*verum* and *factum reciprocantur*) for the scholastic *convertuntur* (*verum* and *factum convertuntur*). As a result several scholars have argued for the historical origin of the *verum-factum* in the transcendentals of the scholastics. The shortcomings of this interpretation have been masterfully treated by Benedetto Croce. In his analysis of Vico's philosophy he shows in great detail the essential differences between Thomas Aquinas's metaphysical claim that the condition of making a thing is to know it and Vico's theory that the condition of knowing a truth is to make it. Croce concludes: "Ficino, Cardano, Tommaso, Cornelio, Scotus and Occam may have anticipated this or that element of Vico's formula and yet . . . Vico takes an old rusty sword and makes of it at last a glittering and trenchant weapon."[46]

More recently, Max Fisch has refined Croce's interpretation.[47] Fisch agrees with Croce that Vico's principle is original—or, as he ably puts it: "Vico poured the new wine of the *Factum* in the old wineskin of the transcendentals." But Fisch disagrees with Croce by arguing that the principle belongs logically and historically to the tradition of the transcendentals. The formula states an analytical relation, namely, that only as made is something interchangeable, or convertible, with the true—and thus intelligible to its maker or doer. But it can also have some degree of intelligibility to any being who could make or do it and who *would*, under specifiable circumstances, make or do it. The formula is not a case of the correspondence theory of truth. *Verum* does not mean "true" as the function of a proposition (whose opposite is "false"); rather, it means true as intelligible. Fisch's interpretation clarifies the metaphysical underpinning of Vico's epistemology and avoids the temptation to render Vico's *verum* as "truth" and his *factum* as "fact." The history of nineteenth-century Vichian historiography shows how easy it is to give in to that temptation.

Yet the metaphysical interpretation seems not completely supported by historical evidences. Although Vico studied Scotist philoso-

---

[46]B. Croce, *La filosofia di Giambattista Vico*, translated by R. G. Collingwood as *The Philosophy of Giambattista Vico* (London, 1913). This discussion appears on pp. 279–301; the quotation is on p. 291.

[47]Fisch, "Vico and Pragmatism," p. 407.

phy, he appears to have been ignorant of any type of Thomism. He considers Scotism the most Platonic of the scholastic systems, and there are traces of this belief in parts of the *De Antiquissima*. Given that Vico is always anxious to mention his sources (whether real or imaginary), it seems unusual that he would fail to mention in the *De Antiquissima* the historical sources of his fundamental principle.[48] Instead he insists that he has recovered it in the ancient wisdom of the Italians, and when pressed by reviewers he offers examples from two passages of Terence's poetry and one of Plautus's.

If one wants to dwell on the historical origin of the principle in addition to its philosophical significance and the use Vico makes of it in his system, it is perhaps fruitful to consider that even in his early inaugural addresses Vico had stressed the Renaissance concept of the human mind as divine and therefore creative and productive. As early as 1699 he had related the creative power of the mind to the activity exemplified in constructing mathematics and geometry, as well as in painting and building. In 1708, in *The Study Method*, he had praised synthetic linear geometry in contrast to Descartes's analytic geometry. There, in relation to physics, he had also emphasized the constructive making involved in geometry. Thus one may surmise that, reflecting on what people do when they involve themselves in mathematics, Vico arrived at the view in the *De Antiquissima* that that which is made (mathematics) or done (the plastic arts) is fully intelligible *only* to its maker or doer.

The *verum-factum* principle is followed by an analysis of three epistemic activities: *intelligere, cogitare,* and *ratio*. Vico understands the first two as marking the essential difference between divine and human knowledge and the third the distinction between human and animal knowledge. God's knowledge is an *aperte cognoscere*, a perfect reading of the elements of things. It is the type of knowledge which Kant attributes to the *intellectus archetypus*, not the type of knowledge with which Descartes endowed his God. Man's knowledge is a *co-agere*, the action of bringing together the elements that make up an object of knowledge. It is a constructive making but not an *aperte cognoscere*. Divine and human knowledge differ in kind and degree. Divine knowledge is a comprehension of the external and internal

---

[48]It is worth noting here that so far as I know there is no mention in Vico's works of the *verum-factum* principle in the form that appears in the *De Antiquissima*.

elements of things. Human knowledge is horizontal and limited. *Ratio* is also an activity, a cognitive moment that intends calculation and mathematical operation.

It follows that human knowledge in its activity is involved only with "the outside of things." Thus human knowledge is, as Vico puts it, "abstractive."

Descartes had attempted to internalize and thus to know external reality by refining the idea of *res extensa* until it became so clear and distinct that it could not be doubted. Yet the ghost of skepticism remains. In the long run, until God is introduced to guarantee the existence of the external world, it must be taken on faith. Vico's refutation of skepticism takes a different route than did Descartes's.[49]

We realize that nature is bound to remain external to the human mind. Rather than trying to internalize it via the apprehension of ideas, we create a science in which its elements are transparent to us. From knowledge of our limitations and by imitating God's creative activity, we construct mathematics and perform experiments in physics. Mathematics does not need God for its validation, as is the case in Descartes's metaphysics.

Geometricians imitate God's creativity. They define the point, and by defining it they make it. From the point a line is generated, and from a line a figure, and from it theorems and problems, and so on. In geometrical construction the human mind arranges the elements of that construction and hence causes it.

In the hierarchy of sciences, geometry and mathematics are the clearest and most certain. They alone prove from causes and they alone are completely demonstrative. Thus they satisfy to the fullest the criterion of the convertibility of the true with the made. The more imbued with empirical elements a science is, the more opaque it is and hence the less certain. In the case of physics and mechanics, natural scientists, unlike geometricians, are limited in their making by the externality of physical nature. Yet physics can be partly demonstrative if the natural scientist can recreate natural structures through experiments. Hence experiments are "demonstrations" and not, as Descartes maintains, ways of checking the validity of deductions.

---

[49]Vico utters a very different criticism against the "skepticism" of Descartes's metaphysics in a passionate letter to Francesco Saverio Estevan. See G. B. Vico, *L'autobiografia*, pp. 212–18.

At first glance Vico's hierarchy of science, guaranteed by the *verum-factum* principle, appears similar to Descartes's system, which is grounded on the criteria of clarity and distinctness. Both endow mathematics with the highest certainty and the moral sciences with the lowest. But they differ significantly in the matter of justification. For in Descartes's system ultimately it is God who validates the truths of mathematics and of the natural sciences. Even the laws of motion, and consequently the sciences of physics and mechanics, are derived from the a priori premise of God's immutability.[50] Consequently, the logic of Descartes's metaphysics demands the coherence of the on-tological and causal proofs for the existence of God. In Vico's system there are levels of truth depending on levels of constructiveness. Mathematics is truer than physics and mechanics because in mathe-matics and geometry the mind puts together the ultimate element of a figure and thus makes it, and in the process of constructing it comes to know it. Physics is less constructive and thus less certain than mathematics because the ultimate elements of natural things are cre-ated by God and thus only clear to Him. Physicists, like mathemati-cians, imitate the creative action of God, and the success of their scientific activity depends on how successful their mimicking is. Vico accepts the traditional view of God, the perfect knower and maker, as a fact of revelation. His system demands that the divine model de-scribe and prescribe what it is like to know with certainty.

Vico proceeds to assess the extent to which Descartes's *Cogito*, with its concomitant criteria of clarity and distinctness, succeeds as a scien-tific principle and as bulwark against skepticism. Descartes reaches the *Cogito ergo sum* through a process of analysis. Any empirical and rational element of consciousness which can be doubted is rejected and considered downright false. The *Cogito* alone remains the only indubitable truth that is clear and distinct. From this primary truth Descartes establishes the truth of the existence of God and of the existence of *res extensa*. Vico acknowledges that the method of analy-sis yields Descartes's *Cogito ergo sum*. But he denies that the *Cogito* offers scientific knowledge of existence. The Cartesian principle is

50This position is made clear in several of Descartes's letters. See *Descartes' Philosoph-ical Letters*, trans. and ed. Anthony Kenny (Oxford: Clarendon Press, 1970): Letter to Mersenne, 15 April 1630, pp. 12–13; Letter to Arnauld, 29 July 1648, pp. 233–37; Letter to Mesland, 2 May 1644, pp. 146–52.

neither original nor "scientific." Even the simpleminded Sosia in Plautus's comedy manages to establish his existence from the simple fact that he is thinking. Descartes has mistaken a common psychological experience for a scientific principle. A distinction must be drawn, Vico argues, between certainty and truth, between being conscious that one exists and knowing it. Hence, whereas Descartes makes certainty coextensive with truth, Vico sharply distinguishes the two. Consciousness and knowledge, certainty and truth, are two irreducible modes of knowledge. If one knew that one existed, one would know the mode and genus of one's existence and thus one would literally make oneself. Because one exists as mind and body, thinking would have to be the cause not only of mind, but also of body. But neither matter nor pure mind thinks. One thinks because one is made of mind and body. One is not made of mind and body because one thinks. Thinking is thus only a sign that one has a mind, but not its cause. Vico applies the same type of argument to Descartes's proof of the existence of God. To know that God exists, one would have to know the genus and mode of God; hence, Vico boldly argues, one would have to be God's maker.

Thus the *Cogito* is not to be trusted as the foundation of all other sciences because it is a psychological principle and not a model of scientific knowledge. Descartes's metaphysics is dogmatic—his *Cogito* is not a principle of demonstrative knowledge—and his hope to refute skepticism and reassure certainty remains a dream. For skeptics do not deny that they think or that they exist. Nor do they doubt that they perceive appearances or that they are cognizant of mathematical truths. What they doubt and thus are skeptical of is the causes of appearances.

Where Descartes's *Cogito* fails, the *verum-factum* principle succeeds. First, it disengages mathematics from physics. Second, by reducing mathematics to a true human construction, it opens the domain of physics to an equally human reconstruction through experiments.

The *verum-factum* principle, as Vico carefully explains in his reply to his reviewers, "is guaranteed for me by God's science, which is the source and standard of all truths. This criterion guarantees for me that the only human sciences are the mathematical ones, and that they prove from causes. Beyond that, it gives me the way of classifying the nonscientific disciplines that are either certain on the basis of indubitable signs or probable on the basis of good arguments or true-like on the basis of powerful hypothesis."[51]

Some commentators have suggested that by appealing to God as "the comprehension of all causes," and thus as the limit of skepticism, Vico is inconsistent and his whole argument against skepticism is a form of *petitio principii*. In fact, the argument would be a form of *petitio* if Vico used it to prove the existence of God. But the appeal to God and God's comprehension of all causes is offered as a limiting model or an ideal of perfection against which the truths of all human sciences must be measured.

It is interesting to speculate on how Descartes would reply to Vico's objections. Perhaps to the fundamental criticism that the *Cogito* can be the criterion neither of self-knowledge nor of other truths, Descartes would have replied with the same phrases he used to respond to Gassendi, Mersenne, Hobbes, and Bourdin. Descartes might have reminded Vico that "it is the wise person alone who knows how to distinguish rightly what is so perceived and what merely seems or appears to be clear and distinct."[52] To the objection that "existence" cannot be deduced from "thinking," Descartes might have replied that Vico, like all anti-Cartesians, misunderstood the meaning of *ergo* in the *Cogito ergo sum*. If Vico had read the phrase as meaning that only through thinking do people constitute themselves, then he would have recognized a kinship between his own theory and that of the *Cogito*.[53] But Descartes would have considered Vico's mathematical views ambiguous and would have found Vico's rejection of analytic geometry in favor of linear synthetic geometry in need of explanation.

Vico's mathematical theory is in fact far from being clear. In the first chapter of the *De Antiquissima* Vico argues, like Hobbes and Locke, in favor of conventionalism. Geometry is made by people and is a fully human construction. Geometricians freely make the elements of their

[51]See below, p. 167.

[52]Descartes, *Philosophical Works*, 2:267.

[53]Jaakko Hintikka offers persuasive arguments that Descartes's *Cogito* is not an inference but a performatory act. See J. Hintikka, "*Cogito Ergo Sum:* Inference or Performance?" *Philosophical Review* 71 (1962):3–32. He uses this argument to stress interesting analogies between Vico and Descartes. See idem, "Practical vs. Theoretical Reason—an Ambiguous Legacy," in *Practical Reason*, ed. Stephan Körner (New Haven, Conn.: Yale University Press, 1974), pp. 83–102.

system just as God makes the elements out of which He creates the world.

As is shown above, Vico argues that the human intellect is essentially discursive. In order to know, it must have recourse to divide and anatomize nature. Yet it is endowed with the special power of turning its limitations to advantage. In the process of investigating the nature of reality we realize we cannot acquire complete knowledge of nature because we have not within ourselves the elements of things. Hence we imitate God and create a world of figures, lines, and numbers. Definitions, postulates, and rules of deductions—the whole furniture of mathematics—is a human construction. Because mathematicians themselves construct all the theoretical primitives necessary for their science, they have full knowledge of it. Arithmetic and geometry are possible, Vico claims, because not only their problems but also their theorems, which were hitherto considered objects of contemplation, are operations of the human mind. Because in the course of putting together the elements of truth it contemplates, the mind cannot do otherwise than make the truth it knows. Mathematics is a fundamental form of human activity. The mathematician invents a name, defines it, and in so doing creates out of nothing, that is to say out of the definition, the point, the line, the surface. The primitives of this science are constructed out of nothing. These primitives, Vico argues, are *ficta*. They have no referent. In fact, if the point or the one would refer, they would contradict their definitions: there would be something that has parts; there would be a one that is no longer a one. Mathematical definitions are nominal but creative, conventional but extremely useful creations of the mind. To define the point, the line, and the surface entails for Vico to construct them, hence to know them, and to deduce from them an unlimited number of uncontroversial ideas. Because they are constructions, the fundamental propositions can hardly be taken as strictly analytical. And because they are not a prescribed mechanical procedure but the product of the exercise of *ingenium*, they can hardly be called arbitrary. The game they generate is one whose validity lies in the utilization of the pattern and play allowed under given rules. In short, for Vico, mathematics is a spontaneous production of the human mind.

In this respect, there seems to be no doubt that Vico's position is analogous to that of Hobbes and Locke. The only significant difference between Vico's theory and that of the British philosophers is that, for Vico, mathematical constructions are useful. Mathematical science is born of human ingenuity, our ability to turn the limited capacity of the mind into a virtue, just as, in the *New Science*, the making of human institutions is born of our inability to have clear and distinct ideas of ourselves. Vico's position is therefore consistent with his criticism of Descartes's application of geometry to the world of nature. Mathematics may be used to investigate nature, but in itself it has no ontological significance and does not offer any insight into the world of things.

When, in the second, third, and fourth chapters of the *De Antiquissima*, Vico moves on from his constructive epistemology to an ontology of Neoplatonic forms and to a metaphysics of Zenonian points, his mathematical nominalism seems to give way to a quasi-metaphysical realism.

Several issues are at stake in this debate over nominalism versus realism. First, there is the internal consistency of the *De Antiquissima*, especially in those sections in which Vico speaks of geometrical definitions as the product of human creativity, then proceeds to consider them "real." Second, there is the issue of metaphysics itself. On the one hand, Vico insists that metaphysical knowledge is denied humans; yet on the other, his metaphysics is supposedly presented in order to understand the ultimate elements of natural things which are precluded from physics. Third, the nominalism-realism issue raises the vexing problem of the relation between the *facere* of the *De Antiquissima* and the *facere* of the *New Science*. In other words, how does the *verum-factum* principle that establishes the certainty of mathematics and the probability of the natural sciences in the *De Antiquissima* differ from the *verum-factum* principle that establishes the truth of human institutions in the *New Science*?

The orthodox view of Croce, Gentile, and Fisch, mentioned earlier, is that Vico makes a transition from the nominalism of the *De Antiquissima*, where human creative power is confined to the "fictions" of mathematics, to the realism of the *New Science*, where people create the real objects of their institutions—and through the making, make themselves. As Fisch puts it, "Out of the historical philological studies that the Cartesian disdained, using anti-Cartesian criteria of both the true and the certain, and passing now from nominalism to realism, he [Vico] has created a new science of history which supersedes mathematics as the exemplary science of the humanly true or intelligible."[54]

Recently some American scholars, following the German school of Otto and Viechtbauer, have developed interesting arguments in favor of a metaphysical realism in the *De Antiquissima* which they claim is congruent with the realism of the *New Science*. David Lachterman points out that Vico's defense of synthetic geometry in the *Study Method*, and even more, his remarks in the second chapter of the *De Antiquissima* clearly indicate that for Vico geometrical constructions are validated by a divine archetype. In addition, when Vico develops his metaphysics of Zenonian points, he rejects any alternative definition of the point. Therefore, Lachterman argues, Vico's definitions cannot properly be considered arbitrary; they have a necessity that precludes a nominalistic stance. This necessity, says Lachterman, "shows up in Vico's central attempt [in the *New Science*] to exhibit the order and configuration of *le cose umane* as they unfold and will always unfold."[55] Lachterman's argument requires careful consideration, for it is a serious attempt to solve some of the textual inconsistencies of the *De Antiquissima* and to relate the *facere* of this work to the *facere* of the *New Science*.

Lachterman is correct when he suggests that the epistemic grounds of Vico's preference for synthetic geometry have never been fully investigated. Those scholars who favor the thesis of Vico's mathematical nominalism either disregard his allegiance to synthetic geometry,[56] or explain it on purely pedagogical grounds.[57] Thus Antonio Corsano endorses Vico's position in the *De Nostri* and considers the mathematical theory of the *De Antiquissima* a forerunner of contemporary mathematical game theory.[58] The mind of the young, Vico ar-

---

[54] M. Fisch, "Vico and Pragmatism," p. 414.

[55] David Lachterman, "Vico and Marx: Notes on a Precursory Reading," in *Vico and Marx: Affinities and Contrasts*, ed. Giorgio Tagliacozzo (Atlantic Highlands, N.J.: Humanities Press, 1983), p. 57; idem, "Vico, Doria and Synthetic Geometry," *Bollettino del Centro di Studi Vichiani* 10 (1980): 10–35 (trans. B. Arcangeli).

[56] Isaiah Berlin, *Vico and Herder: Two Studies in the History of Ideas* (New York: Viking, 1977), pp. 11–21, and Bertrand Russell, *Wisdom of the West* (London: Crescent, 1959), pp. 206–7.

[57] Corsano, *G. B. Vico*, pp. 107–16.

[58] Corsano has modified his interpretation of Vico's nominalism in his "Vico and Mathematics," *Giambattista Vico: An International Symposium*, ed. Tagliacozzo and White), pp. 425–37.

gues in the *De Nostri*, is stimulated by the forms and figures of Euclidean geometry but not by the species of Cartesian analytics. In this
early work he does not offer any other explanation as to why geometry taught by forms is preferable to that taught through species. In the
second and third chapter of the *De Antiquissima* Vico moves on to
show how his theory of truth validates an ontology of Neoplatonic
forms and relates to a theory of causal knowledge. In the context of
discussing the utility and specificity of forms versus Aristotle's generic universal, he explains why synthetic geometry is more certain than,
and thus preferable to, Cartesian geometry. The former proceeds
from the "indefinite power" of known postulates to the unknown.
Analytic geometry starts from the "infinite" and descends to *minima*.
Hence, Cartesian method is bound to be foundationally uncertain in
so far as it assumes a given—and then proceeds to divide it into
simpler figures until it reaches a minimum element. The *product* of
analytic geometry is certain, but its starting point is not. Synthetic
geometry, on the other hand, begins with starting points that, as
made and constructed, are images of divine creativity. The mind
makes the elements—point, line, plane, and so on—then proceeds
constructively to demonstrate theorems and solve problems. It causes
the whole system. Synthetic geometry is a paradigm of generative
knowledge and its primitives are imitations of metaphysical
archetypes.

At this juncture, Vico's nominalism appears to lose its force; it must
be qualified in accord with how much significance one is willing to
give to the exemplaries of geometrical constructions. If one stresses,
as Lachterman does, the divine archetype as the source of the possibility of geometry, then one is bound to see Vico's mathematical
theory as a form of metaphysical realism. The problem with this
interpretation lies in viewing the archetype as making geometry possible rather than as being a paradigm that the human mind considers
and on which it meditates. Unfortunately, the text is ambiguous and
open to various interpretations. Often Vico argues that geometry and
arithmetic are "rooted" in metaphysics; but he also claims that the
"powers" or "virtualities" both sciences exemplify are "borrowed"
from metaphysics. Ultimately, he remains firm in the belief that the
relationship between mathematics and metaphysics is circular. "Geometry," Vico states in Chapter Four, Section II, of *De Antiquissima*,
"accepts its truth from metaphysics and gives back to the very same

metaphysics what it receives. In other words," he continues, "geometry shapes human knowledge on the model of divine knowledge, and corroborates divine knowledge, in its turn, with human knowledge."[59] This statement has escaped the attention of those scholars who argue that Vico is a mathematical realist and of those who opt for Vico's nominalism.[60] The circular relationship between metaphysics and geometry, so reminiscent of a transcendental argument, disallows any clear-cut argument in favor either of unqualified realism or unqualified nominalism.

The Metaphysical Points and Descartes's *Res Extensa*

Although the *De Antiquissima*'s subtitle is *Liber Metaphysicus*, there is no mention of metaphysics in the first three chapters we have considered. The identity of the true and the made establishes the truth of the mathematical sciences and the probability of physics and morality. It also undermines Descartes's a priori proof of the existence of God and of the certainty of self-knowledge and it solves the problem of whether scientific knowledge is of the Platonic individual or of the Aristotelian universal. But Vico has not spoken yet of metaphysical knowledge or considered whether metaphysics as a science is possible.

Chapter Four, "De Essentiis Seu de Virtubibus," contains Vico's metaphysics proven *more geometrico sive arithmetico*. The chapter opens with the claim that for the ancient Latins, "force," "power," and "immortal gods" are identical in meaning to that of the scholastics' "essences." Because Aristotle and the scholastics considered essences as indivisible and individual entities and Plato as immutable and eternal causes, Vico argues that the ancient philosophers of Italy must have understood essences to be the eternal and infinite powers of nature. Hence, the proper subject matter of metaphysics is the power of extension and conatus, and the subject matter of physics is body and motion. This argument represents the core of what Vico calls Zenonianism, namely, the theory of metaphysical points. On the

---

[59]See below, p. 75.

[60]The exception is Croce who considers the "Vichian circle" incoherent and contradictory. See Croce, *Filosofia di G. B. Vico*, 4th ed. p. 12.

assumption that *punctum* is synonymous with *momentum*, one arrives at the hypothesis that *punctum* is not extended but generates extension. Just as the unit in arithmetic generates the numerical series without it being a number, and the geometrical point generates the extension of a line, without it being extended, so Vico argues that the ultimate elements of nature are points generating bodies without them being bodies.

When the reviewers of the *De Antiquissima* complained that this theory "envelops the whole treatise in a darkness that is almost palpable," they echoed, just as in the case of the *verum-factum* principle, the general refrain held by the majority of Vichian scholars. The theory bristles with difficulties ranging from the issue of its historical origin to that of its philosophical significance and to the explanatory role Vico attributes to it.

In his autobiography Vico tells how his interest in metaphysics developed under the influence of the Zenonist Giuseppe Ricci. In the same work he mentions Doria as the only philosopher among his contemporaries with whom he could discuss metaphysical matters. By 1710 Doria had published his treatise on the theory of motion and on the mechanics of sensible and insensible bodies. Vico dedicates the *De Antiquissima* to Doria and in several passages recognizes him as the author of his theory that "there are metaphysical powers and physical acts."

Recently Badaloni has returned to a detailed study of the intellectual European environment of the *De Antiquissima*. He argues convincingly for the similarity of Vico's topical logic to that of Herbert of Cherbury and of the theory of metaphysical points to Galileo's dynamics. Commenting on the expansive force of Vico's points, Badaloni argues that "it is as if Galileo's theory of dynamics is brought into metaphysics and motion alone is left in the domain of physics."[61] Corsano[62] and Robert Flint[63] suggest analogies between Vico's metaphysical points and Leibniz's early theory of the monads, understood as centers of forces. There are, however, more than analogies between Vico and Leibniz. Both philosophers are equally aware of the need in physics for a theory of matter different from that of the Cartesians. Both use their respective metaphysics in polemics with

[61]Badaloni, *Introduzione a Vico*, p. 20.
[62]Corsano, *G. B. Vico*, p. 125.
[63]Robert Flint, *Vico* (Edinburgh: Blackwood, 1984), p. 127.

Descartes and both reformulate Zeno's theory of mathematical points in an identical fashion. Vico attributes his theory to Zeno, confusing the Eleatic with the Stoic. He claims to deliver that doctrine from the misinterpretations of Aristotle. Hence, he argues that the theory is far different from the way it was understood by his contemporaries. Namely, extension is not composed of geometrical points; rather, the geometrical point is an example of the metaphysical point endowed with the power to contain and support extension and thus named by Zeno "metaphysical point." The only difference between Leibniz's position and Vico's is that Leibniz criticizes Zeno because he derives physical matter from mathematical points. Vico attributes to Zeno the metaphysical theory of the points as if it had been revised by Leibniz.

The theory has two functions, one epistemological and the other cosmological. Although Vico remains faithful to his fundamental claim that metaphysical knowledge is a human impossibility, he proceeds to argue that by understanding how mathematics works, one can have indirect knowledge of the fundamental elements of the physical world. Descartes claims that the only properties that really belong to things are those that it is possible to know a priori. For Descartes this is an essential postulate in physics. Accordingly, in his system what physics should imitate in mathematics is not its precise quantification, but its deductive method of discovery. For Vico the only properties that really belong to things are those it is possible to know by understanding the *facere* of mathematics. As Vico puts it, "One knows the metaphysical foundations of physics by meditating on how mathematics proceeds."

Hence, one arrives at the hypothesis of metaphysical points by reflecting and meditating on the mind's ability to construct mathematics. Just as the geometrical point possesses the capacity to produce a world of figures, so the metaphysical point has the expansive power to generate extension and motion. In addition, just as the point defined as "that which has no parts" solves the paradoxes of concentric circles and that of the incommensurability of the line, so the metaphysical point and its conatus solves the Cartesian paradox of absolute rest and communication of motion. Rest is not of the physical world and extension or space is not the essence of matter.

In Descartes's metaphysics God creates by two distinct acts: matter and motion. Furthermore, the relationship between God as an uncreated substance and *res extensa* as a created substance remains unexplained; as Vico puts it, "in the manner of the analysts he [Descartes] simply assumes that matter has been created and goes on to divide it." But Vico "aimed to treat the world of solids, which God created, on the basis of the world of forms, which man establishes for himself by synthesis from points."[64] The metaphysical points and their conatus explain the origin of nature as extended and in motion. With reference to the world of solid things, metaphysical points are the grounds of existence, primary matter, and substances. They are substances in the sense that substance "is what lies underneath and sustains things; though in itself indivisible, it is divided in the entities it sustains."[65] With reference to God, the points are mere acts and effects. Their conatus is not, like motion, measurable; it is in fact a pure metaphysical force. Hence, by considering the substance of body immaterial and the cause of motion motionless, Vico avoids Descartes's dualism without resorting to Spinoza's monism or to Malebranche's intellectualism.

Ingenium and Descartes's *Res Cogitans*

In Vico's physical universe there are no rectilinear motions, no principle of inertia. The force of conatus keeps the universe alive and in motion.

In the final chapters of *De Antiquissima*, where Vico develops his psychology and his theory of mental activities, the same force becomes the unifying principle of the human mind. Earlier he had argued against Descartes's failure to account adequately for the world of extension and motion. Now he uses the unifying principle of life to reject Descartes's dualism of mind and body. He concludes the *De Antiquissima* by developing his philosophy of mind grounded on *ingenium* and on a logic of discovery based on topics.

Contrary to what several commentators have argued, there is a strong relation between the *verum-factum* principle, the metaphysics of Zenonian points, and the psychology based on the gradual development of thinking from feeling and sensing. Just as the *verum-factum*

---

[64]See below, Chapter Four, Section II, p. 76.
[65]See below, p. 176.

principle validates the metaphysics of points and refutes Cartesian mechanicism, so in Vico's psychology the *verum-factum* certifies a view of the human mind at variance with any form of Cartesian phenomenalism. In addition, just as conatus explains the origin and conservation of the physical world, so in these final chapters the principle of life—what Vico calls air—explains the origin and development of thinking.

Badaloni offers ample evidence of the debates among members of the Academy of the Investigators on the theory of air as a cosmological principle.

He correctly traces the obvious naturalism of these final sections to the "modern Platonism" that characterizes the school of the followers of Galileo at the beginning of the eighteenth century. This form of Platonism, well known to Vico, centers around the theory of the continuous creation of the world's soul and of human nature. As mentioned earlier, Vico never wrote the projected volume on physics, but summarized his views on the science of nature in the *De Aequilibrio Corporis Animantis*, of which he gives a sketch in his autobiography. In this work he argues that the Latins used the word *anima* for air as the principle that gives the universe motion and life and on which the ether acts as male on female.

> The ether insinuated into living beings the Latins called *animus;* hence the common Latin distinction *anima vivimus, animo sentimus,* "by the soul we have life, by the spirit sensation." Accordingly, the soul—that is, the air insinuated into the blood—would be the principle of life in man, and the ether insinuated into the nerves would be the principle of sensation. To the degree that ether is more active than air, the animal spirits would be more mobile and quick than the vital spirits. And just as soul is acted on by spirit, so spirit would be acted on by what the Latins called *mens,* or thought; hence the Latin phrase *mens animi,* the mind of the spirit. And this thought or mind would come to men from Jove, who is the mind of the ether.

Vico repeats almost verbatim this argument at the beginning of his analysis of mental activities, and he uses it to conclude his criticism of Descartes's *res cogitans* and to reject the hypothesis of the pineal gland. The view Descartes presents is that of the mind directly moving the pineal gland. This gland is suspended in the center of the brain, and thus it affects the "animal spirits," which are the causes of mechanical changes in the body. Using his theory of the conservation of motion, Descartes postulates that the direction of motion of these spirits is affected by the soul, but not the direction of their speed.

To Vico this hypothesis is "the invention of a man entirely ignorant of metaphysics" and poorly acquainted with medicine. Descartes introduces the device of the pineal gland because he is ignorant of the causes and origin of thinking. He fails to distinguish animus from anima and he misunderstands the function of the animal spirits. Thus Descartes does not see how improbable it is for the mind to reside in that part of the body which is the most inert and passive, nor can he explain how people with a damaged brain are able to reason and argue correctly. Because air, or ether,[66] is the vehicle of both vital and animal spirits, the difference between animus and anima is a difference in degree and not in kind. Animus is autonomous, free, and immortal. From animus mind originates as *mens animi*, the most subtle part of spirit and life. The faculty of desire which is "for everyone his God" pushes animal spirits into vital spirits, and from these thinking originates. As Badaloni remarks, in this theory of mind thinking is no longer an a priori datum, but "the result of an objective force." It is, in fact, the expression of the divine conatus which moves the physical universe.

Vico's view of the divinity of the mind differs from that endorsed by some of Descartes's followers. Malebranche, for example, accepts Descartes's *Cogito* and argues that ideas are created by God. To Vico this form of spiritualism places conditions on God. Hence he argues that if Malebranche were to be consistent, he would have to accept the logical implications of his theory, namely, when "I think," it is really God who thinks in me and in God "I recognize my mind." Malebranche remains, in the long run, a Cartesian; but Vico detaches himself from this tradition and introduces a view of thinking conditioned by its divine nature, which is therefore action, invention, and *ingenium*. As many commentators have pointed out, the view of the creative powers of mental faculties can be traced historically to the

[66]In Chapter Five of the *De Antiquissima* and in the *Risposte*, Vico seems to collapse the distinction between ether and air which he makes in the *De Aequilibrio* and in the *New Science*. See Vico, *The Autobiography*, p. 149, and *New Science* (hereafter NS), 695–702. [Unless otherwise noted all references to Vico's *New Science* are to *The New Science of Giambattista Vico*, rev. trans. of the third edition, Thomas Goddard Bergin and Max Harold Fisch (Ithaca: Cornell University Press, 1968) hereafter NS].

tradition of Herbert of Cherbury and to several British empiricists, including Locke and Berkeley. Yet the path Vico takes to refute Descartes's phenomenalism and its concomitant skepticism is original with him.

There are no traces in his theory of the Cartesian view of the mind as a substance whose essence is thinking. Neither *res extensa* nor *res cogitans* is given—one to be mathematized, the other to be analyzed. The mind is active, constructive, and productive in all of its functions. As Vico ingeniously puts it, the faculties of the mind are "facilities to make." We create colors in seeing and flavors in tasting. We represent and make images of things in imagination. Even understanding is a "facility" because through the process of understanding a thing we make it true. Thus mathematics, geometry, and mechanics are products of human faculties because in these sciences we make the truths we demonstrate.

Finally, *ingenium* is the original and natural faculty of humans; it is the proper faculty with which we achieve certain knowledge. It is original because it is the first "facility" young people untouched by prejudices exemplify upon seeing similarities between disparate things. It is natural because it is to us what the power to create is to God. Just as God easily begets a world of nature, so we ingeniously make discoveries in the sciences and artifacts in the arts. *Ingenium* is a productive and creative form of knowledge. It is *poietic* in the creation of the imagination; it is *rhetorical* in the creation of language, through which all sciences are formalized. Hence, it requires its own logic, a logic that combines both the art of finding or inventing arguments and that of judging them. Vico argues that topical art allows the mind to locate the object of knowledge and to see it in all its aspects and not through "the dark glass" of clear and distinct ideas. The logic of discovery and invention which Vico uses against Descartes's analytics is the art of apprehending the true. With this Vico come full circle in his arguments against Descartes.

We are the makers of truths because it is only when we produce that we become like God. There is a difference between God's knowledge as the model for human knowledge and God being the foundation and ultimate guarantor of human knowledge, as in Descartes's system. In the latter, human nature is bound to be passive; in the former, it had better be creative if it wants to be fully human. The idea of the origin and development of institutions as a way of saving humans from dissolution is not far off.

ON THE
MOST ANCIENT WISDOM
OF THE ITALIANS

UNEARTHED FROM THE

ORIGINS OF THE LATIN LANGUAGE

THREE BOOKS

First Book: Metaphysics

Second Book: Physics

Third Book: Moral Philosophy

1710

PROEM

The occasion of the work—Learned languages [derived] from the philosophers of the [gentile] nations—Origins of the learned Latin language from the Ionians and Etruscans—The wisest Italian school of philosophy—The Etruscans very learned in metaphysics—Etruscans earlier geometricians than the Greeks—This work modeled on Plato's *Cratylus*. Different from the works of Varro, Scaliger, Sanchez, and Scioppio

As I was studying the origins of the Latin language, I noticed that [the origins of] many words were so learned as to seem derived from some inward learning rather than from the vernacular usage of the people. Certainly, there is nothing to prevent any language from being filled with philosophic expressions, if philosophy is much renowned in that people. From my own memory, I can draw the fact that when philosophers of Aristotle's school and physicians of Galen's flourished, it was common for unlettered men to speak of the "abhorrence of the vacuum," "natural antipathies and sympathies," "the four humors," "qualities," and countless similar expressions. Afterward, in fact, as the new-fashioned technique of physics and medicine had come into use, one might occasionally hear the man in the street mention the "circulation of the blood" and its "coagulation," "helpful and harmful fermentation," "air pressure," and other such phrases.[1] Before the time of Hadrian, the words *ens, essentia,*

[1]The slow development from the old scientific method of the late seventeenth century to the new science of the early eighteenth century is exemplified by two distinct

substantia, and *accidens* had never fallen on Latin ears because Aristotle's *Metaphysics* was not known.[2] After this time, learned men paid attention to this work and these terms became common. For this reason, then, since I had noticed that the Latin language abounded in quite learned phrases, and since, according to historical evidence, the ancient Romans had devoted themselves down to the time of Pyrrhus[3] to nothing but farming and war, I conjectured that they had taken these expressions from some learned nation and used them unaware of their meaning.

---

types of languages, the old language of "hidden qualities" and the new language of "circulation of blood" and the like. Vico is presenting factual evidence for his theory that linguistic expressions may be used to determine the world view of a historical period. This central thesis, which Vico never rejects, is found in a different form in the *New Science.* In that work, it is the poets of the *gens,* not the learned men of an earlier *gens,* whose recondite wisdom is embodied in the vulgar tongue. See *NS,* 444–455.

[2]Vico has in mind M. Fabius Quintilianus, to whom he refers elsewhere, and his work *Institutio Oratoria* (Rhetorical Instruction), written under the emperor Domitian (ca. A.D. 95), a generation before Hadrian's reign (A.D. 117–138). Vico is interpreting two passages on *essentia* as the Latin translation of the Greek *ousia* (with *essentia*) while overlooking a third. In II, 14, 1–2, Quintilian cites the coining of *essentia* (being) and *queentia* (i.e., *potentia,* power) by Plautus. Since Radermacher's edition of Quintilian (Leipzig, 1907), *queentia* has been accepted for the manuscript *entia.* See A. Ernout and A. Moillet, *Dictionnaire étymologique de la langue latine,* 4th ed. (Paris: Klincksieck 1959), s.v. *ens*). However, Vico's text must have read *entia.* In III, 6, 23, Quintilian again mentions Plautus's translation of Aristotle and discusses Roman methods of translating Greek philosophical terms. However, later in *Institutio Oratoria* (VIII, 3, 33), Quintilian ascribes the *essentia* and *queentia* (for Vico *ens* or *entia*) to Sergius Flavius. Clearly, the Plautus of the two earlier passages is either a manuscript error or the third name of Sergius Flavius. In any case, this Plautus is not the comic playwright of ca. 200 B.C. whom Vico frequently uses to support his contentions about the archaic usage of philosophical terms. Thus, Vico's argument here rests partly on a case of mistaken identity and on a faulty manuscript tradition. Aristotle's surviving works were not generally known in the last two centuries before Christ. In Rome, Cicero knew and used Aristotle's rhetorical works and his dialogues. Around 85–84 B.C., Cornelius Sulla appropriated an Aristotelian library (see Plutarch's *Sulla,* 26) which became the basis of the published text of our Aristotelian corpus sometime after the middle of that century, when Andronicus edited and published it. Vico's statement that the *Metaphysics* was not known in Rome before Hadrian is true only to the extent that new interest in Peripatetic philosophy brought about learned discussion and commentary on Aristotle's works *after* Hadrian.

[3]Pyrrhus (318–272 B.C.), king of Epirus, whose costly military success gave rise to the phrase "Pyrrhic victory." Modern students of Roman history still assert that Roman contact with the Greeks of southern Italy was intensified when Pyrrhus was the ally and protector of Tarento, in Italy's "instep." Earlier Roman contacts with Greek cities such as Naples and Marseilles can be proved, but no contact with a city of great renown in classical Greece. The Romans found Greek resistance to their armies relatively weak or nonexistent before Pyrrhus entered Italy.

Of learned peoples from whom they could have borrowed these phrases, I discovered two: the Ionians and the Etruscans. There is no need to say much about Ionian culture, since an Italian school of philosophy—and a very learned and outstanding one at that—flourished among the Ionians. Moreover, the Etruscans' doctrine of magnificent sacred rites, a subject in which they excelled, proves that they were a very erudite people. For it is only when natural theology is cultivated that civil theology is ennobled; whenever worthier opinions of the Supreme Being are held, religious institutions become more august. And hence, by the same token, among us Christians ceremonies are the purest of all because the doctrines concerning God are the holiest of all. Moreover, the fact that the architecture of the Etruscans is simpler than that of any other people affords weighty proof that they had knowledge of geometry before the Greeks. Etymologies testify to the fact that a good and large part of the Latin language was imported among the Latins from the Ionians. It is further agreed that the Romans derived from the Etruscans the rites of their gods and, along with them, also the sacred phrases and priestly language. Therefore, I take it as certain that the learned origins of Latin words came from these two peoples. For this reason, I have directed my attention to unearthing the most ancient wisdom of the Italians from the etymologies of the Latin language itself. As far as I know, this is something no one has attempted hitherto, and perhaps it deserves to be numbered among Francis Bacon's desiderata.[4]

Plato sought to unveil the ancient wisdom of the Greeks by the same method in his *Cratylus*.[5] But the notable achievements of Varro

[4]Vico is claiming that a philosophical study of language should be added to the list of "desiderata" that Bacon introduced in the Appendix of his *De Dignitate et Augmentis Scientiarum* (1623). (The Appendix bears the title *Novus Orbis Scientiarum sive Desiderata*, Montague edition [London, 1823], pp. 129, 131.) For the most accurate study on Vico's debt to Bacon, see Enrico De Mas, "Bacone e Vico," *Filosofia* 10 (1959):505–59. Also, for useful references on the relation of Vico to Bacon in the broad perspective of seventeenth-century Europe, see Paolo Rossi, *Francesco Bacone: Dalla magia alla scienza* (Bari: Laterza, 1957); and Antonio Corsano, *G. B. Vico* (Bari: Laterza, 1956), pp. 196–200.

[5]Although Plato, with Bacon, Tacitus, and Grotius, is one of Vico's four authors, a study of Plato and Platonistic influences on Vico is still to be written. The relevance of the *Cratylus* on Vico's theory of language is carefully treated by A. Pagliaro. See *La dottrina linguistica di G. B. Vico*, *Atti dell' Accademia Nazionale dei Lincei, memorie della classe di scienze morali, storiche, critiche e filologiche* 8, 8 (1959):379–486; reprinted as "Lingua e poesia secondo G. B. Vico" and "Omero e la poesia populare in G. B. Vico," in *Altri saggi di critica semantica* (Messina and Florence: D'Anna, 1961), pp. 299–474.

in his *Origins*,[6] Julius Scaliger in the *Causes of the Latin Language*,[7] Franciscus Sanctius in *Minerva*,[8] and Gaspar Scioppius in his *Notes*[9] to that work are far removed from our undertaking here. These men busied themselves in unearthing the causes of language and in formulating it into a system on the basis of the philosophy to which they were devoted, and in which they were learned. Whereas I, not being an adherent of any school of thought, shall seek out the ancient wisdom of the Italians from the very origins of their words.

[6]Marcus Terentius Varro (ca. 116–27 B.C.), student of the earliest Roman philologist Antiochus of Ascalon. Varro wrote on agriculture, Roman antiquities, philosophy, and astronomy. Unfortunately, most of his works are lost. Of his *De Lingua Latina*, originally in twenty-five books, only five have survived. Vico had read a great deal of Varro, and despite what he says here, he owes him more than he is willing to acknowledge. Much of Varro's religious investigation was utilized by Augustine, especially in Book IV of *The City of God;* also by Arnobius, and by Tertullian in his *Address to the Pagans.* Varro's education may be viewed through Cicero's *Academica*, Book I.

[7]Julius Caesar Scaliger (1484–1558), a well-known Italian humanist, wrote the earliest Latin grammar based on scientific principles. *De Causis Linguae Latinae* and *De Comicis Dimensionibus*, a brief treatise on comic meters, were the only literary works published in his lifetime. Vico reiterates his opinion of Scaliger in the *New Science* (384, 455, 807) and in an unduly complimentary note on one of the mediocre works of his pupil. See *Idea di una grammatica filosofica*, in *Vico, Opere*, ed. F. Nicolini (Milan: Ricciardi, 1953), p. 944. Leibniz, in *Preface to an Edition of Nizolius* (1670), recognizes Scaliger as the grammarian who best deduces the usage of words from their origin by continuous sorites of figures of speech. See G. W. Leibniz, *Philosophical Papers and Letters*, trans. and ed. L. E. Loemker (Dordrecht: Reidel, 1970), p. 122.

[8]Francisco Sanchez El Brocense (1523–1600), Spanish humanist and professor of rhetoric at the University of Salamanca. The work mentioned here is *Minerva, sive de causis Linguae Latinae* (Salamanca, 1587).

[9]Gaspar Scioppius of Neumark (1576–1649).

THE FIRST BOOK

OR

BOOK OF METAPHYSICS

DEDICATED TO THE MOST

NOBLE GENTLEMAN

AND

OUTSTANDING PHILOSOPHER

PAOLO MATTIA DORIA

To begin with, then, I shall treat in this first book those locutions that provide a basis for conjectures regarding the opinions that those early sages of Italy held on the first truth, on God and on the human mind, and I have resolved to dedicate the book to you, Paolo Matteo Doria.[10] Or better, I have decided to discuss in these pages metaphysical matters under your auspices. For you take pleasure in these very lofty studies beyond other philosophical matters, as befits so able and learned a philosopher, and you cultivate them with a generosity and wisdom of the highest order. It is the mark of loftiness of

[10]Here and in *The Autobiography* Vico confesses that the only learned gentleman in Naples with whom he could discuss metaphysical problems was Paolo Mattia Doria. Vico, *The Autobiography*, trans. M. H. Fisch and T. G. Bergin (Ithaca: Cornell University Press, 1963), p. 138. Doria was born in 1666 in Genoa and in 1696 came to Naples, where he stayed until his death in 1746. Several times president of the Academy of Medinaceli, at first a convinced Cartesian, he adopted in his mature years a more conservative way of thinking. He defended the synthetic method in geometry and people's innate goodness in social philosophy, and dreamt of a synthesis of Plato, Augustine, and Descartes. His works include *La vita civile* (Augusta, 1710); *Considerazioni sopra il moto e la meccanica dei corpi sensibili e dei corpi insensibili* (Augusta, 1711; perhaps already in print in 1709); *Discorsi critici filosofici intorno alla filosofia degli antichi e dei moderni* (Venice, 1724); and *Difesa della metafisica degli antichi contro il Signore Giovanni Locke*, 2 vols. (Venice, 1732–33). For an interesting view on the Vico-Doria relation, see Jules Chaiz-Ruy, *La formation de la pensée philosophique de G. B. Vico* (Gap: L. Jean, 1943). Salvatore Bono's critical analysis (1955) of Doria's works has generated a great deal of research and scholarship. See *Rassegna di filosofia* 4 (1955):214–32. The best study in English on Doria and his relation to Vico is an essay by David Lachterman, "Vico, Doria and Synthetic Geometry," *Bollettino del Centro di Studi Vichiani* 10 (1980):10–35 (trans. B. Arcangeli). See also Harold Stone, "Vico and Doria: The Beginnings of Their Friendship," *New Vico Studies* 2 (1984):83–91.

spirit that you admire and praise the exceptional meditation of other sublime philosophers, but you expect still greater things of yourself and you produce them. And it is a mark of no lesser wisdom that you alone of all men of this generation have applied the primary truth (i.e., metaphysics) to human uses, adapting it in one way to mechanics and in another way to civil doctrine, and so forming a prince untouched by all the evil arts of rule with which Cornelius Tacitus and Niccolò Machiavelli endowed their prince. No teaching is more conformable than yours to Christian law, none more conducive to the prosperity of republics. But these are common merits of yours, recognized by all to whom even the mere fame of your most noble and illustrious name has reached. To these common merits are to be added your special merits in regard to me, in that you regard me, and all my affairs, most kindly in accordance with singular humanity; and you have most strongly encouraged me toward studies of this kind.

Last year, over dinner at your home, I put forth a discourse in which, starting from the very etymologies of the Latin language, I made nature consist in a motion through which all things are driven to the center of their respective movements by the force of a wedge, and expelled from the center to the edge by a converse force; and I held that all things come to be, live, and perish through a kind of systole and diastole.[11] Afterward you and Agostino Ariani,[12] Giacinto di Cristoforo, and Nicola Galizia,[13] citizens of our state, illustrious for their learning, adjured me to go to the root of the matter and present it as a thesis established with due order and method. And, therefore, I have developed this metaphysics by persisting on the same route of Latin origins, a metaphysics I hereby dedicate to you particularly among their company. For I shall dedicate something from my later studies to these three illustrious gentlemen in testimony of my gratitude and special deference.

[11]This theory was to appear in Vico's second book the *Liber Physicus*, of his projected philosophical system.

[12]Agostino Ariani (1672–1748), a teacher of mathematics and mathematician in his own right, is principally remembered for having introduced the theories of Newton to the University of Naples. See *Memorie della vita e degli scritti di Agostino Ariani, raccolti da Vincenzo Ariani, giureconsulto* (Naples, 1778).

[13]Nicola Galizia (1663–1730) and Giacinto di Cristoforo (1650–1725), both lawyers and mathematicians of an extremely modern and revolutionary cast of mind, were persecuted by the Holy Office as atheists and atomists. See Nicola Badaloni, *Introduzione a G. B. Vico* (Milan: Feltrinelli, 1961), pp. 192, 194, 235.

CHAPTER ONE

I. *Verum* and *Factum*

Latin "true" and "made" are the same—On understanding, thinking and reason—Man called "participant of reason"—The true is precisely the made—Why the first truth is in God—Why it is infinite and most complete—What knowing is—Thought is proper to man, understanding to God—Divine truth is a solid image of things, human truth a plane image—Science is cognition of how something is made—Why for the ancient Italian philosophers the true is the same as what has been made—The thing to be distinguished in our religion—Why divine wisdom is called the "Word"

For the Latins, *verum* (the true) and *factum* (what is made) are interchangeable, or to use the customary language of the Schools, they are convertible.[1] For them, the verb *intelligere* is the same as "to read perfectly" and "to have plain knowledge." In addition, their *cogitare* was the same as our vernacular "to think" (*pensare*) and "to gather" (*andar raccogliendo*). And for them, *ratio* meant the reckoning of arith-

[1]For the literary meaning of the terms, see Lewis and Short, s.v. *verum:* what is true or what is real and also a fact. Also s.v. *factum*, whose significance ranges from "done, performed, accomplished, prepared, produced, brought to pass, caused, effected, created, committed, perpetuated, formed, fashioned, made." For a possible etymological derivation of *verum* from the Hebrew *davur*, see Andrea Battistini, "Vico e l'etimologia mitopoietica," *Lingua e stile* 9 (1974):31–66. For the historical origin of the principle, see Rodolfo Mondolfo, *Il "verum-factum" prima di Vico. Studi Vichiani*, no. 1 (Naples: Guida, 1969). For the philosophical significance of the principle in Vico's development, see Ada LaMacchia, *Il verum-factum prima della Scienza nuova* (Bari: Ecumenica, 1978).

metical ratios as well as man's endowment by which he differs from and surpasses brute animals. Also, they commonly described man as an animate being, *rationis participem*, that is, as partaking of reason, but not always having full possession of it. Moreover, as words are symbols and signs of ideas, so ideas are symbols and signs of things. Therefore, just as *legere* (to read) is applied to one who combines the written elements of which words are composed, so *intelligere* (to understand) may be the combining of all parts of an object from which its most perfect idea may be expressed.

Hence, it is reasonable to assume that the ancient sages of Italy entertained the following beliefs about the true. "The true is precisely what is made" (*Verum esse ipsum factum*).[2] And, therefore, the first truth is in God, because God is the first Maker; this first truth is infinite, because He is the Maker of all things; it is completed truth, because it represents to Him all the elements of things, both external and internal, since He contains them.

But to know (*scire*) is to put together the elements of things. Hence, discursive thought (*cogitatio*) is what is proper to the human mind, whereas intelligence (*intelligentia*) is proper to God's mind. For God reads all the elements of things whether inner or outer, because He contains and disposes them in order, whereas the human mind, because it is limited and external to everything else that is not itself, is confined to the outside edges of things only and, hence, can never gather them all together. For this very reason it can indeed think about reality, but it can not understand it fully. On that account, the human mind partakes of reason, but does not possess it fully.

This can be illustrated by an analogy. Divine truth is a solid image like a statue; human truth is a monogram or a surface image like a painting. Just as divine truth is what God sets in order and creates in the act of knowing it, so human truth is what man puts together and makes in the act of knowing it. Thus, science is knowledge of the genus or mode by which a thing is made;[3] and by this very knowledge the mind makes the thing, because in knowing it puts together the elements of that thing. As we said, God makes a solid thing

---

[2]Literally, "The true is the thing made [or done] itself."

[3]See *NS*, 147: "The nature of institutions is nothing but their coming into being (*nascimento*) at certain times and in certain fashions. Whenever the time and fashion is thus and so, such and not otherwise are the institutions that come into being."

because He comprehends all the elements, man a plane image because he comprehends the outside elements only.

In order that the matters under discussion may be more easily reconciled with our own religion, we must recognize that the ancient sages of Italy considered the true and what is made convertible. For the gentile philosophers held the world to be eternal, and they worshiped a god who operated always from the outside—a tenet denied by our theology. In the context of our own religion, therefore, where we proclaim the world to have been created in time out of nothing, we need to make here the following distinction: created truth is interchangeable with what has been made, uncreated truth with what has been begotten. For this reason, Sacred Scripture, with its truly divine elegance, called the wisdom of God "the Word," in which the ideas of all things—as well as the elements of all ideas—are contained. For, in the divine Word, truth is identical with the comprehension of all the elements that constitute this universe of things, and which could, if He should wish, found countless worlds. And from these elements known to Him in His divine omnipotence, the real and most complete Word stands forth which since is known by the Father from eternity likewise from eternity was begotten by Him.[4]

II. The Origin and Truth of the Sciences

Why revealed theology is the most certain of all sciences—Human science is a kind of anatomy of nature—Objects of science differ in God and man—God is a being and creatures belong to being—The truly one is that which is unmultipliable—The infinite is without relation to body and is not bound by space—What are reasonings in man's mind are works in God's—Man has choice, God ineluctable will—For the Latins "separation" is the same as "diminution"—The method of division is useless with syllogisms; merely magical with numbers; blind guesswork with fire and solvents—Abstraction results from a defect in the human mind—Abstraction is the mother of human science—Man feigns for himself a world of numbers and forms—

[4]In the Christian tradition, the *verbum* is the *comprehensio elementorum et idearum*. It is the knowledge that stands forth from the holding together of elements and ideas, and *ideae* are generated from *elementa*. Then the *res* are created by the free motion of the *comprehensio*, the *verbum*.

Mathematics a productive science—God defines things according to the true; man defines names—Formal definition and nominal definition were the same for the Latins—The same fate has overtaken both human science and chemistry—The sciences that are most useful to the human race are those that are the most certain—The science in which the true is synonymous with what is made is similar to divine science—The criterion of the true is to have made it—The reason sciences are less certain the more they are immersed in matter—Those physical theories are approved which have something similar to our operations in them—When human truth is convertible with human good

On the basis of these tenets about the true maintained by the ancient sages of Italy and this distinction between what is made and what is begotten, which is adhered to in our own religion, we can take it as a principle that since truth is complete in God alone, we ought to proclaim as wholly true what God has revealed to us; and we ought not to ask what the genus and mode of that truth is, because we cannot wholly comprehend it. Starting from the same premise, we can trace the origin of the human sciences, and finally we can have the standards and a criterion for distinguishing what the true sciences are. God knows all things because in Himself He contains the elements with which He puts all things together. Man, on the other hand, strives to know these things by a process of division. Thus, human science is seen to be a kind of anatomy of nature's works.

For, by way of an enlightening example, human science has dissected man into body and mind, and mind into intellect and will. And from body it has picked out or, as men say, abstracted figure and motion, and from these, as well as from all other things, it has extracted being and unity. So metaphysics examines being; arithmetic, the unit and its multiplication; geometry, shape and its dimensions; mechanics, motion from the periphery; physics, motion from the center; medicine, the body; logic, reason; and moral philosophy, the will.

This anatomy of nature produces the same results as the everyday anatomy of the human body. The more acute physicians are in no little doubt about the location, structure, and function of the bodily parts and as to whether, for example, upon death the position and structure of the living body may not have altered, because of the solidification of the liquids, the cessation of motion, and the cutting up [in the autopsy]. Consequently, the functions of these same parts can no longer be explored.

For this being, this unity, this shape, motion, body, intellect, and will are different in God, in whom they are one, from what they are in man, in whom they are divided. In God they live, in man they die. For God is all things "eminently," as Christian theologians say, and the uninterrupted generation and corruption of beings do not affect Him at all, because they neither increase nor decrease Him. Limited and created beings are nothing but dispositions of the unlimited and everlasting being. Only God is truly a being, whereas all the rest belong to being. On this account, when Plato speaks of "being" absolutely, he understands the Supreme Deity.[5] But what need have we of Plato's testimony when God Himself defines Himself for us? "I am who am" or "I am who is,"[6] as if to say each and every thing *is not* in comparison with Him. And our own ascetics or Christian metaphysicians preach as follows: no matter how great we are, and whatever the reason for our greatness, before God we are nothing. And since God is uniquely one because He is infinite (for an infinite being cannot be multiplied), a created unity perishes with respect to Him. For the same reason, body perishes with respect to Him, since the immeasurable does not suffer measure; motion, which is defined by space, perishes because body perishes, inasmuch as space is filled with body. Our human reason perishes because, what are reasonings in us are works in God who has within Himself what He comprehends and to whom all things are present. Finally, our will is pliable, whereas that of God is ineluctable since He has no other goal set before Him than Himself alone, since He is perfectly good.

We can observe in Latin idioms the traces of what we have been talking about. For the same verb *minuere* means both to lessen and to separate;[7] as if what we separate may not fully be any longer what had been put together, but is diminished, changed, and corrupted. Is this perhaps the reason the so-called method of division (*via resolu-*

[5]The validity of this quotation is dubious. Probably Vico has in mind Plato's *Parmenides*, as sifted through the Neoplatonic tradition.

[6]A variation of Exodus 3:13–14.

[7]Vico's two senses are indeed the frequent metaphoric sense, "to lessen," and the rarer literal one, "to chop into smaller bits." See Lewis and Short, s.v. *minuere*.

tiva)[8] is found useless when it is employed by the Aristotelians upon genera and syllogism, or why it is mere magic when it proceeds in algebra by means of numbers? Or why it leads nowhere when it is used in chemistry for experimentation with fire and solvents?

For these reasons, then, when man embarks on the investigation of the nature of things, he realizes at length that he cannot arrive at that nature by any means, because he does not have within himself the elements from which composite things are constituted, and that this lack arises from the limitations of the human mind, to which everything is external. Man then turns this fault of his mind to good use and creates two things for himself through what is called "abstraction": the point that can be drawn and the unit that can be multiplied. Yet these are both fictions. For the point is no longer a point if you draw it; and the unit is no longer fully one if you multiply it. In addition, man has arrogated to himself the right to proceed from these fictions to infinity, so that he is allowed to project lines indefinitely and to multiply the unit countlessly. By this device,[9] man has created a kind of world of shapes and numbers which he can embrace entirely within himself, and by lengthening, shortening, or putting together lines, by adding, subtracting, or reckoning numbers, he achieves infinite effects because he knows infinite truths within himself.

Nor is it only in problems, but in the theorems themselves, which

[8]The logical process of indicating the species within a genus, the subspecies within the species, and so on. It is generally to be understood as a classificatory scheme constructed on the principle of genus and species. Historically, this method was first used by Plato as a substitute for the dialectic method, and it finds its best illustration in the *Sophist*. See W. M. Kneale, *The Development of Logic* (Oxford: Oxford University Press, 1962), pp. 9ff. It is interesting to note that Vico appeals to etymology to criticize the Aristotelian scholastic method of classification, which has reduced mathematics to magic and which is completely useless for any serious scientific investigation. It still is not clear to what this reduction amounts. Descartes, Pascal, and Newton are moderns who would not concede that the *via resolutiva* in algebra is mere divination.

[9]*Hoc pacto*, literally "by this convention," "on this assumption," also "on this basis." Almost all Italian translators disregard the specificity of the expression and render it "così," "in questo modo," "analogamente," "per tale modo" ("in this way"). *Opere filosofiche*, ed. P. Cristofolini, with an introduction by Nicola Badaloni (Florence: Sansoni, 1971) pp. 66, 68. See also *Giambattista Vico: Opere*, ed. F. Nicolini (Milan: Ricciardi, 1953), p. 263. For an important discussion on the significance of Vico's use of the expression *hoc pacto*, see Antonio Corsano, "Vico and Mathematics," in *Giambattista Vico: An International Symposium*, ed. Giorgio Tagliacozzo and Hayden White, (Baltimore: Johns Hopkins University Press, 1969), pp. 425–37.

are commonly supposed to involve contemplation alone, that there is need for construction.[10] For when the mind gathers the elements of the truth that it contemplates, it cannot do so except by making the truths it knows. Of course, the physicist cannot truly define things, that is, he cannot assign to each its own nature and thus truly make it, for that is God's right but is unlawful for man. So he defines the names themselves, and on the model of God[11] he creates from no substrate the point, the line, and the plane, as if from nothing and as if they were things.[12] Thus, he understands by the name "point" that which has not parts; by the designation "line" the extension or length of the point devoid of width and depth, and by the expression "plane" he understands the conjunction of two different lines at one point only, or a length and breadth with the depth cut off. On this basis, even though it is denied to him to have hold of those elements of things from which the things themselves exist for certain, he can feign for himself the elements of words from which ideas are stimulated without any controversy. And this, too, the wise authors of the Latin language perceived well enough. For we know that the Romans talked in such a way that they could speak indifferently of "what the name is" (*quaestio nominis*) or of "what the definition is" (*quaestio definitionis*). They considered that they were asking for a definition when they asked what response was stimulated generally in men's minds when a word was uttered.

From here you can see that the same fate has befallen both human

---

[10]Proclus (*Euclid*, 1:125) recorded a difference of opinions among the mathematicians of the academy on the distinction between "problems" and "theorems," claiming that Speusippus and Anphinomous held that all mathematical propositions should be called theorems, whereas Menaechmus wanted to call them problems. Vico knew Proclus's *Institutio Theologica* (see below, p. 181 and p. 173, n. 47). He must have read Proclus's *Commentary on Euclid* in the Italian translation by Francesco Barozzi (Padua, 1560). For an enlightening discussion on the distinction between theorems and problems, compare Alan C. Bowen, "Menaechmus versus the Platonists: Two Theories in the Early Academy," *Ancient Philosophy* 3, no. 1 (Spring 1983):12–29.

[11]*Ad Dei instar* (on the model of God); that is, we make truth as an image only of God's speaking word.

[12]Because God alone knows the nature of things, God alone offers a real definition of things. Aristotle's and, indirectly, Plato's theory of real definition, by means of which what is defined is the form or common nature of things, applies to God's knowledge only. Human knowledge must rest on a nominal definition in which we invent names, but Vico points out that because names are human inventions they are the source of noncontroversial ideas.

knowledge and chemistry. For just as chemistry in its pursuit of a vain goal has unintentionally given birth to an art that is effective and most beneficial to mankind—pharmaceutics—so likewise the quest of human curiosity for a truth denied to man by nature has begotten two sciences that are most useful to society—arithmetic and geometry—and from these, in turn, it has begotten mechanics, the parent of all the arts necessary to mankind. Therefore, human science was born of the vice of our mind, specifically from its extremely narrow compass, in that it is outside of everything and does not contain what it affects to know, and because it does not contain them, it does not actualize the truths it aims at. The most certain sciences are those that wash away the blemish of their origin and that become similar to divine science through their creative activity inasmuch as in these sciences that which is true and that which is made are convertible.

From what we have said thus far, you may quite rightly gather that the criterion and norm of the true is to have made it. Hence, our clear and distinct idea of the mind cannot be the criterion of the mind itself (let alone of other truths). For the mind does not make itself as it gets to know itself, and since it does not make itself, it does not know the genus or the mode by which it knows itself. Since human knowledge is purely abstractive, the more our sciences are immersed in bodily matter, the less certain they are. For instance, mechanics is less certain than geometry and arithmetic, because it deals with motion, but with the aid of machines; physics is less certain than mechanics, because mechanics treats the external motion of circumferences, whereas physics treats the internal motion of centers; morality is less certain than physics because the latter deals with those internal motions of bodies which are by nature certain, whereas morality examines the motions of minds which are most deeply hidden and arise mostly from desire, which is infinite. Hence, too, those theories are approved in physics which have some similarity to what we do.[13] For this reason, hypotheses about the natural order are considered most illuminating and are accepted with the fullest consent of everyone, if we can base experiments on them, in which we make something similar to nature.

Thus, to sum up in one word, when a known truth owes its existence to the mind that knows it, then the true coincides with the

---

[13]"Atque indidem in physica ea meditata probantur, quarum simile quid operemur."

good. In this way, human knowing can be a copying of divine knowledge, in which God as He knows the truth generates it *inwardly* from
eternity and creates it *outwardly* in time. In the case of God, the
criterion of truth is His having communicated goodness to His
thoughts in the process of creation, for "God saw that they were
good";[14] to this may be compared on man's side our having made the
truths that we know.

But in order that these things may be more firmly established in
their places, we must defend our position against the dogmatists and
the skeptics.[15]

III. The First Truth Meditated by René Descartes

Metaphysics assigns the subjects to every other science—Dividing line between dogmatics and skeptics—Descartes's tricky demon same as Stoics'
divinely sent dream and similar to Mercury's impersonation of Sosia in Plautus's *Amphitruo*—Consciousness different from knowledge—What knowledge and consciousness are—Hidden causes of thought also hidden in our
religion—Human mind feigned to be like a spider by our metaphysicians—
Whether knowledge of being arises from consciousness of thought—What
knowledge is according to the skeptics

The dogmatists of our troubled times consider all truths doubtful
until metaphysically justified—not only those that are established in
practical life, such as the truth of morality and mechanics, but also the
truths of physics and even those of mathematics. For these philosophers teach that metaphysics alone provides us with an indubitable
truth and from it, as from a wellspring, flow in the other sciences
secondary truths. This is because no truths of the other sciences can
demonstrate what [kinds of] being there are and that, of those kinds,
mind is one and body another. So these other sciences cannot be
certain what are the subjects of which they treat. For this reason, the
metaphysicians deem that metaphysics alone gives to each science its
proper foundations. Therefore, the great Meditator bids the postulant

[14]Genesis 1:12.
[15]For a Kantian reading of this passage, see G. Gentile, *Studi Vichiani* (Florence: Le
Monnier, 1927), pp. 107–46.

for initiation to approach the holy of holies of metaphysics with minds purified not only from those convictions or prejudices that arise in thought from infancy because of those deceitful messengers, the senses, but even from all the truths he has learned from other sciences. And since he cannot forget and so cannot attend to the metaphysicians with a mind like a blank tablet, let him do so with a mind like a rolled scroll, a scroll that he can later unroll in a better light. The dividing line between skeptics and dogmatists is, therefore, the primary truth that the metaphysics of Descartes has unveiled to us. And that dividing line is, the mighty philosopher teaches us, as follows.

Man can call into question whether he feels, lives, occupies space, and even whether he exists at all. In support of this argument, our philosopher adduces the aid of a certain tricky demon who can deceive us, just as the Stoic in Cicero's *Academica*[16] resorts to a device, and uses a god-sent dream to prove the very same things. But in no way at all, Descartes claims, can anyone remain unaware that he thinks, and from this awareness of his thinking, he can gather for certain that he is. So our René has revealed this to be the primary truth: "I think, therefore I am." And just as we are put in doubt by Descartes's tricky demon and by the god-sent dream of the Stoic, so likewise the character Sosia in Plautus was brought to the point of doubting whether he was, by Mercury, who had assumed the form of Sosia. Sosia meditated on his double and found peace of mind in this primary truth:

> By Pollux I recognize my own form when I regard him.
> He is as much like me as my own reflection in a mirror.
> He wears the same hat and garb; he is my spit and image.
> Legs, feet, stance, haircut, eyes, nose, teeth, lips,
> cheeks, chin, beard and neck are, one and all, my own.
> Need I say more? If his back is scarred, there is nothing
> more like to this likeness [than me]. But when *I think*,
> *I am for certain* the same man I have always been.[17]

Yet the skeptic does not doubt that he thinks. On the contrary, he professes that what he seems to himself to see[18] is certain; and he

---

[16]*Academica*, II, 15, 47.
[17]Plautus, *Amphitruo*, 441–47.
[18]*Quod sibi videre videatur* (of what he seems to himself to see [as the truth]).

professes so obstinately that he defends his view by chicanery and insults. Nor does he doubt that he exists. Rather, he assures his well-being by suspending judgment in order not to add the burdens of opinion to the burdens already inherent in things themselves. But he contends that the certainty that he thinks is consciousness (*conscientia*),[19] not knowledge (*scientia*). It is an ordinary cognition that happens to any unlearned person such as Sosia, not a rare and esoteric truth, which requires for its discovery such deep meditation by the greatest of philosophers. For to know is to grasp the genus or the form by which a thing is made, but consciousness is of those things whose genus or form we cannot demonstrate. So throughout the course of our daily living, we may invoke our consciousness as evidence for things for which no [causal] sign or [genetic] explanation (*argumentum*) is granted to us.[20] But although the skeptic is conscious that he thinks, he nevertheless is not conscious of the causes of thought or of how thought originates, and he emphatically proclaims in our days that he is unaware of this, since we proclaim in our religion that the human soul is a thing quite devoid of all corporeality.

This is where those thorns and brambles come from, with which the subtlest metaphysicians of our time scratch one another and get pricked in turn, when they inquire how the human mind acts on the body or the body on the mind, since only bodies can touch other bodies and be touched by them. Driven by these difficulties, they resort to a mysterious law of God as to a device, explaining that the nerves arouse the mind when they are moved by external objects and the mind pulls on the nerves when it wishes to act. Thus, they feign the human mind to be in a pineal gland, like a spider resting in the middle of its web. When a thread of the web is moved in any direction, the spider feels it. However, when the spider feels a thunderstorm coming on, the web being still, she can make all the threads move with it. They cite this mysterious law because they do not know the genus through which thought is produced, and for this reason the skeptic will assert stubbornly that he has no knowledge of thinking.

The dogmatist, in contrast, would answer that the skeptic acquires knowledge of his being from awareness of his thinking, since the unshakable certainty of existence is born from his awareness of thinking. And, of course, no one can be wholly certain that he exists unless

---

[19]*Conscientia.* I have used consciousness and awareness interchangeably.

[20]I take *signum* and *argumentum* to refer to the genus and form held by one who has true knowledge.

he makes up his own being out of something he cannot doubt.[21] Consequently, the skeptic cannot be certain that he is because he does not gather his existence from a wholly undoubted principle.

To all this the skeptic will respond by denying that knowledge of being is acquired from consciousness of thinking. For, he argues, to know (*scire*) is to be cognizant (*nosse*) of the causes out of which a thing is born. But I who think am mind and body, and if thought were the cause of my being, thought would be the cause of the body. Yet there are bodies that do not think. Rather, it is because I consist both of body and mind that I think; so that body and mind united are the cause of thought. For if I were only body, I would not think. If I were only mind, I would have [pure] intelligence. In fact, thinking is the sign, and not the cause, of my being mind. But the sure sign (*techmerium*)[22] is not the cause, for the clever skeptic will not deny that certainty of sure [rational] signs, but just the certainty of causes.

IV. Against the Skeptics

God is the comprehension of all causes—Divine knowledge is the norm of human knowledge

To be sure, there is no other way in which skepticism can indeed be refuted, except that the criterion of the true should be to have made the thing itself. For the skeptics profess that things do appear to them, but they say that they are ignorant of what these appearances are in reality. They admit the effects and, hence, concede that these effects have their own causes. But they deny that they know the causes, because they are ignorant of the genera, or forms, from which each thing is made. You may turn their own argument against them in this way.

This comprehension of causes, in which all genera are contained, or all the forms whereby all effects result, whose likeness the skeptics admit to be presented to their minds even though they do not know

---

[21]Vico pairs *conficio* with *conscientia* and *facio* with *scientia*.

[22]Here is an example that explains the meaning of *signum*, above. (See n. 20.) Also see Liddell and Scott, s.v. Τεχμήριον (II, esp. II, 3).

what they are [likenesses of] in reality, is the first truth. It is the first truth because it comprehends all [causes] in which the ultimate ones also are contained.[23] Because it comprehends all, it is infinite, for it excludes none. And because it comprehends all, it is prior to body, of which it is the cause, and hence it is something spiritual. Therefore, it is God and, indeed, the God whom we Christians confess. We ought to measure human truths by the norm of this truth. For, of course, those truths are human truths, the elements of which we shape (*fingamus*) for ourselves, which we contain within ourselves, and which we project ad infinitum (to infinity) through postulates; and when we combine them, we make the truths that, by combining them, we come to know. And because of all this we have hold of the genus and form by which we make [these things].

[23]*Omnes* could signify *omnes causas*. But Vico seems to use *formal* for the intermediate causes of appearances.

CHAPTER TWO. GENERA OR IDEAS

For the Latins *genus* (kind) and *forma* (idea) synonymous—*Species* signifies an individual entity and a copy—How genera are infinite—Metaphysical form is the potter's form; physical form, the seed's form—Physical forms are formed from the metaphysical ones—The utility of forms—Why geometry through forms is very certain both in procedure and results—Why geometry through species is uncertain in its procedure but certain in its results—Why fine arts attain their goal with certainty—Why conjectural arts are not like that—The uselessness of the Aristotelian genera—Why sciences are less useful the more general they are—The advantages of experimental physics—Jurists rated by the exceptions [they make], not by [their use of] rules—Best pleaders stick to the particulars of a case—Who are the useful historians?—Imitators good when circumstances improve—Origin of the Platonic hierarchy of ideas—Wisdom is not concerned with those things contained in a genus—How genera are metaphysical matter—Noteworthy difference between physical and metaphysical matter—Wrongs produced by the universals in jurisprudence, medicine, and practical life—All errors are due to homonymy of reference to genera—Men avoid homonymy by natural instinct—Whether genera have led philosophers into error more than the senses have led the vulgar into prejudices—The meaning of *certum* for the Latins—*Verum* and *aequum* synonymous for the Latins—Because man is neither nothing nor everything, he can perceive neither—The universals have a certain function as archetypes

When the Latins say *genus* (kind), they understand form. When they say *species* (appearance), they mean two things, namely, what the Schoolmen call *individuum* (individual) and *simulacrum* (copy) or

appearance.[1] Every school of philosophy agrees that genera are infinite. It follows, therefore, that the ancient philosophers of Italy must
have held that genera are forms infinite not in amplitude, but in
perfection and that because they are infinite, they are in one God.
They also must have held that species, or singular things, are likenesses in accord with these forms.[2] Indeed, if for the ancient sages of
Italy the true is identical with that which is made, then genera must
for them have been forms and not the universals of the Schoolmen.

By "forms" I understand metaphysical forms, which differ from
physical forms in the same way that the form of the potter differs
from that of the seed. For the form of the potter remains the same
while something is being modeled on it, and it is always more perfect
than its copy. But the form of the seed changes and improves as it
unfolds day by day. As a result, physical forms are themselves
formed from metaphysical forms. We can easily conclude that genera
are to be considered infinite for their perfection and not for their
range, once we have compared the utility of both [genera and univer-
sals].[3] Geometry, which is taught according to the synthetic method—that is, by means of forms—is most certain both in its process
and in its results. Through its postulates, geometry proceeds from the
smallest elements to infinity, and in this way teaches us how to combine the elements out of which the truths that it demonstrates are
formed. Thus, it shows us the way to combine the elements because
man possesses within himself those elements that geometry teaches.
But for that reason analytic geometry, even though it produces results
that are certain, is nevertheless procedurally uncertain, because it

[1]Here Vico reduces the Aristotelian genus to the Platonic form and the Aristotelian
species to the individual. To his own satisfaction, Vico solves the problems of the
universals by reducing the universal to the Platonic individuals.

[2]The introduction of singular general ideas replacing abstract general ideas is not
completely foreign to the influence of Augustine and Malebranche and is also one of
the most interesting points on which Berkeley differs from Locke. A comparison can be
made between what Vico says here and what Berkeley claims in the introduction to his
Treatise: "Now if we will annex a meaning to our words, and speak only of what we can
conceive, I believe we shall acknowledge that an idea which considered in itself is
particular, becomes general by being made to represent or stand for all other, particular
ideas of the same sort." Berkeley, Introduction, *A Treatise Concerning the Principles of
Human Knowledge,* in *The Works of G. Berkeley,* ed. A. A. Luce and T. E. Jessop (London:
Nelson, 1949), 2:31.

[3]I read *utrorum* as referring to *genera* and *universalia* because every other possible pair
is feminine. None of the Italian translators makes this clear.

takes its subject matter from the infinite and descends from there to the smallest element. That all things can be found in the infinite is evident, but in what way you are to find them there is not.[4]

The arts that teach the genera, or modes, by which their subject matter comes to be—such as painting, sculpture, ceramics, and architecture—achieve the goals they have set for themselves with greater certainty. These arts are more certain than those that do not teach the modes, and hence are all conjectural, such as rhetoric, politics, and medicine. The former surely do teach securely these modes because they are molded on prototypes the human mind possesses within itself; the latter do not, because man does not have within him any form of the things he conjectures. And because forms are individual in the sense that, for example, a single line—more or less long, wide, or deep—deforms a figure so that you would not recognize it as the same one. Hence, it happens that the more the arts and sciences are founded upon Aristotelian instead of Platonic genera, the more they confuse the forms; and the more magnificent they turn out, the less useful they become.

That is why Aristotelian physics has a bad reputation nowadays for its extreme generality. In contrast to this, the experimental use of fire and machinery as instruments in recent physics which brings about effects similar to the singular works of nature herself has enriched mankind with countless truths. Similarly, in jurisprudence it is not the jurist who because of his strong memory masters "thetic" or positive law,[5] the highest and most general law, who is well thought of; it is, rather, the jurist who can see with acute judgment the distinctive characteristics[6] in his cases, the circumstances through which they deserve the application of equity, or the exceptions through which they escape from the general law. The finest orators are not those who wander among common places, but those who "stick to particulars" (to echo a verdict and a phrase of Cicero).[7] Again, the useful historians are not those who crudely narrate the facts and their general causes, but those who hunt out the ultimately distinctive

---

[4]Analytic (Cartesian) geometry assumes the whole, without questioning it, and proceeds to divide it. Synthetic (Euclidean) geometry construes and makes its figures; hence it alone satisfies the limit placed on the science by the *verum-factum*.

[5]The thetic law (*jus theticum*); positive and dogmatic.

[6]*Ultimas peristases* (distinctive characteristics).

[7]The phrase here is not Cicero's.

circumstances of the situations and uncover the causes peculiar to them. And in the arts, which thrive on imitation—such as painting, sculpture, ceramics, and poetry—those men excel who can embellish an archetype taken from common nature with traits that are not common, or with new and marvelous features; or those who set off an archetype first expressed by another artist, with better features of their own, and so make it theirs. Some of these archetypes can be better feigned in effigy[8] than others, because the models always surpass their copies; hence the Platonists construct a hierarchy of ideas; and by way of ideas of increasing perfection, they ascend by a flight of steps, so to speak, right to the supreme, best, and greatest God, who contains within Himself the best ideas of everything.

In fact, wisdom itself is nothing but the skillful care of what is fitting, which enables the wise man to speak and act in every new situation in such a way that nothing equally apt for the purpose could be derived and adapted from elsewhere. Consequently, the wise man has a mind disciplined by such long and frequent practice upon right and useful things that he receives the impressions of new situations exactly as they are, and just as he is always ready to speak and act with dignity in all situations, so also he is brave and has a mind equally ready for all unexpected terrors. But new, surprising, and unexpected situations are not provided for by those universal genera [of the Schools]. The Schoolmen speak neatly enough in this connection when they call genera "metaphysical matter," but only if this is taken to mean that the mind becomes in a certain way formless through the genera, so that it can more easily take on the specific forms. This is quite true to be sure, for the man who possesses the genera, or simple ideas of things, perceives facts and events as they ought to be perceived more easily than the man who has equipped his mind with peculiar forms and looks at other, different forms in the light of his own odd ones; for it is only with difficulty that one formed thing is adjusted to another; and for this reason it is hazardous to make decisions on the basis of examples, since the factual circumstances of two situations never, or hardly ever, coincide. This is the

---

[8]*Confingi.* Again *confingo* goes with *conscientia,* just as *fingo* goes with *scientia.* The mathematician *feigns* intellectual elements of God's spiritual activity; the artist only feigns the phenomenal things of ordinary natural consciousness. If imitating God's creative activity is feigning, then it seems appropriate to call copying God's created works "feigning in effigy."

difference between physical and metaphysical matter. Physical matter evolves the best form for itself, no matter how peculiar that form may be, since the way it evolved was the only possible way. Because all peculiar forms are imperfect, however, so metaphysical matter contains the best form in the kind itself or in the idea.

We have seen the usefulness of the forms. Now let us survey the harmfulness of the universals. To speak with universal words is proper to babies and savages. On the whole, in jurisprudence errors arise most frequently under the influence of positive law or under the authority of rules. In medicine, those who carefully follow the book work harder at keeping their medical systems intact than at healing the ill. How often men sin in the business of living, because they arranged their life according to their maxims (*themata*)! Just for them we have brought into our vernacular a Greek word so that we can label them "thematics."

All philosophical errors arise from homonyms, which are commonly called equivocations. Yet equivocations are nothing but words that signify more than one thing. For without genera equivocations would not exist, since men are naturally averse to homonymy. For instance, if you were to tell a boy to summon John and to say nothing else in a case where there were two people named John, the boy, because nature heeds particulars, would ask at once, "Which John do you want me to summon?" So I do not know whether [universal] genera lead the philosophers into errors more than the senses lead the vulgar into false convictions or prejudices. For in our way of speaking, [universal] genera confuse the form or, as [the dogmatists put it], they produce confused ideas, no less than prejudices produce obscure ones. And in fact all the sects in philosophy, medicine, jurisprudence, and all controversies and quarrels in daily life arise from [universal] genera, since those homonymies or equivocations that are said to be caused by mistake arise from them. This is the case in physics because the nouns *matter* and *form* are generic; in jurisprudence because the term *just* ranges far and wide; in medicine because the words *healthy* and *sick* are far too broad; and in practical life because the expression *useful* has not been defined.

Traces survive in Latin of the fact that the ancient philosophers of Italy had the same view. Latin *certum* (certain) means two things: both what is explored and indubitable, and the peculiar as opposed to the common—as if what is peculiar [to me] were certain [for me], but what is common were, so to speak, dubious. And for the Latins *verum* (true) and *aequum* (equitable) were synonymous,[9] for the latter concerns the ultimate circumstances of cases, whereas *iustum* (just) concerns the genus itself; as if those things constituted in a generical manner were false, and the ultimate species of things were true. But the truth is that those genera are only nominally infinite, since man is neither nothing nor everything. Consequently, he cannot think about nothing, except by the negation of something; nor can he think about the infinite, except by the negation of the finite. Yet every triangle has angles equal to two right angles. Quite right! But this is not for me[10] an infinite truth. Rather, I know it because I have the form of the triangle imprinted on my mind and I recognize this property of that form, which is for me the archetype of other triangles. If [the universalists] argue that this truth[11] is an infinite kind because countless triangles correspond to this archetype, I will let them have their own way. For I will gladly give in to them about the word[12] if they will agree with me about the thing.[13] But all the same, those who want to say that the yardstick is infinite because every extension can be measured by that standard are talking nonsense.

[9]See *NS*, 324.

[10]For me as a human thinker generally, not as a sectarian philosopher.

[11]" . . . et ea mihi est archetypus ceterorum. Si vero id contendant esse infinitum genus . . ." I refer *id* to *verum*. Perhaps the gender is only accommodated to *genus* following, but there is *ea [forma] est archetypus*, so it is unlikely that Vico would let ambiguity in here.

[12]*Universal*.

[13]Singular genus or form.

CHAPTER THREE. CAUSES

For the Latins *causa* and *negotium* are synonymous—Why what arises from cause is called effect—To prove something from causes is to effect it—Effect is the true synonymous with that which is made—Genera of causes—To prove from causes is to gather the elements of things—Arithmetic and geometry truly prove from causes—Physics cannot be proved from causes—Any finite entity at all is produced by an infinite power—Christian sages recognize God's infinite power in the smallest body—It is impious piety to want to prove God from causes—The clarity of metaphysical truth the same as that of light—The most appropriate analogy for this

For the Latins the terms *causa* (cause or case) and *negotium*[1] (business and activity) are synonymous. And what is born of a cause they call the effect. This, too, appears to be consistent with what I have argued regarding the true and the made. For if the true is what is made, to prove something from causes is the same as to make it. Thus, cause and business will be the same, namely, activity, just as the true and what is made will be the same, namely, the effect. Furthermore, matter and form in the natural sciences, value in moral

[1]The term *nec-otium* literally signifies being in a state of not-idleness—hence, operation and activity. In addition, *negotium* is synonymous with cause, only, however, when it indicates a litigation in court. Therefore, it is only in the legal and business sense of "case" and "affair" that *causa* is identical with *negotium*. Vico is arguing that the word *cause* in nature is identified with *case* in social affairs because, in these affairs, we are the cause. This is not an intelligible identity, but an identity of experience; hence Vico says *confundo*.

[64]

philosophy, and the author in metaphysics are all considered principal causes. Therefore, it is likely that the ancient philosophers of Italy believed that proving from causes consists in giving order to the matter or the chaotic elements of a thing, and composing its scattered parts into a whole; for from that order and composition of the elements a definite form of the thing arises which induces a peculiar nature in the matter.

If this is true, arithmetic and geometry, which commonly are not considered proven from causes, do truly supply proof from causes. And they do so because the human mind contains the elements of the truths that it can order and compose; and it is through the disposition and composition of these elements that the truth they demonstrate arises; so that demonstration is the same as construction, and the true is the same as the made. And for that very reason, we cannot prove physical facts from causes, because the elements of natural things are external to us. For although they are finite, an infinite potency (*virtus*) is required for their ordering and composition, and to make them effectively exist. Indeed, if we were to consider the first cause, it would require no less potency to produce an ant than to have created this universe of things; for the motion by which this world was created out of nothing contributes no less to the formation of an ant out of its substrate matter than to the genesis of the world itself.

Just see how often the sage of our religion (I mean those who have been most illustrious both for their cognition of the Deity and for the sanctity of their morals) have arrived at the thought of God in their ascetic sermons through meditations on a little flower because they acknowledge the infinite power involved in its generation.[2] (And this was what I said, too, in my essay *On the Method of Studies of Our Time*: "We demonstrate geometrical truths because we make them; if we could demonstrate physical facts, we would make them."[3] On this account, those who strive to prove the existence of God Almighty a priori must be found guilty of impious curiosity. For to do this would be equivalent to making themselves the God of God and denying the God whom they seek. The clarity of metaphysical truth is equal to

[2]Saint Francis's "Song of Brother Sun" could be an example of the mystic approach to the discovery of God through the humblest of His creatures. See *I fioretti di San Francesco*, ed. Adolfo Padovan (Milan: Ulrico Hoepli, 1915), pp. 236–37.

[3]*De Nostri Temporis Studiorum Ratione*, in *Opere di G. B. Vico*, ed. F. Nicolini and G. Gentile (Bari: Laterza, 1968), p. 85.

that of the light that we can only apprehend through opacity. Try, after having gazed long and hard at a leaded window that lets in the light, to direct your line of vision on an entirely opaque body; you will seem to see the shining panes but not the light. This is the way a metaphysical truth is luminous, bounded by no limit and distinguished by no form; for it is the infinite principle of all forms. Physical facts are opaque, that is to say, they are formed and finite, and in them we see the light of the metaphysical truth.

CHAPTER FOUR

I. Essences or Powers

Essence called *vis* and *potestas* by the Latins—Science is about eternal and unchangeable things—The *dei immortales* of the Latins are the infinite powers of all things—Why metaphysics is the truest of all sciences

What the Schoolmen designate as *essentia* (essence) the Latins call *vis* (force) and *potestas* (power). And all philosophers agree that essences are eternal and unchangeable. Aristotle explicitly asserts that they are individual or, as the Schoolmen say, they consist of the indivisible; and Plato, following Pythagoras, considers that science deals with the eternal and unchangeable.

Thus, we may fairly surmise that the ancient philosophers of Italy held that individual essences were the eternal and infinite powers of all things. The vulgar used to call them "immortal gods," whereas the wise acknowledged in them the One Supreme Deity. For this reason, the Latins considered metaphysics to be the only true science, because it alone treats of the eternal powers. Hence, we may legitimately question whether, whenever motion and conatus (which is the power of motion) are given, extension and the power by which something is extended are given likewise. Moreover, just as matter and motion are the proper subject of physics, so conatus and power of extension belong to metaphysics. You are my authority, most illustrious Paolo, for this tenet that there are actions in physics and powers in metaphysics.[1]

II. Metaphysical Points and Conatus

For the Latins *momentum* and *punctum* are synonymous, and signify indivisibility—The theory of metaphysical points was [first] asserted in Italy—After metaphysics, geometry and mathematics have the greatest truth—Metaphysics is the source of all truths—The way truth flows from metaphysics to geometry—The power of extension is prior to the extended body, and hence it is unextended—The power of number is not a number—How the definition of a point is nominal—Geometry treats the simple matter that metaphysics supplies to it—The geometrical point is the symbol of the metaphysical point; and the metaphysical point is the power of physical matter—Verdict upon Pythagorean and Zenonian physics—Four types of philosophers—Zeno's type, Descartes's type—Why Descartes and Epicurus are mistaken on the principles of physics, but make successful progress—Whether Aristotle's demonstrations hurt or help Zeno—God is the accumulation of all perfections—In God conatus is rest, and the power of extension is mind—Division is a physical motion and thing—Divisibility is a power and a metaphysical essence—Aristotle disagrees with Zeno about other things, but agrees with him here—Aristotle's demonstrations against the metaphysical points are based on the definitions of a geometrical point—Zeno contemplates a metaphysics that has come down from geometry to physics—The power of extension is indivisible and for this reason it is spread out equally under unequal extensions—Conatus equally underlies unequal motions—Conatus is the attribute of a point—Nature began to exist through conatus; conatus is the mean between rest and motion—The point is the mean between God and the extended thing—God is rest—Matter is conative—Extended bodies are moved—Basis of Descartes's arguments on the reflection and refraction of motion—Both small and large entities are equally distant from nothing—Division is an evil; goodness is indivisible—There is in metaphysics a kind of unextended thing that is capable of extension—Descartes brings analysis into physics; Zeno views physics synthetically—Aristotle introduces metaphysics into physics without any hypothesis—Descartes raised physics to the level of metaphysics—It is fallacious to think about physics

---

[1]This should be taken not only as a token of respect, but also as a sincere recognition of Doria's influence on Vico's metaphysics. See David Lachterman, "Vico, Doria and Synthetic Geometry," *Bollettino del Centro di Studi Vichiani* 10 (1980):22–35.

metaphysically and about metaphysics physically—How the infinite descends to finite entities is incomprehensible—It is a fault of the human mind to know distinctly—The clarity of metaphysical truth is the same as that of light—Metaphysical light or the leading powers into action is produced by conatus

For the Latins, *point* and *momentum* were synonymous. But momentum is a thing that moves, and hence for them both *point* and *momentum* meant an indivisible something.[2] Is it the case, then, that the ancient philosophers of Italy held the view that there is a certain indivisible power of extension and motion? And did this theory, like so many others, cross the seas from Italy to Greece, where Zeno[3] later reshaped it? For, to my mind, no one felt more correctly about this indivisible power of extension and motion[4] than the Stoics, who treated it in the hypothesis of the metaphysical point.

To begin with, there is no doubt that geometry and arithmetic, above all the other sciences that are called subaltern, are either absolutely true or certainly bear in themselves quite an exceptional resemblance to the truth. And yoked with this is the other primary truth, that metaphysics is the source of all truth, the fount from which it flows to all the other sciences. Everyone realizes that geometricians derive their synthetic constructions from the point and rapidly progress to the contemplation of infinity by means of those frequent postulates of theirs, with the result that it is possible for them to project lines indefinitely. So if someone asks how truth, or the near

[2]*Momentum* for *movimentum* from *moveo*. Also *Momentum staterae*, a particle sufficient to turn the scales. See Isaiah 40:15 (Vulg.). Hence, a particle, a point. It is Vico's inference, however, that both *momentum* and *punctum* mean an indivisible something.

[3]There has been common agreement among scholars that Vico makes the mistake, so common in his time, of confusing Zeno the Eleatic (fl. 464 B.C.), founder of the dialectic, and Zeno the Stoic (d. 264 B.C.), founder of the Stoic school. Vico combines Eleatic principles with Stoic elements and creats a pseudo-Zeno, who becomes the forerunner of his own metaphysics, and who explained the origin of multiplicity from the One by the hypothesis of indivisible metaphysical points. The whole discussion actually is minimized, because as Vico later confesses, the only true authority for the metaphysical points is Vico himself.

[4]This specific reference to the Stoics is correct, as they maintained a pantheistic, materialistic physics and granted the existence of forces (*vires*) or tensions that were not separated from material substance, but lived and coexisted with it. It was force that caused the ebb and flow of the universe. Vico accepts this motion from the Stoics in general and from Zeno in particular.

semblance of truth, flows from metaphysics into geometry, there is to be sure no other road save the perilous gateway of the point. For geometry has borrowed from metaphysics the power of extension, which, because it is a power, is prior to extension—in other words, it is unextended. In like manner, the arithmetician has borrowed from metaphysics the power of number, namely the one, which because it is the power of number is not a number. And even as the one, which is not a number, generates number, so the point, which is not extended, gives birth to extension. The geometrician's definition of the point as that which has no part is a nominal definition,[5] since no thing exists that has no parts, and yet you can draw it in your mind or with your pencil. Likewise, the definition of the one among mathematicians is also nominal because they present us with a unit that is multipliable and, therefore, is not in reality a one.

The Zenonians, instead, consider that definition of the point as the definition of a real thing, inasmuch as the point is the image of what the human mind is capable of thinking in regard to the indivisible power of extension and motion.[6] Therefore, the common belief that geometry purifies or, as the Schoolmen say, geometry "abstracts" its major concepts from matter is false. For the Zenonians believed that no science treated matter more exactly than geometry—meaning the simple matter that metaphysics supplies to geometry, namely the power of extension. Nor would Aristotle's[7] demonstrations about metaphysical points against the Zenonians have such great weight among his followers if the geometrical point were not a symbol for the Stoics like the metaphysical point and the metaphysical point were not the power of physical body.[8] For that matter, neither Pythagoras nor his followers (among whom we know of Timeus through Plato) believed, when they examined natural matters by means of numbers, that nature truly consists of numbers. Rather, they aimed to explain

---

[5]*Euclid's Elements*, trans. Thomas L. Heath (New York: Dover, 1956), Book 1, def. 1, p. 153.

[6]In other words, both the Euclidean "point" and "unit" are theoretical constructs; their definitions are nominal insofar as neither term denotes any existing thing. But the definition of "the Zenonian" (actually Vico's) is real insofar as it connotes what the mind can think about the "indivisible power of extension and motion."

[7]For the arguments against Zeno's paradoxes, see Aristotle, *Physics*, vi, 9, 239 b11 (Dichotomy), vi, 9, 239 b16 (the Achilles), vi, 239 b5–7 (the Arrow), vi, 9, b33–240 a18 (the Stadium).

[8]On *vis* according to the Stoics, see n. 4, above.

the world external to them in terms of the world they contained within themselves.[9] We must pass the same judgment on Zeno and the Zenonians, who held that points were the principles of things.[10]

Truly, throughout all human memory, we can establish four classes of philosophers. The first were outstanding geometricians who discussed physical principles on the basis of mathematical hypotheses. Such was Pythagoras. The second are those educated in geometry and devoted students of metaphysics who thought about the principles of things on the basis of no hypothesis, but discuss the things of nature in the metaphysical mode. Such was Aristotle. The third class, ignorant of geometry and hostile to metaphysics, devised a simple extended body for use as matter (i.e., the atomic theory). And although they made grave mistakes right at the outset in their explanation of principles, still they thought more successfully about the specific phenomena of nature. Such was Epicurus. Finally, the fourth class claimed that the principles of everything were body in its quantity and quality. Among the ancients such were those who spoke of earth, water, air, and fire, either singly or coupled or as group; and among the moderns, such as the chemists.[11] Yet these men have made no worthwhile contribution to the discussion of principles. Explanations of specific natural phenomena upon their principles were successful only in those few instances where daring rather than forethought gave them the answer.

Zeno, the supreme metaphysician, adhered to the hypotheses of the geometricians and explained the origin of things by means of points, just as Pythagoras did it by means of numbers. But Descartes, equally eminent, both in metaphysics and in geometry, adhered to the teaching of Epicurus. Descartes makes up for his blunders of principle about motion and the formation of the elements in the plenum, just as Epicurus makes up for his blunders about the void and the swerve of the atoms by his success in explaining specific natural

[9]Vico relies on a Neoplatonic reading of the *Timaeus* as a document of the Pythagorean doctrine. Hence, this interpretation of conceptual and supersensible numbers, which has Platonic as well as Augustinian overtones.

[10]The forces of the Stoics.

[11]A probable reference to some members of the Academy of the Investigators. For a detailed discussion of the history of the academy, see Max H. Fisch, "The Academy of the Investigators," in *Science, Medicine, and History: Essays on the Evolution of Scientific Thought and Medical Practice Written in Honour of Charles Singer*, ed. E. Ashworth Underwood, 2 vols. (London: Oxford University Press, 1953).

phenomena. May the reason [for success and failure] be that both of them explain natural things by means of shapes and mechanisms? For the specific effects of nature are formed and mobile things, whereas for principles and powers there is no explanatory shape because they are shapeless, and no mechanism because they are indefinite.

What we have said so far has been for the propounding and validating of Zeno's view.[12] Let us now present the arguments implicit in our problem.

Aristotle proves by geometrical demonstrations that the smallest possible particles of an extended entity may be divided to infinity.[13] But Zeno remains unmoved by these demonstrations of Aristotle; indeed, he finds in them a confirmation of his own metaphysical points.[14] For it is fitting that the power of this physical thing should be granted in metaphysics; otherwise, how can God be the sum of all perfections? Obviously, extended entities do exist in nature, but it is sinful to speak of something extended in God. We measure the extended, but the infinite defies measure. Indeed, it is entirely right for the power of extension to be contained in God "eminently," as our theologians say. Therefore, just as conatus is the power of motion, and in God as author of conatus, it is rest, so too primary matter is the power of extension, which in God as the founder of matter is the purest mind. There is, therefore, a substance in metaphysics which is

[12]Vico is imitating Aristotle's method. All naturalists preceding him were lisping cosmologists. They fell short of the Zenonian synthesis of the geometrical with the metaphysical principle of the metaphysical points.

[13]Reference to Aristotle's claim that the infinite and unlimited exist only "potentially" and not "actually." "Being means either being potentially or being actually, and the infinite is possible by way of addition as well as by way of division. Now, as we have explained, magnitude is never actually infinite, but it is infinite by way of division, for it is not difficult to refute the theory of indivisible lines; the alternative that remains is that the infinite exists potentially." *Physics* III, 6, 206a, 13–19 (my translation). Aristotle, therefore, recognizes the infinite in the direction of the smallest, that is, in the form of infinite divisibility. He believes that he has answered Zeno's paradoxes, which assume the infinite divisibility of magnitude, by distinguishing between potential and actual divisibility and by insisting that, though magnitude is potentially divisible to infinity, in actuality it is not, but its essence and reality is continuity. See *Physics*, 263a23–263b3.

[14]Given what Vico says here, it is difficult to claim that there is no confusion of the two Zenos in Vico. Here, according to Vico, Zeno uses Aristotle's notion of the "power" of extension to construct his metaphysical points. Since the Zeno of Plato's *Parmenides* was "about forty" when Socrates was young, we must at least grant that Vico was confused about the Eleatic's dates.

the power of the indefinite division of extension. Division is a physical thing, the power in virtue of which a thing can be divided is a
metaphysical reason (*argumentum*). For division is an action of body,
whereas the essence of body, as of all other things, consists in its
indivisibility. And even Aristotle ought to admit this, for he teaches
it. [So it seems] to me that Aristotle is contending with Zeno about
something else, but that he agrees with him on this matter. For Aristotle is talking about act and Zeno about power.[15] And when Aristotle
insists on the division of parts into infinity by the demonstration of a
diagonal that intersects with a lateral line at the same points (and the
resulting two lines are incommensurable), he is then no longer dividing a point, but rather some extended entity, for he is drawing it. But
this very demonstration—like those about the concentric circles that
intersect with their certain points, and about the parallels that, when
drawn obliquely to the horizontal, would never divide the entire
perpendicular that they intersect—and other such demonstrations,
depend on their establishment upon the definition of the point that
has no parts. Nor are these wondrous things demonstrated to us
through a geometry among whose definitions the point is said to be
the least particle divisible into the immeasurable,[16] but by a geometry
for which the point constitutes an indivisible entity. It is from the
point so defined that these wondrous demonstrations are arrived at.
Wherefore, far from being refuted by these very demonstrations,
Zeno was, rather, confirmed in his own position. For just as this
nominal definition, this fictitious thing without parts, equally underlies unequal extensions in this world of forms which man feigns for
himself and in which he is in a way the god, so likewise on this same
model in the true world that God founded[17] there is a certain indivisible power of extension which, because it is indivisible, stretches
equally under unequal extensions. Thus, powers are indefinite and,
therefore, we may not speak of their being "so many" or of "how
many" there are; it is not possible to think of their being "more" or

---

[15]This is an example of Vico's theory of equivocation. For Aristotle, matter, or extension, was potentially divisible ad infinitum; for Zeno, power, or substance, though
indivisible, produces infinite divisibility. (See below, Vico's First Response, section 3,
pp. 133–32.)

[16]For probable sources of the first two of these geometrical problems which Vico
wrongly attributes to Aristotle, see Pierre Bayle, *Dictionnaire historique et critique*, 3d ed.
(Rotterdam, 1720), 4:2910.

[17]*Verum:* true, i.e., the world God really made from nothing.

"fewer"; they do not tolerate this "more" and "less." And these very demonstrations, which prove this, also go to show[18] that conatus, or the power of motion, inasmuch as it is a metaphysical thing, equally underlies unequal motions.

First, it is much more fitting to the most complete facility of Divine Omnipotence[19] that He should have created a matter that is simultaneously the power of both extension and motion than that He should have created first matter and then motion in two separate operations. Good metaphysics leads us to this view also.[20] For since conatus is not itself a thing but a "way of being,"[21] that is, a mode of matter, it had to be created when matter was created. Our view fits in physics too, for all things are in motion when nature once exists or, as the Schoolmen say, when nature is brought to completion (*in facto*). Before it existed, all things were at rest in God. Therefore, nature began to exist through conatus, or as the Schoolmen also say, the conatus is the mean between rest and motion. In nature, there are extended things, but before all nature there is a thing that abhors all extension—God. Therefore, between God and extended things, there is a mediating thing, unextended certainly, but capable of extension; and this mediation is the metaphysical point.

In fact, from no other point of view would the following correspond to each other with the highest symmetry or, as the Schoolmen say, "quantity": rest to God, conatus to matter, and motion to the extended body. God, the mover of all, remains at rest within Himself; matter exercises the power of conatus; and extended bodies move. And just as motion is a mode of the body and rest an attribute of God, so conatus is the legacy of a metaphysical point. And just as the metaphysical point is the indefinite power of extension that equally underlies unequal extended bodies, so conatus is the indefinite power of moving that equally unfolds unequal motions.

As the foundation of all his most illuminating meditations on the reflection and refraction of motions, Descartes says that motion is different from its determinations, so that more motion can exist under

---

[18]Vico says *conficiunt*, i.e., they prove the proposition in his sense of "making up" and "bringing together" the rational elements of which it is constituted.

[19]Notice that *expeditissima facilitas*, which below will be claimed to be synonymous for *facultas*, creates a matter that is all alive.

[20]That is, Vico's metaphysics.

[21]Vico wrote *quid non sit, sed cuius* (is not a what but an of what).

the same mode or quantity of determination. From this assumption. he derives the consequence that there is more motion in oblique than in straight directions. And in this he has found the way in which a body, moved in an oblique direction, satisfies two causes at one and the same time. The first cause is that of its own weight, which tends to carry it downward, and the second is that of its direction, which tends to carry it obliquely toward the horizon. And thus, when it falls on a completely impenetrable plane, it displays the effects of both causes at one and the same time, and it reflects its motion in such a way that the angle of reflection equals the angle of incidence. But if it were to fall on a penetrable plane, it would refract its motion, and in proportion to the greater or lesser fluidity of the surface it penetrates, it would depart either more or less from the perpendicular than it would if it were carried down through a surface that was uniformly penetrable. Descartes saw the truth, in fact, that under the same mode of determination there can be more motion.[22] But he mistakes the reason for it because he agrees with Aristotle and not with Zeno. He is mistaken, I say, because, just as an equal power of extension underlies a diagonal and a lateral line, so too an equal power of motion underlies the rectilinear motion and the motion oblique to the horizon.

Unless I am mistaken, the basis of all the phenomena (*rerum*) that we have discussed up to now is that, at the very beginning, things begin to exist out of their own nothingness through points and conatus; and both the least and the greatest things are equally distant from nothingness. For this reason, geometry accepts its truth from metaphysics and gives back to the very same metaphysics what it receives. In other words, geometry shapes human knowledge on the model of divine knowledge and corroborates divine knowledge, in its turn, with human knowledge. How aptly all the following points fit in with our doctrine.

Time is divisible and eternity belongs to the indivisible. Unless other things move, one does not have the means to measure rest. Hence, the anxieties of the mind are lessened or increased, but tranquility knows no degree. Extended things are corrupted, and immor-

---

[22]It is difficult to determine with precision what Cartesian proof Vico is using to show the inadequacy of Descartes's physics. The only possible candidate is that in the Second Discourse of Descartes's *Dioptrique* (in *Oeuvres de Descartes*, ed. Charles Adam and Paul Tannery, 12 vols. [Paris: L. Cerf, 1897–1910], 6:97–98).

tal ones consist of indivisible [substance]. The body allows divisions, but the mind is intolerant of parts. The opportune moment comes just at one point, whereas contingencies surround us on every side. Truth is absolutely precise; falsity is in all directions [from it]. For knowledge is not divisible, whereas opinion begets diverse sects. Virtue is not on that side or on this [but in the mean], whereas vice stretches far and wide. The right is unique; evils are countless. In every genus, what is best is based on the indivisible thing. And so the physical world is made up of imperfect things that are infinitely divisible. The metaphysical world is made up of ideas, the best things, to wit, indivisible powers whose efficacies are infinite.

In metaphysics, then, there is a kind of thing that is not extended and yet is capable of extension. Descartes does not see this because, in the manner of the analysts, he simply assumes that matter has been created and goes on to divide it. But Zeno saw it because he aimed to treat the world of solids, which God created, on the basis of the world of forms, which man establishes for himself by synthesis from points. Aristotle did not see it because he introduced metaphysics directly into physics; and hence, he discusses physical questions in a metaphysical manner, appealing to powers and faculties. Descartes did not see it because he directly raised physics to the level of metaphysics and thought about metaphysical matters in a physical manner by appealing to actions and forms. Both courses [Aristotle's and Descartes's] inevitably lead to error.[23] For if defining means mapping the limits of things, and the limits are the edges of formed bodies, and all formed bodies are drawn out of matter by motion, then, since nature exists already, they must be referred to what has been accepted as already existing. It is improper to define things by appealing to their powers once the nature from which we get their actualities already exists, and it is impertinent to describe things by appealing to actuality before nature exists and things are formed. Metaphysics transcends physics because it deals with powers and the infinite; physics is a part of metaphysics because it deals with forms and determined things. But even if God were to explain it to us, we could not follow the path by which the infinite has descended to the

---

[23]Both philosophers, Vico claims, have committed a mistake of categories. Aristotle, in explaining physical phenomena, uses the metaphysical language of essences and powers. Descartes explains metaphysical notions by using the physicist's language of motion.

level of our finite [world], because this is a truth of the divine mind, for which to know and to make are unconditionally equivalent. But man's mind is finite and has a [definite] form. Hence, we cannot understand the limitless and formless, though we can think about them. As we say in Italian, "Può andarle raccogliendo, ma non già raccoglierle tutte" (One can keep on picking things up, but never get them all together). Even to think this is to confess that what one [can] think is formless and has no limits. And for this very reason, knowing distinctly is a vice of the human mind, rather than a virtue, because it means knowing the limits of things. God's mind sees things in the sunlight of His truth. In other words, while it sees a thing, it knows an infinity of things along with the thing that it sees. When man's mind knows a thing distinctly, it sees it by lamplight at night. For while the mind sees it thus, the thing's circumstances are lost from its sight. For instance, I am in pain and yet I do not know any form of pain, and I know no limits of the soul's illness. This cognition is indefinite and, being indefinite, it is fitting for man. The idea of pain is vivid and illuminating like nothing else.

But this clearness of the metaphysical truth is, in number, just like that of a light, which we cannot distinguish unless it is in the midst of opaque objects. Metaphysical truths are illuminating because they cannot be bounded by any limit and distinguished by any formed body. But physical truths are the opaque bodies by means of which we distinguish the light of metaphysical things. This metaphysical light or, as the Schoolmen say, the transition from potentialities into actualities (but not vice versa), is generated by conatus, that is, by the unlimited power of motion which equally underlies unequal motions. This is the legacy of the point or of the indefinite power by which something is extended; and it is stretched equally under unequal extensions.

III. There Is No Conatus in Extended Things

Either extended things are not subject to conatus or the truest motion belongs to them—Light arises by true motion—It is improper for the physicists to explain natural phenomena by appeal to virtues and potencies—The word *conatus* should be restored from the schools of physics to those of metaphysics—Nature is motion; principle of motion is conatus; God starts conatus

For extended things seem manifestly incapable of any conatus. This is evident if there is a plenum of homogeneous bodies which resist one another mutually with equal force; for the power of movement cannot be set off in a plenum where there is equilibrium of forces; [or] it is evident also if there is a plenum of heterogeneous bodies, some of which resist while others relent. For it is in these bodies that truly genuine motions occur. And I would not truly produce a conatus if I tried to put a hole in a wall with my arm; for that is a true motion of the nerves, which from being relaxed become very tense. The motion of a fish when it swims against the current toward a river bank is precisely like that. For a flow of the animal spirits follows upon this tension of nerves, and hence, there is true motion until, with fresh spirits arriving, the nerves grow weak and relax. Now, if conatus generally is the inhibited power of motion through which extended things become existent, is it able to unfold itself in any way when it is maximally inhibited? Or will it be unable to unfold itself in any way? If it can do so in some way, then it is the truest motion; but if it cannot, what kind of force is this that is always frustrated? There cannot be a force that is not expressed at the moment it comes into being, so that what produces the force is tensed or moved. Hence, if we were to run through all natural effects, we would find that they are born of motion and not of conatus. Even light, which seems to be diffused instantaneously, comes into being, according to the teaching of the best physicists, over an interval of time and by true motion. If only that light were to come into being in an instant, we would have the most splendid work of nature born from a point. For if light is generated in an instant of time, then this effectiveness of the [meta-physical] point is necessarily present in nature. For a temporal instant correlates to a spatial point. Therefore, if light is directed motion of corpuscles in a ray, yet comes to be in an instant, the corpuscles could not be directed toward any part of their range which is extended. For extensions are delineated by their boundaries, which are held apart by what lies between. And the extreme and middle parts are traversed in a time interval and by true motion. So for light to be generated by conatus, and in an instant, the corpuscles must be directed at the points that have no parts. But then, lo and behold, there would be in nature a thing that would have no extension. But those points, over which light is diffused, or darkness looms up, as they say, are much too material and are not nullified by the graceful ingenuity of geometry, or better, they are not denuded of all extension by the subtlety of metaphysics.[24]

Therefore, once a nature exists in which there are different kinds of extended things—some hard and some penetrable—there is no conatus, but just true motions. Consequently, the phenomena of an already existing natural order cannot be explained [physically] by appeal to powers and forces. Thanks to the better physicists, the language of "natural sympathies and antipathies" and of "nature's secret designs," called "hidden qualities," has already been expelled from the schools of physics. The word *conatus* survives as a holdover from metaphysical language. So in order for the language of physics to be perfected, conatus should be taken out of the schools of physics and restored to the metaphysicians.

Let us sum up our argument. Nature is motion. The indefinite power to move underlying this motion is conatus. The infinite, and in itself motionless, mind that excites this power is God. The works of nature are brought into being by conatus and brought to perfection by motion. In sum, the genesis of things presupposes motion, motion presupposes conatus, and conatus presupposes God.

IV. All Motions Are Composite

The composite mode of composite things—Figure, space, time—Latins' indiscriminate use of temporal and spatial particles—No motion is rectilinear—Straightness and sameness are metaphysical things; crookedness and otherness physical—Motion consists of indefinite conatus just as a curved line consists of countless straight lines—No motion in the void because no environment in the void—Feigning a body in motion in the void is the same as inventing imaginary space—Bodies are stable because they are moved in the plenum—Why the Latins opposed nothingness and straightness

---

[24]The example of light offers empirical evidence that there is no conatus in extended bodies. If light were produced by conatus it would be manifested instantaneously so that luminous corpuscles would originate from empty spaces because metaphysical points are unextended. But light corpuscles are extended and thus are neither geometrical nor metaphysical.

The mode of a composite object is of necessity composite. For if the mode is the things itself disposed in such and such a way and if an extended thing has parts, then the mode of the extended thing comprises the many parts arranged in this way. And in truth, a figure is a composite mode because it consists of at least three lines. Place is a composite mode because it consists of three dimensions. A position (*situs*) is a composite mode because it is the relation (*ratio*) of two or more places. Time is a composite mode because it involves two places, one of which stands still while the other is in motion. The originators of the Latin language knew this very thing too. They used the particles indicating time and space interchangeably. For instance, *ibi* (there) for *tunc* (then), *inde* (hence) for *postea* (afterward), *usquam*, *nusquam* (everywhere and nowhere) for *unquam* and *nunquam* (ever and never), and so forth. From these examples it emerges that motion is composite, for it consists of terms such as *unde* (whence), *qua* (by what way), and *quo* (whither).

Because all motions are produced by air pressure from all sides, they can in no way be simple and in a straight line. Bodies that fall through the air or cross the surface of land or sea do seem to describe a straight line, but in reality that line is not straight. For "straightness" and "sameness" are metaphysical things. I seem to myself to be the same person, but from one moment to the next I am a different person because of the constant coming and going of the things that enter and leave me. So, too, the apparently straight motion is crooked at every moment.

But if someone were to regard these things from the geometric standpoint, he could easily link metaphysics with physics. For the truer hypothesis is the one by which we descend from metaphysics to physics. Just as crooked lines are composed of straight lines, so that curved lines consist of an indefinite number of straight lines because they consist of an indefinite number of points, so the composite motions of extended things are composed of the simple conatus of [metaphysical] points. In nature, things are crooked and imperfect, whereas the straight against which crooked things are measured is supranatural.[25]

[25]Straight lines are perfect and intermediate between metaphysics and physics because they can appear in nature but are not there. All real lines are crooked by physical necessity, and heavenly orbits, for example, are not circular, though self-perpetuating, and in that sense "infinite."

Nowadays the belief that extended bodies have conatus toward straight motions is based on the assumption that if a body were to move freely (i.e., through a nonresistant [medium]), it would move in a straight line indefinitely. But to begin with, the feigning of this hypothesis is ruled out by the fact that those who construct it define motion as change in the location of nearby bodies. But what nearby bodies are there in the void? Someone might say that the environment of a place whence a body was first moved must be considered. But if it is considered, how does the immeasurable exist? How can there be a "nearer" and a "farther" in the immeasurable void? If someone admits that there is, how does he differ from the scholastic, with his "imaginary spaces"? For it typifies the same mentality to imagine that there is an empty space in the farthest reaches of the highest heavens and to feign the motion of a body farther and farther through the immeasurable void from a place whence it was first moved.

Nature does not allow this kind of feigning. For bodies subsist stably [only] because they are moved in a plenum; and hence, they are [only] more or less stable because they resist other bodies and are resisted by them more or less. Were it not for this resistance, a body would not even move, let alone move in a straight line ad infinitum. But just as the walls of a space would come together if all the air within were withdrawn from the place, so too a body that was withdrawn into the void would be dissipated.

The wise originators of the Latin language knew this to be true: that straightness was metaphysical and crookedness physical. For on religious grounds, the Latin called *nihil* (nothing) the opposite of *recte* (straightly or rightly), as if the straight, the exact, the perfect, and the infinite were opposed to the nothing; and the finite, the crooked, and the imperfect were almost nothing.

V. Extended Bodies Are in Motion

Rest is a metaphysical thing, motion physical—To be composite is to be moved—The life of things is like a river—Physical form is the continual change of the thing—There is no perfect rest in nature

Rest is a metaphysical thing, motion a physical one. Physics does not admit the feigning of a body that is self-contained or, as they say, "indifferent" to motion and rest. For the feigning of something that is at the same time both inside and outside of nature is not allowed. For nature is the motion by which things are composed, live, and are dissolved. At every instant something is composed within us and something is dissolved by us. Hence, to be composed is to be moved. For motion is change of environment or position. Bodies near other bodies never stop changing their position. They flow in and out all the time. This is the life of things, just like the river that seems the same, yet is forever the flowing of different waters. Therefore, nothing in nature holds on to the same place and bodily environment, even for an instant.

The opinion that things steadily pursue the form with which they have once and for all been endowed befits the scholastics, who regard these principles of self-conservation as belonging among the causes of natural things.[26] In fact, what form is [i.e., could be] the property of each natural thing when something may be added or subtracted at every moment? Therefore, a physical form is nothing but the continuous change of the thing. Therefore, [the notion of] perfect rest must be entirely eliminated from the science of physics.

VI. Motion Is Not Communicated

Communication of motion is penetration of bodies—Communication of motion seems to be the same as attraction—All motion is generated from impulse—God is the author of all motion—Man can [only] determine motion—Common to all motion is the surrounding impulse of air—How the common motion of the air becomes proper to each [moving body]—All motions by impulse are spatial and of one kind

Motion is nothing but a body in motion; in more accurate metaphysical language, it is not so much a "what" (*quid*) as an "of what"

[26]On Vico's Heracleitean view of nature, there cannot be a self-preservative or teleological principle in the natural or physical order. There is Spinoza behind his Heracleiteanism. The water makes a stable river, but only the totality of all possible arrangements of elements is logically conserved. Organic order comes from the creative intelligence.

(*cuius*). For the mode of a body is that which cannot be distinguished—not even mentally—from the thing of which it is a mode. Therefore, communication of motion is exactly the same as penetration of bodies.

The opinion that motion can be communicated from one body to another seems no less objectionable than the common scholastic doctrine that explains attractions and motion by appealing to the abhorrence of a vacuum. For, to my mind, the view that a projectile carries with it the full force of the throwing hand appears similar to the opinion that air sucked up out of pumps draws up the water after itself. For through most illuminating experiments on the basis of the new improved physics, these attractions have now been discovered to be truly the pressure of the surrounding air. And it is now steadily maintained that all motion is born of impetus.

Anyone who thinks that some extended bodies are at rest comes to grief upon these rocks. But anyone who understands that all things are moved by perpetual motion and that there is no rest in nature understands also that a body that seems to be at rest is not roused to motion by the impulse of the hand, but it is determined by a different type of motion. Indeed, it is not within our power to move anything. God alone originates all motion and arouses conatus, which is the beginning of motion. It is the determination of motion that is truly within our power. Other determinations arise from one kind of mechanism or another. Air is the mechanism common to all motions, and its pressure is God's perceptible hand, by which all things are moved. But every single thing is moved, each in one way or another by its own specific device. And since every motion is a local motion and is born of impulse, he [who understands this] would, of course, never admit any distinction between the motion by which water rises in a siphon, where it is beyond doubt that the water is driven out by air pressure, and the motion by which projectiles are hurled through the open air. Indeed, he will not judge that there is any difference between this motion of missiles and that by which fire burns, plants grow, and animals frolic in the meadows. For all of them are due to air pressure. And just as the common motion of the air is transformed by means of specific devices in the motion of fire, of plants, and of animals, so there is a motion proper to projectiles. Surely, the heat that is generated by a ball in motion is not communicated to it by the hand; nevertheless, the heat quite certainly belongs to the ball. And what is heat but motion? The hand, therefore, is the device peculiar to projectiles; and by it the nerves, which move according to the intention of the hand, are determined as well. The body, also, which is already in motion, is determined to move in another way. And the surrounding air, already in motion, is determined to advance the missile. This common mechanism of air pressure becomes proper to the thrown body, and hence heat and often fire are proper to it.

CHAPTER FIVE

I. The Spirit and the Soul

With the soul we live, with the spirit we sense—Air called soul—Air of blood the vehicle of life—Air of nerves the vehicle of sensation—Vital spirit is less active, animal spirit more active—Motion of blood due to nerves—According to the Latins, spirit is immortal, but not soul

The elegance of these two words, *animus* (spirit) and *anima* (soul), whereby *anima vivamus, animo sentiamus* (with the soul we live, with the spirit we feel), is so well known that Titus Lucretius laid claim to it as if it had been conceived in Epicurus's Garden.[1]

But we must remark that the Latins also called the air anima, which is recognized as the most plastic of all bodies; and we have argued, in the last section, that air is the only body that is moved by a motion common to all bodies, a motion that thereafter becomes by the operation of special mechanisms the motion proper to each. Thus, we may surmise that the ancient philosophers of Italy defined soul and spirit by reference to the motion of air. And truly air is the vehicle of life which, by its inhalation and exhalation, moves the heart and arteries

---

[1]Lucretius, *De Rerum Natura*, II, 137. Also Augustine, *De Civitate Dei*, VII, 23. For the elaboration of the present theory see *NS*, 695–702. In these sections M. Fisch translates *anima* and *animus* as "soul" and "spirit." See *NS*, 695, 696. For stylistic reasons I have followed Fisch's rendition rather than the obvious alternatives "the principle of life" and "the principle of feeling."

and the blood in them. This movement of the blood is life itself. Moreover, the vehicle of sensations is the air that insinuates itself into the nerves and stirs their sap, and distends, inflates, and twists the fibers. Nowadays in the Schools the air that moves the blood in the heart and arteries is called *spiritus vitales* (vital spirits), and that which moves the nerves and their sap and filaments is called *spiritus animales* (animal spirits).[2] But the motion of the animal spirit is far quicker than that of the vital spirit, for as soon as you want, you can move a finger, whereas the blood takes a long time—some physicists calculate that it takes a third of an hour to pass from the heart to the finger in its circulation. What is more, the heart muscles are contracted and dilated by nerves, so that through systole and diastole the blood is made to circulate continuously, receiving from the nerves its own motion. Therefore, they called this masculine and strenuous motion of air through the nerves the animus; but the feminine submissive motion of air in the blood which overlies it, so to speak, they called the anima.

So when the Latins argued about immortality, they were speaking of the immortality of spirits, not of souls. Perhaps the origin of this locution may be that the inventors of the language noted that the motions of the animus are free and relative to man's will, whereas those of the anima cannot happen apart from the mechanism of the body, which is corruptible; and because it moves freely, the animus yearns for infinity and, hence, immortality. This argument is so important that even Christian metaphysicians have considered freedom of choice the quality by which man is distinguished from beast. Certainly, the Church Fathers invoke the fact that man desires infinite duration to support [the dogma] that man was created with an immortal spirit and was made immortal on God's own account.[3]

---

[2]The ancients were in disagreement as to the exact location of the vital spirit and the animal spirit. Aristotle and Galen claim the heart as the seat of the vital spirit and the brain as the seat of the animal spirit. Harvey's discovery of the circulation of blood did not destroy the belief in the existence of the vital spirits as vital forces, and the debate continued for about eighty years after Harvey's experiments. Among the members of the Academy of the Investigators, the nature of the blood was subject to much experimentation. Many investigators accepted the hypothesis, as Vico does, that animal spirits run through the whole nervous system. This is why Vico calls animus that produces thought *animus mentis*. See N. Badaloni, *Introduzione a Vico* (Milan: Feltrinelli, 1961), pp. 347–54.

[3]*Propter Deum:* on God's own account; for God's sake; because God is his goal.

II. The Soul of Brutes

For the Latins *brutum* signifies "immobile"—Brutes are moved by attendant objects serving as devices

The word *bruta*, by which the Latins designated animals devoid of reason, is in agreement with what we have just set forth. For to them brute meant the same thing as immobile, yet they saw that brutes were moved.[4]

So the ancient philosophers of Italy must have held that brutes were immobile because they [were not self-moved but] were moved only by external objects serving as a mechanism, whereas men have an inner principle of motion, namely the animus, which moves freely.

III. The Seat of the Spirit

The Latins located prudence in the heart—*Acetum pectoris. Cor hominis. Excors. Vecors. Cordatus. Corculum.*—Ancient opinion on the origin of nerves—Why we appear to think in our head—The seat of the soul in the pineal gland?—Men with damaged brains reason successfully—Mechanics denies that the mind in the head is in charge of the body—In plants, the seat of life is in the seed—The heart is the first to be produced, the last to die—Whether the principle of life is in the heart and the principle of reason in the principle of life—"Deficiency of spirit" and "feeling ill"—Who is wise—The mind of spirit—Two appetites are the fuel of the passions—Seat and vehicles of the appetites—Mind is dependent on the spirit—Whether it is safer to cast off passions, for meditating on the truth, or prejudices

The ancient philosophy of Italy maintained that the heart was the seat and abode of the spirit. For the Latins commonly spoke of prudence as lodged in the heart, or of plans and worries as turned over in

[4]Cf. *Sexti Pompei Festi de verborum significatu quae supersunt cum Pauli epitome*, ed. Wallace M. Lindsay (Leipzig: B. G. Teubner, 1913), p. 28: "*Brutum* antiqui gravem dicebant"; and p. 201: "*Obbrutuit*, obstupuit, a bruto, quod antiqui pro gravi, interdum pro stupido dixerunt"; and Lucretius, *De Rerum Natura*, VI, 105: "bruto deberent pondere." Actually, *brutus* means "heavy" in these contexts, not "immobile."

the heart, and of keenness of insight as lodged in the breast. Or, to use a Plautine idiom,[5] they used to say *e pectore acetum* (from the breast springs sharpness of wit). Also, they had these other expressions: *cor hominis* (man's heart) and *excors* for stupid; *vecors* for mad; *socors* for a slow thinker and *cordatus* for wise,[6] whence Publius Scipio Nasica was called Corculum (little heart) because he had been adjudged to be the wisest of all Romans by an oracle. Did these expressions perhaps derive from the fact that the Italian school agreed with the rest of antiquity that the nerves have their beginning in the heart?

And the grounds for our seeming to think with the head is, perhaps, the fact that the organs of two senses are in the head: of which hearing is the most trainable of all senses and sight by far the most perceptive. But the belief that the nerves originate in the heart has been found to be false by contemporary anatomy; for the nerves are observed to spread out through the entire body from the brain, as if from a tree trunk. Hence, the Cartesians situate the human spirit in the pineal gland, as if it were an observatory (*specula*); they hold that it receives there all the motions of the body via the nervous system and, through these motions, it relates cognitively (*speculari*) to outer objects.[7] Yet persons with damaged brains are often observed alive, moving, sensing, and reasoning with success.

But it seems improbable that the spirit would be situated in that part of the body where there is a lot of mucus and very little blood (and hence, what is there is thick and sluggish). For mechanics teaches that in a clock the wheels directly put in motion by the [animal] spirits are the finest [nerves] and quickest [wheels] of all.[8]

The seat of life in plants is in the seed, and from there it is dispersed through the upper trunk into the branches and through the stocks [below] into the roots. Did [the Latins] make the heart the seat of the soul or of life because they observed that in the generation of an animal the heart was the first thing to grow and to beat and the last to lose heat and motion in death? Or was it because they believed that

---

[5]See Plautus's *Bacchides*, 405; also *Pseudolus*, 739–40.

[6]*NS*, 702. Also Horace, *Odes*, 16, 13–16.

[7]See Descartes, *Les passions de l'âme*, in *Oeuvres de Descartes*, ed. Charles Adam and Paul Tannery, 12 vols. (Paris: L. Cerf, 1897–1910) 11, articles 31, 32, pp. 351–52.

[8]What Vico says here is clear. How it is to be interpreted is not. He seems to have collapsed his comparison. The animal spirits move the nerves in the way that the spring moves the wheels of a watch. This entire sections calls to mind Collingwood's *New Leviathan*. But for Vico's source, compare Plato's *Republic*, IV.

the flame of life burns in the heart? Or because they saw that when someone is overtaken by a fainting spell (a fainting, which we Italians call precisely *uno svenimento di cuore*), not only the motion of nerves stops, but so does that of the blood? Was it then that they considered and said of the man that "his spirit is failing" or "he is sick in spirit"? And did they decide that in the heart resides the principle of life or of soul or that in the life principle resides the principle of the spirit or of reason? Or was it because it is the wise man who thinks what is true and wills what is just that they posited spirit in the passions and mind in the spirit, which they, therefore, called the mind of spirit?[9]

Certainly, the twin stimuli of all the perturbations, or feelings, of the soul are the appetites of desire and anger; blood seems to be the vehicle of desire, bile of anger. The seat of both humors is in the vicinity of the heart. Consequently, [the ancient philosophers] would have held that the mind depends on the spirit because how one thinks reflects one's spiritual state, and men hold different opinions on the same subject because of their different concerns.

I might almost say that it is a greater safeguard for meditation on the truth to put off one's passions than to shed one's prejudices. For you can never destroy prejudice while passion remains, but once passion is extinguished, the mask we have put on things is torn from them and only the things themselves remain.

IV. The Civil Skepticism of the Romans

Roman formulas for decisions, judgments, and oaths

Did the Romans make their solemn declarations with words like *videri* (seem) and *parere* (appear) and their oaths with *ex animi sui sententia* (according to his state of spirit)[10] because they thought that no one could make his spirit quite empty of passions, and because they had a religious awe in judging and swearing, lest they perjure themselves if matters stood otherwise than they thought?

---

[9]Lucretius, *De Rerum Natura*, IV, 758; NS, 696.
[10]Quintilian, *Institutio Oratoria*, VIII, 5.

CHAPTER SIX. MIND

Latin *mens* same as Italian *pensiero*—The mind is given by the gods—Ideas are created by God in the spirits of men—The mind of the spirit—Active intellect of the Aristotelians—Etheral sense of the Stoics—*Daemon* of the Socratics—Malebranche's teachings confuted—God the first origin of every motion—The origin of evils—What is man's free choice—God shines even in the darkness of errors—Why metaphysics treats indubitable truth

The Latins meant by "mind" what we call *pensiero,* "thought"; and they claimed that mind is "given" or "imparted" to humans "by the gods." What this amounts to is that those who thought out these phrases believed that ideas were created and activated in the mind of men by God; and hence, they spoke of the mind of the spirit (*mens animi*); also they attributed to God the unlimited (*liberum*) right and choice of the spirit's motions, so that desire (*libido*) or the capacity to desire everything is for each man his own God. This God, peculiar to each man, would seem to be the *intellectus agens* (active intellect) of the Aristotelians, the *sensus aethereus* (etheral sense) of the Stoics, and the *daemon* of the Socratics. The metaphysicians of our present age have discussed this problem very cleverly and at length.[1]

But if that most acute man, Malebranche, contends that these propositions are true, I wonder why he agrees with René Descartes's

[1]See P. Gassendi, *Opera* (Sumptibus Laurentii Anisson, 1658), Tomus Tertius, quo continentur Syntagmatis. . . .

primary truth, *Cogito ergo sum.*[2] Since he recognizes that God creates ideas in me, he should rather put things as follows: "Something thinks in me; therefore, it exists. However, I acknowledge no idea of body in my thought; therefore, what thinks in me is an absolutely pure mind, namely, God." On the other hand, perhaps the human mind could be so structured that, after having begun from things that were quite indubitable for it, and having arrived at the knowledge of God as best and greatest, when once it knew him it would recognize for false even what previously it held to be quite indubitable. And indeed, quite generally, all ideas derived from created things are, in a way, false in the face of the idea of the Supreme Deity because they concern things that, when put in relation to God, do not seem to exist truly. For it is only of God that there is a true idea, because He alone truly is. So if Malebranche wanted his doctrine to be consistent, he ought to have taught that the human mind acquires from God knowledge, not only of the body to which it belongs, but of itself as well; so that it does not ever know itself, unless it knows itself in God. Mind exhibits itself in the act of thinking. God thinks within me and, therefore, I know my own mind in God. This would be the case if Malebranche's teaching were consistent.[3]

What we receive inwardly thus is this: that God is the first originator of all motions whether of bodies or of spirits. But here come those shoals and reefs, because if God is the mover of the human mind, how is it possible that there are so many evils, so much ugliness, so many errors and vices? If God has the truest and most absolute knowledge, how is it that there is in man free choice of what to do?

Certainly we know that God is omnipotent, omniscient, and perfect; what He understands is truth, what He wills is good, His understanding is absolutely simple and completely present, His will fixed and ineluctable. Yet more, according to Holy Scripture, no one of us can go to the Father unless the same Father has drawn him.[4] How does He drag one who wants to come? Here is Augustine's answer:

---

[2]N. Malebranche, *De la recherche de la vérité,* in *Opera,* ed. Genevieve Rodis-Lewis, 2d ed. (Paris: J. Vrin, 1972), vol. 1.

[3]Vico agrees with Malebranche that human knowledge derives from God. But God is logically prior to the activity of the human mind. Man has the potentiality for thinking God and only the desire for it can make such a potentiality actual.

[4]John 6:44.

"He drags not only a willing man but one gladly willing, and He drags him by joy."[5] What could be more apt both to the consistency of the divine will and to the freedom of our choice?

It follows from this that, even in our errors, we cannot lose sight of God. For we embrace falseness under the guise of truth and evil under the likeness of goodness. We see finite things, we feel ourselves finite, but this means that we think of the infinite. We seem to see motions started and communicated by bodies, but this very stirring of motion, these very communications, assert and prove God—God as mind and as author of motion. We perceive evil as goodness, many as one, difference as identity, activity as rest. But since in nature there is neither straightness nor unity, neither sameness nor rest, to make mistakes about these things means nothing else save that men who lack foresight or are deceived about created objects contemplate the perfect and almighty God in these very imitations.

On this account, metaphysics treats of indubitable truth because it concerns a subject matter of which you can be certain even when you doubt, go astray, or are mistaken.

---

[5]In the Latin edition of G. Gentile and F. Nicolini this passage is given as in *Augustine: Tractatus in Iohannem* 4. See *Opera di G. B. Vico*, ed. G. Gentile and F. Nicolini (Bari: Laterza, 1914), pp. 301–2. Probably Gentile and Nicolini have used the ancient edition of Augustine: *Sancti Aurelii Augustini . . . operum tomus primus. . . . Opera et Studio Monachorum Ordinis Sancti Benedicti e Congregatione Sancti Mauri . . .* (Antuerpiae; Sumptibus Societatis, 1700). This is the edition of Augustine which was available to Vico through the library of Giuseppe Valletta. See G. Valletta, *Opere filosofiche*, ed. M. Rak (Florence: Olschki, 1975), p. 523. Vico might have paraphrased a similar passage in another work by Augustine. See *Sancti Aurelii Augustini in Iohannis Evangelium tractatus* cxxiv (Turnholti: Brepols, 1954), p. 261.

CHAPTER SEVEN

I. Faculties

Etymology of *facilitas*—"Faculties of soul" an elegant expression of the Schools—Faculties are of the things that we make—Outer senses—Things have smells and men make them perceptible—Imagination—Inner senses— True intellect—Arithmetic, geometry, and mechanics are within the human faculty—Physics within God's faculty—True faculty in God—How all things are divine thoughts

The word *facultas* is a contraction from *faculitas*, from which comes the later word *facilitas*, which signifies an unhindered and ready disposition for making (*facere*).[1] Hence, faculty is the ability to turn power into action. The soul is power, sight an activity, and the sense of sight a faculty. Therefore, the scholastics speak quite elegantly when they call sensation, imagination, memory, and intellect the faculties of the soul. But they spoil that elegance when they declare that colors, flavors, sounds, and touch are in things. For if the senses are faculties, we make the color of things by seeing, flavor by tasting, sound by hearing, and heat and cold by touching. An undistorted trace of this tenet of Italy's ancient philosophers survives in the words *olere* (to have a smell) and *olfacere* (to perceive a smell). For a thing is

---

[1]Cicero, *De Inventione*, 1, 27, 41. Also, Quintilian, *Institutio Oratoria*, I,3.

said to have a smell and the animate sense is said to perceive a smell because the sense makes the scent by smelling the smell (*olfactus*).[2]

Undoubtedly, the imagination is a faculty, for we use it to feign images of things. The same obtains for inner sense, for those who withdraw from the fight feel pain when they become aware of their wounds. In keeping with these examples, true intellect is a faculty by which we make something true when we understand it. Therefore, arithmetic, geometry, and their offspring, mechanics, are human faculties, since in them we demonstrate a truth because we make it. Physics, however, is within the faculty of the perfect and almighty God, in whom alone there is true faculty because this faculty is the most unhindered and the most ready; what is only disposition in man is the purest act in God.

It follows from these arguments that, just as man by activating his mind brings the modes and images of things into being and generates human truth, so God generates divine truths by exercising His intellect and makes a created truth. Thus, what we say improperly in the vernacular language when we call statues and pictures "the thoughts of their authors" should be said properly of God; that all those things that are, are "the thoughts of God."

II. Sense

Latins called all activities of the mind sensation—This was the pagan metaphysics—Christian metaphysics teaches the opposite

Under the word *sensus*, the Latins included not only such external

---

[2]Vico reads *olfacere* as *facere olere*. By this etymology, to smell a scent is to make it smellable, to make the potential scent into a real one. Democritus, Epicurus, and Lucretius agree on considering secondary qualities to be relations. Whether Vico's source is Galileo's *The Assayer* (trans. Stillman Drake [New York: Doubleday, 1957], pp. 273ff.) or, as Badaloni suggests (*Introduzione a G. B. Vico* [Milan: Feltrinelli, 1961], p. 352), Herbert of Cherbury, or, for that matter, Locke and Democritus, the whole argument on the use of the term *faculty* is a corollary of the *verum-factum*. This principle becomes here the criterion of truth for elementary cognition. We create sound, smells, and everything else through the faculty of smell, sight, etc.

senses as, for instance, the sense of sight[3] and the inner sense, which was called the sense of the spirit (such as grief, pleasure, and boredom), but also judgments, deliberations, and prayers. They said *ita sentio* (I feel thus) for "this is my judgment"; *stat sententia* (the feeling stands) for "it is certain"; *ex sententia evenit* (it turns out according to my feelings) for "as I desired"; and this was one of their formulas: *ex animi tui sententia* (according to the feeling of your spirit). Was it the case that Italy's ancient philosophers (like the Aristotelians) believed that the human mind perceived nothing except through the senses, or that the mind was nothing but sense (like the Epicureans), or that reason was a kind of ethereal and very pure sense (as the Platonists and Stoics held)? In fact, there was no sect of gentile philosophy that recognized that the human mind was free from all corporeity. Hence, they thought every work of the mind was sense; that is, whatever the mind does or undergoes derives from contact with bodies. But our religion teaches that the mind is quite incorporeal, and our metaphysicians confirm that when the bodily organs of sense are moved by bodies this is an occasion for the mind to be moved by God.

III. Memory and Imagination

What memory and reminiscence are—For among the Latins memory is equal to imagination—Man cannot feign anything save what is given to him by nature—Why the Muses are the daughters of Memory

The Latins called the faculty that stores sense perceptions "memory"; when it recalls perceptions they called it "reminiscence." But memory also signified the faculty that fashions images (which the

---

[3]The text reads *sensus vivendi*. This is probably a misprint for *sensus videndi*. Cristofolini's text reads *sensus videndi* (*Opere filosofiche* [Florence: Sansoni, 1971], p. 115). Nicolini, however, translates it with *senso di vivere* (*Giambattista Vico: Opere* [Milan: Ricciardi, 1953], p. 293). Otto translates it with *Gesichtssinnes* (*Liber Metaphysicus* [Munich: Wilhelm Fink Verlag, 1979], p. 123).

Greeks call *phantasy* and the Italians call *immaginativa*).[4] For in ordinary Italian, *immaginare* is equivalent to the *memorare* of the Latins. Is this because we can feign only what we remember and can remember only what we perceive through the senses? Certainly no painter has ever painted any kind of plant or animal that nature has not produced. The hippogryphs and centaurs are true to nature but falsely mixed. Nor have poets thought up any form of virtue that does not exist in human affairs. On the contrary; they elevate some form of courage chosen from reality beyond belief and mold their heroes on it. Therefore, the Greeks have handed down in their myths the tradition that the Muses, forms of imagination, were the daughters of Memory.

IV. *Ingenium*

What *ingenium* is—Why it is called acute and obtuse—*Ingenium* is synonymous with nature—*Ingenium* is the nature peculiar to man—Only man sees the measures or proportions of things—God is the artificer of nature, man is god of artifacts—Why "known" is used for the beautiful—Why among the sciences arithmetic and geometry are the most well established— Why engineers are so named

Ingenium is the faculty that connects disparate and diverse things. The Latins called it acute or obtuse,[5] both terms being derived from

---

[4]Probably a reference to *firma animi et rerum ac verborum ad inventionem perceptio.* Cicero, *De Inventione*, I, 7. Also *NS*, 699, 819. See also D. Verene, *Vico's New Science of Imagination* (Ithaca: Cornell University Press, 1981), pp. 96–126, 169.

[5]*Ingenium*: ingenuity, inventiveness, mother wit. Together with *verum* and *factum*, *ingenium* is one of Vico's most difficult expressions to render in appropriate English. I have decided to let the Latin stand in the heading of this section, although in other sections of the *De Antiquissima* I have opted for "wit" and "mother wit" rather than the usual translation of "ingenuity." There are several reasons, but most of all because "wit" is the customary term used in many treatises of the period to denote an original mental activity distinguishable from understanding. It is found in John Locke and Thomas Hobbes and is discussed in the works of John Lily, Emanuele Tesauro, Antonio Persio, Jan Huarte, and Baltazar Gracian. For Locke, see *An Essay Concerning Human Understanding*, ed. Campbell Fraser (New York: Dover, 1959), 1:202–3. For Hobbes, see *Leviathan* (New York: Dutton, 1950), 1:54–60. For the most recent discussion of Vico's *ingenium* as it is used here and in the *New Science*, see Michael Mooney,

geometry. An acute wit penetrates more quickly and unites diverse things, just as two lines are conjoined at the point of an angle below 90 degrees. A wit is obtuse because it penetrates simple things more slowly and leaves diverse things far apart, just as two lines united at a point lie far apart at the base when their angle is greater than 90 degrees. And so an obtuse wit joins diverse matter more slowly, an acute wit more rapidly. Furthermore, *ingenium* (mother wit) and *natura* (nature) were one and the same to the Latins. Is this because human wit is man's nature inasmuch as our wit can see the symmetry of things and recognize what is apt, fitting, beautiful, and ugly, whereas brutes are denied this? Or is it because, just as nature generates physical things, so human wit gives birth to mechanics and, as God is nature's artificer, so man is the god of artifacts?[6]

Certainly *scientia* (knowledge) comes from the same roots as *scitum* (the known). And the Italians render these no less elegantly as *ben inteso* (well understood) and *aggiustato* (arranged).[7] Is this because human knowledge is nothing but making things [in the mind] correspond to themselves [in the world] in beautiful proportion, which only those endowed with wit can do?

Therefore, geometry and arithmetic, which teach these things [proportion, etc.], are the most certain of sciences. Those who excel in their application we Italians call *ingegneri* (engineers).

V. The Faculty of Certain Knowledge

The three mental operations (perception, judgment, reasoning) are directed by the three arts (topics, criticism, method)—Why the ancients did not have any peculiar art of method—Geometrical method is useful neither to morality nor to public speaking—Cicero's order of argumentation. Demosthenes' confusion—Demosthenes' force of eloquence is contained in the disturbed order

---

Vico in the Tradition of Rhetoric (Princeton, N.J.: Princeton University Press, 1985), pp. 135–69. See also *NS*, 699, 819. For some arguments in favor of the use of *ingenuity* for Vico's *ingenium*, see Enrico Nuzzo, "Ancora su Vico in Inglese." *Bollettino del Centro di Studi Vichiani* 16 (1986):397–403.

[6]*NS*, 331.

[7]Even if this argument were valid, it would remain a feeble one. Vico tries to demonstrate that what happened with *natura* and *ingenium* in Latin happened with *scientia* and *scitum* in Italian.

of his argumentation—Method is not the fourth operation of the mind, but the art of the third—All ancient dialectic is divided into topics and critics—Without topics, Cartesian critics are not precise—How Aristotle's topics and categories are useful to discovery—The arts are the laws of the community of letters—Why the Greeks separated topics from criticism—*Ingenium* is the proper faculty of knowledge--It develops in man from childhood—What common sense is—Likeness is the mother of all invention—Why argument is so named and who the *arguti* are—What *ingenium* is—Invention is both the procedure and the result of *ingenium*—Ancient dialectic used induction and analogy—What syllogism and sorites are—What type of argument is acute and what subtle—Why the geometrical method is useful for discovery in geometry, but only useful to organize inventions outside of it—In physics demonstration, not geometrical method, must be applied—When geometry sharpens *ingenium*—Synthesis finds truths, analysis makes them—Imagination is the eye of *ingenium*, judgment the eye of understanding

These thoughts afford us the opportunity to investigate which proper faculty for knowledge has been given to man. For man perceives, judges, reasons, yet often he perceives falsely, judges rashly, and reasons fallaciously. The Greek schools of philosophy maintained that these were the faculties that had been given to man for knowing, and that each one was governed by its own set of rules: the faculty of perception by topics, judgment by criticism, and reason by method. But they have not handed down any teaching on method in their dialectics because children learned more than enough method through practice itself while studying geometry. With the exception of geometry, the ancients believed that the ordering [of studies] should be left to prudence, which is not governed by any art; indeed, practical wisdom is prudence because it is not governed by art. Only artisans instruct [apprentices] that you do this first, that next, and then the other things in order: this method (*ratio*) does not mold a man of practical wisdom, but some type of craftsman.

Truly, if you were to apply the geometrical method to practical life, "you would no more than spend your labor on going mad rationally,"[8] and you would drive a straight furrow through the

---

[8]Terence, *Eunuchus*, 62–63. Michael Mooney correctly notes that the idiom from Terence was suggested by Grotius (*De jure belli ac pacis*, prol. 4), who used it to characterize his opponent's view that warfare and law are irreconcilable. Mooney, *Vico in the Tradition of Rhetoric*, p. 4.

vicissitudes of life as if whim, rashness, opportunity, and luck did not dominate the human condition. To compose a public address according to the geometrical method would be the same as excluding everything clever from it, carefully demonstrating nothing but what is quite obvious, treating the audience like children and putting nothing but pap in their mouths, and to sum up in one word, playing the part of pedant instead of being the speaker at an assembly.

And indeed, I cannot help but marvel that those who recommend the use of the geometrical method in public speaking so vigorously propose Demosthenes as the one paragon of eloquence. For—may God help us!—Cicero is dismissed as imprecise, disorderly, and all mixed up. Yet the world's most learned men have all, till now, admired the order and cogency that they have noticed in his work; this is such that what he says first opens itself in a certain way and embraces what he says next; so that what comes later in the speech seems not so much to be asserted by him, as to emerge from and flow out of the facts themselves, while Demosthenes, for heaven's sake, offers nothing but hyperbata from beginning to end, as Dionysius Longinus, the most discriminating rhetorician of all, rightly remarks.[9] To his opinion, I might add this: that in Demosthenes' disturbed order of speaking, the whole enthymematic capacity of speech is strained like a catapult. For he usually sets forth his argument to give his listeners notice of what is at issue; but soon he is running on about things that seem to have nothing to do with the matter announced, so that, to some extent, he alienates and distracts his audience. Then, at the end, he explains the analogy that links the subject now under discussion with what he first set forth, so that the thunderbolts of his eloquence fall all the harder the more unforeseen they are.

We must not think that all antiquity employed only a crippled [faculty of] reason because the ancients did not recognize the operation of the mind which is today counted as the fourth. For method is not the fourth operation of the mind, but rather the art of the third, by which reasoning is ordered. So all ancient dialectic is divided into the art of discovery and that of judgment: the Academics were concerned only with the former, the Stoics only with the latter. Both were

---

[9]A conflation of Dionysius of Halicarnassus, who wrote a treatise on great Greek orators, part of which has survived, and Longinus Cassius, to whom the Greek work *On the Sublime* was for a long time wrongly attributed.

wrong, because there is no invention without judgment and no judgment without invention. Thus, how can a clear and distinct idea of our mind be the criterion of truth unless it has seen through all [of the elements] that are in the things, or are germane to it? And how can anyone be certain that he has seen through all of them completely unless he has examined all the questions that can be asked about the matter at hand. And first, he must examine the question "Does the thing exist?" so as to avoid talking about nothing. Second, the question "What is it?" so as to avoid arguing about names. Third, "How big is it?" either in size, weight, or number. Fourth, "What is its quality?" under which he considers color, taste, softness, hardness, and other tactile matters. Fifth, "When was it born, how long has it lasted, and into what [elements] does it break down?" On this pattern, he must take it through the remaining categories comparatively and set it beside everything that is somehow germane to it. The causes from which it arose and the effects it produces or what it does must be compared with other things like it, or different, with contraries, with things greater, smaller, and equal to it.[10]

Thus, Aristotle's *Categories* and *Topics* are completely useless if one wants to find something new in them. One turns out to be a Llull[11] or Kircher[12] and becomes like a man who knows the alphabet, but cannot arrange the letters to read the great book of nature. But if these

[10]By "putting it beside everything in any way germane to it," one "puts together" all the elements of a mental construction (a fiction) of the object itself. For this comparison places the thing on every categorical scale in relation to the other things on the scale. Here Vico expresses his theory so that its relation to the Cartesian rules of method is evident. But the crucial thing is that the answer to the first two questions (whether it is, and what it is) is given only by proceeding to the fifth question. He stops his own progress through the categories at that one because it is only when we have the answer to that question that we have a properly real object before us. This is the "different concern" of his method, which Vico now goes on to point out. He fits Aristotelian logic, Cartesian analytics, and Bacon's "new logic" of observation and comparison into the context of his own theory of knowledge. If this analysis is correct, there is much more in this chapter than the strong influence of Bacon, as M. Mooney claims. Mooney, *Vico and the Tradition of Rhetoric*, p. 57, n. 62.

[11]Ramon Llull, or Lullus Ramundus (1235–1315), the famous and controversial Catalonian logician. For a more articulate criticism of Lullus's method, see F. Bacon, *De Augmentis Scientiarum* in *The Works of Francis Bacon*, ed. J. Spedding (London: Longmans, 1879), 6:669.

[12]Vico calls Athanasius Kircher a haughty, learned man, *NS*, 605. Lynn Thorndike quotes from John Webster, *Metallographia* (London, 1671), p. 30, as an example of the opinion that people of this time had of this Polish scholar (1601–80): "Athanasius Kircher, that Universal scribbler and rhapsodist, who, after a great many huge and barren volumes, did promise the world a work by him styled *Mundus subterraneus*,

tools were considered the indices and ABC's of inquiries about our problem [of certain knowledge] so that we might have it fully surveyed, nothing would be more fertile for research. And from the same founts from which well-equipped speakers spring, there also might come forth the best [scientific] observers. But if someone is confident of having looked all through a thing in a clear and distinct mental idea [of it], he can easily be mistaken and may often think that he knows the thing distinctly when he has still only a confused knowledge of it, because he does not know all [the elements] that are in the thing and which distinguish it from others. But if he will scrutinize all the "places" distinguished in the *Topics* with a critical eye, then he will be certain that he knows the thing clearly and distinctly because he has turned the matter over in his mind and answered all the questions that can be asked with respect to the subject under discussion. And by completing this process of questioning, topics itself will become criticism.

For the arts are, in a way, the laws of the republic of letters. For they are the observations of nature made by all learned men, which have gone away into the rules of the disciplines.[13] A man who makes something in accordance with the art can be certain to be in agreement with all learned men; but one who does not have the art is easily mistaken because he puts his trust in his own nature.

Oh, my most wise Paolo, you too agree with me when, in the education of your prince, you do not send him straight to the critical art, but have him imbued with examples for a long time before he is initiated in the art of making judgments about them. Why else is this but first to bring his mother wit into full bloom and then to let it be cultivated by the art of judgment?

This division between invention and judgment arose first among

---

which put all the learned into great expectations of some worthy and solid piece of Universal knowledge. But alas, when it appeared every reader may soon be satisfied that there is but very little in it except the title that doth answer such conceived exceptions or fulfill such great promises." (Quoted in *A History of Magic and Experimental Science* [New York: Columbia University Press, 1958], 7:568.)

[13]The "going away into rules" would ordinarily be expressed by calling them "abstractions" or "universal rules." But Vico's rules remain singular. They exist properly only in their creative application, which is uniquely specific for the given problem. Hence, his method begins as topics. I take it as obvious that one cannot demonstrate that one's topical examination is exhaustive. One can only exhaust the "places" that the scientific community has so far thought of. Thus, the best result one can arrive at is the universal consensus of others trained in the discipline.

the Greeks just because they did not pay attention to the proper faculty of knowing. This faculty is mother wit, the creative power through which man is capable of recognizing likenesses and making them himself. We see it in children, in whom nature is more integral and less corrupted by convictions and prejudices, that the first faculty to emerge is that of seeing similarities. For example, they call all men fathers and all women mothers and they make likeness: "They build huts, hitch mice to little wagons, play odds and evens, and ride on a great hobby horse of a stick."[14]

Moreover, the likeness of customs among peoples gives birth to common sense.[15] And those who have written about the inventors of things have relayed to us the belief that all arts, and the conveniences with which the crafts have enriched mankind, were discovered either by chance and luck or by some likeness that even inferior creatures could have noted, or in what men had already thought out in their enterprise.[16]

The logical relation that the scholastics call the middle term the Italian school called *argumen* or *argumentum*. This remnant of the ancient language proves that they knew what we have said so far. *Argumentum* is derived from the same root as *argutus* (clear, bright, sharp) or from *acuminatus* (sharpened). Moreover, the sharp men (*arguti*) are the ones who are able to find a likeness or ratio between things very different and far removed from one another, some way in which they are cognate, or who leap over the obvious and recall from distant places the connections appropriate for the things under discussion. This is the type of mother wit that is called acumen. Hence, wit is essential to invention because, in general, to find new things requires both the work and the activity of wit alone.

Since this is the case, it is a likely conjecture that the ancient philosophers of Italy did not prove things by syllogism or sorites, but used induction by analogy in their discussions. Chronology supports this conjecture. For induction was the oldest dialectic and the analogy of like cases, which Socrates was the last to use. After him, Aristotle argued by syllogism and Zeno by sorites.[17] In truth, a man who uses the syllogistic argument does not so much compare diverse things as,

[14]Horace, Satire 3, II, 247–48.
[15]Cf. NS, 141–42.
[16]NS, 217.
[17]NS, 499.

rather, unfold from the very heart of the genus something specific, which is already contained in it, and a man who uses the sorites weaves a chain linking each cause together with the next one. Those who excel in either mode are not joining two lines in an acute angle, but are extending a single line; each, therefore, seems to be more subtle than acute. The logician of sorites is more subtle than the logician of syllogism inasmuch as genera are more inclusive than the peculiar causes of each thing.

Descartes's geometrical method corresponds to the sorites of the Stoics. But Descartes's method is useful in geometry because geometry is adapted to it, in that the defining of names and the postulation of possible [constructions] is allowed. But when it is taken from the discussion of three measures and of numbers, and is imported into physics, the method is not useful for making new discoveries so much as for setting in order the discoveries we have already made. You yourself, most learned Paolo, are a proof of this for me. For why is it that although many others have a practical knowledge of that method, they are not able to discover the things that you think of?

You were already a grown man when you applied your mind to the things of the mind. You had already spent a life in litigation about an immense fortune with princes and magnates who were your relatives. In this unduly demanding generation, you fulfill all duties incumbent on a gentleman all day long and for a large part of the night. Yet, in a short time, you have accomplished so much that hardly any other man could have done it, even if he had devoted his whole life to these studies. Let not your modesty credit the method for the fruits of your inspired wit. Let us conclude finally that demonstration, and not the geometrical method, ought to be introduced into physics. The greatest geometricians saw physical principles in the principles of mathematics. Among the ancients, there were Plato and Pythagoras; among the moderns, Galileo. In this view, we have to explain the particular effects of nature by the special type of experiments which are the distinctive results of geometry. In Italy, this has been the concern of the great Galileo and other outstanding physicists who explained countless natural phenomena of great importance in this way (*ratio*) before the geometrical method was introduced in physics. This is the one thing that the English are today seriously concerned about, and for that reason they are prohibited from publicly teaching physics according to the geometrical method.

This is how physics can be advanced. To that end, in my essay *On the Method of Studies of Our Time* I argued that it is possible to avoid the pitfalls of physics through the cultivation of *ingenium*. This may be surprising to anyone who is concerned with method. Since method inhibits intuitive wit while aiding facility, it dissolves curiosity while providing for truth. Geometry does not sharpen the wit when it is taught by method only, but when it is employed with creative wit upon diverse complicated, different, and disparate [problems]. Therefore, I wanted it to be taught in the synthetic rather than the analytical way, that is, through demonstration by composition, so that we do not just discover the truth, but make it. Discovery is the result of luck; making, the result of hard work. I wanted, therefore, to have geometry taught through forms, not through numbers or species, so that, even if learning did but little to develop the wits, yet it would strengthen the imagination, which is the eye of mother wit, just as judgment is the eye of intellect. In fact, those Cartesians whom you, Paolo, so neatly call "the Cartesians of the letter not the spirit" could well take note that they themselves practice what we preach even though they deny it in words. Except for the one truth that they borrow from consciousness, *Cogito ergo sum*, all of the truths that they use as norms to direct everything else they borrow from arithmetic and geometry and nowhere else, namely from the true that we make. They praise this, saying, "Let a truth follow this model: three plus four makes seven; the sum of any two angles of a triangle is greater than the third angle."[18] This is tantamount to looking at physics from the point of view of geometry. And whoever postulates that in reality postulates this: physical things will be true only for whoever has made them, just as geometrical [proofs] are true for men just because men make them.

[18]An obvious mistake here. See *Giambattista Vico: Opere*, ed. Nicolini, p. 304, n. 1.

CHAPTER EIGHT

I. The Supreme Artificer

Divine will, fate, chance, fortune

In our discussion of the true and the made, we have maintained the following positions: first, the true is the collection of the elements of the thing itself, of all of them in God, and of the extrinsic ones in man['s mind]; and the mental word [of truth] comes to be properly in God and, in an improper sense, in man; second, that "faculty" refers to what we make and to what we make skillfully and with facility. These four Latin words—*numen* (divine will), *fatum* (fate), *casus* (chance), and *fortuna* (luck or fortune)—support our claims.

II. Divine Will

Divine goodness makes matter by willing—Why painters and poets are called divine—What nature is

The Latins call the will of the gods *numen* as if the perfect and almighty God signifies His will by the act of willing, and signifies it with as much speed and facility as in the twinkling of an eye (*nutus oculorum*).[1] Just as Dionysius Longinus[2] admires Moses for worthily and magnificently expressing divine omnipotence in the phrase *dixit et facta sunt* (He spoke and they were made),[3] so the Latins seem to have signified both things in one word. For divine goodness, by willing what it wills, makes things so, and it does this with such facility that they seem to exist on their own account.

So, since Plutarch tells us that the Greeks praised the poetry of Homer and the paintings of Nicomachus because they seemed to have grown spontaneously, rather than to have been made by art, it is my view that poets and painters are called "divine" because of this faculty for feigning. Just as the divine facility in creation is "nature," so what we call "naturalness" is a rare and excellent virtue, as difficult as it is highly praised,[4] and Cicero would render it as "a genius flowing spontaneously and, somehow after a fashion, natural."[5]

III. Fate and Chance

Dictum, certum, fatum—Dictum, factum, casus— Why fate is inexorable

For the Latins *dictum* (said) was the same as *certum* (fixed, certain). For us *certain* is the same as *determined*.[6] Moreover, *fatum* (spoken, i.e., fate is the same as *dictum*; and *factum* (made) and *verum* (true) are interchangeable with *verbum* (word). And when the Latins themselves wanted to express agreement that something could be quickly done, they said *dictum factum* (no sooner said than done). And they

---

[1] If it were not that "facility" should be preserved, it would be better to render this passage as "signifies it as rapidly and easily as in the twinkling of an eye."

[2] *De Sublimitate*, IX.

[3] Genesis 1, passim.

[4] *Sit rara et praeclara illa virtus, tam difficilis quam commendata* is a conscious echo of the last sentence of Spinoza's *Ethics*. Vico seems to have turned Spinoza's intellectual standard of judgment (*claritas*) into his own standard of universal human consent. Spinoza goes from *praeclara* to *rara*; Vico goes from *rara* and *praeclara* to *commendata*. The other possible source of this passage is Plato. See *Greater Hippias*, 304e; *Republic*, 365d.

[5] Cicero, *De Oratore*, II, 15, 54, 77.

[6] See *NS*, 321; see also, 137–41, 163, 325, where the problem of knowledge becomes that of making true that which is certain.

called the final outcome of both deed and word *casum* (fall, chance, case). So the Italian sages who first thought up these words [must have] believed that *fatum* was the eternal order of causes, and that *casum* was the outcome of that eternal order. Thus, the deeds of God are His words, and the outcomes of things are the lot (*casus*) of the words that He speaks, and fate the same as what is made. Hence, they regarded fate as inexorable because what is done cannot be undone.

IV. Fortune

Fortuna from *fortus*—What fortune is—The world of nature is a republic—In what sense fortune is the queen of all things

Fortune was called kind or adverse. Yet *fortuna* was derived from the archaic word *fortus,* meaning "good." Therefore, to distinguish one kind of fortune from another, they later spoke of *fortuna fortis.* Moreover, *Fortuna* is [a] god who operates beyond our hope, but according to certain causes.[7] Did the ancient philosophers of Italy believe, then, that God did what was good, no matter what He did, and that every truth or every deed is identical with a good? Because of our iniquity, through which we consider ourselves, and not this universe of things, we think that what is adverse for us is evil, even though it is good because it contributed to the common good of the world.[8] In this view, the world is a kind of republic of nature in which the perfect and almighty God looks to the common good like a prince, and each of us, like a private citizen, looks to a certain good of his

---

[7] A clear indication of one of the main theories fully developed in the *New Science.* For the theory of providence and the heterogeneity of ends, see *NS,* 132–33, 341–42, 1108.

[8] Vico identifies human weakness with the fact that we are not equal to the world, but only with our own created nature. That is why he always moves from mathematics, our nature or creative capacity, to metaphysics. This is his version of the Cartesian circle. He disagrees with Spinoza and Leibniz, who thought that we can begin from God and so avoid it. Ethically, however, he seems to agree with Spinoza. Our standards of good and evil are those of our own finite self-interest made absolute. Only by seeing what truth is and seeing how our standards of truth are really related to the divine truth can we finally discover what the real standard of goodness is.

own. A private evil may be a public good; and just as in the republic founded by men the safety of a nation is the supreme law, so in the universe established by God luck would be the queen of all. To put it another way, luck is God's will by which He dominates over the private goods of all men and their peculiar natures, while He looks to the safety of the universe. And just as private safety yields to public safety, so the good peculiar to each person must take second place to the conservation of the universe, and in this way the adversities of nature are its goods.

CONCLUSION

Here then, Paolo Doria, for your great wisdom you have a meta-physics compatible with human frailty, which neither allows all truths to men, nor yet denies him all, but only some. It is a meta-physics consonant with Christian piety because it distinguishes divine from human truth and does not set up human knowledge as the rule for divine knowledge, but divine science as the rule for human knowledge. It is a handmaid for experimental physics, which is today cultivated with great profit to humanity; for in this metaphysics we regard as true in nature that to which we make something similar through experiments.

[Summing up] what you have here is this: to make [something] and to verify (*verare*) it are the same (Chapter One, Section I). Hence, God knows physical things, and man mathematical objects (Section II), and thus, the dogmatics do not know everything (Section III) nor the skeptics nothing (Section IV). Hence, too, kinds are the absolutely perfect ideas from [i.e., upon the model of] which God makes [nature][1] absolutely and the imperfect ideas by which man makes truth *ex hypothesi* (Chapter Two). Consequently, to prove from causes is itself to cause (Chapter Three). Because God makes even the smallest things by infinite power; therefore, just as existence is actuality and a physical thing, so the essence of things is power [virtue] and a

---

[1]God does not make truth, he begets it (like other Platonists, Vico accommodates his philosophy with the Bible via the Logos). The truth is not made, it is the mold for all making. The truth about nature is that nature was made.

metaphysical thing. This is the proper topic [metaphysical being] of my treatise (Chapter Four). And so there is in metaphysics a kind of thing that is the power of extension and motion and it subsists equally in unequal extensions and motions. This thing is the metaphysical point that we contemplate through the hypothesis of the geometrical point (Section II). And from the holy mysteries of geometry it is demonstrated that God is the purest infinite mind. The unextended [being] makes extended ones, and arouses conatus (Section III), composes motions (Section IV), and while at rest (Section V), it moves everything (Section VI).

You have here the doctrine that the spirit rules man's soul (Chapter Five), his mind rules his spirit, and that God rules the mind (Chapter Six). The mind makes fictions by paying attention (Chapter Seven), or the human mind makes truths *ex hypothesi*, while the divine mind makes true [things] absolutely (Sections I–III). Hence, man is given his mother wit for knowing or making (Section IV). Finally, you have the doctrine that God wills by a nod or by making (Chapter Eight. Section I). He makes by speaking or by the eternal order of causes, which we, in our ignorance, call chance (Section II), and in our self-interest, we call it fortune (Section III).

I ask you to take under your protection these principles of divinity which the Italians of old professed. For the work is rightly yours, [in general because] you belong by birth to the noblest family of Italy, famed for many monuments of its most glorious achievements; and [specifically because] you are renowned, throughout Italy, as the most learned of all who cultivate the field of metaphysics.

DISPUTATION CONCERNING
the *DE ANTIQUISSIMA*
ITALORUM SAPIENTIA,
1711–12

FIRST ARTICLE

Giornale de' letterati d'Italia,
volume V, article VI (1711): 119–30.

The main goal of this learned gentleman is to recover the philosophy of the ancient peoples of Italy. Because it cannot be ascertained on the basis of their philosophical writings, as none of them has come down to us, he promises to gather it from the origin and meaning of various terms in the Latin language.

In the proem he tells that, while he was studying the origin of the Latin language, he found in it many learned words that could not have originated in colloquial use, but, rather, in some teaching that was intrinsic to the peoples who used those words.[1] In fact, it seems very probable that a natural language becomes enriched with philosophical idioms whenever philosophy itself is much studied. He argues that, although the ancient Romans lacked any science until the time of Pyrrhus, they, nevertheless, used terms pregnant with philosophical meaning without understanding their import. It follows, therefore, that they must have appropriated these words from other neighboring nations. These nations professed the Italian philosophy that had been transplanted from Ionia, as well as from the ancient Tuscans [i.e., Etruscans], whom he shows to have been very learned

---

[1]*Doctrina intrinseca:* teaching that is intrinsic to the mind, that is, constitutive of its structure. Perhaps the reviewer himself does not understand Vico's idea that the Roman mind was structured by the philosophers of Magna Graecia, who built a metaphysical theory into language.

in every type of science, but mainly in theology. Doubtless the Romans received religious doctrine from them and also the language and idioms used by the priests in religious ceremonies.

He divides his philosophical work into three books: *Metaphysics, Physics,* and *Moral Philosophy.* In the *First Book of Metaphysics,* dedicated to the very learned Paolo Mattia Doria, he treats of forms of speech from which we can infer the ancient Romans' beliefs concerning the first truth, God, and the human mind. He divides it into eight chapters; and he confesses that it was three very learned friends— Messrs. Agostino Ariano, Giacinto di Cristoforo, and Nicola Galizia—who first encouraged him to undertake the project.

First, he asserts that among the Latins *verum* and *factum* are reciprocal terms. The verb *intelligere* means "to read perfectly" and "to have plain knowledge." The verb *cogitare* means "to think" and "to gather."

Then he goes on to argue that the ancient wise men of Italy believed that God possessed complete and infinite truth, for he is the maker and creator of everything, and His Truth represents to him the elements of all things, both internal and external.[2] Moreover, because knowledge is nothing but the putting together of the elements of things, he reasons that intelligence is proper only to God, who, because He contains all things in Himself, can read not only the outside of them, but also the inside, whereas only thought is proper to the human mind (which is finite and outside of things), or, in other words, not the integral gathering of things, but only the gathering of their extremities, and of what is on the outside, so to speak.

Then he proceeds to prove that, because the perfect truth is only in God, we have no science more certain than the revealed theology that we have received from God Himself through faith.

God knows everything because He contains in Himself the elements of which everything is composed. Man, likewise, tries to know everything by way of division, so that human knowledge can be called an anatomy of the works of nature. Thus, for example, we are accustomed to dividing man into body and mind and mind into intellect and will; we abstract from body extension and motion and from these, as from everything else, being and unity. Here we have the origin of the human sciences. Metaphysics studies being; arithmetic studies the one and its multiplication; geometry, figure and its mea-

2*Gli elementi delle cose tutte.*

sures; mechanics, motion round the center; physics, motion from the center; medicine, the body; logic, reason; ethics, the will. However, these sciences are, for the most part, very imperfect in man and far from the truth; and having things only outside us, we cannot know them except by way of abstraction, thus turning to our advantage that which is the mere defect of our mind. And by this abstraction are produced two sciences that are the most useful because they are the most certain: geometry and arithmetic; from these two was begotten mechanics, whence all the arts needful to humankind were born. And because these sciences are constructive, they are also the most true, being similar to divine science, in which the true and the made are convertible.

After he has established that the human mind knows many truths at least, if not all, he begins first to confute Descartes, who sets up for his metaphysician the primary canon that he must not only rid himself, to begin with, of every prejudice, but also of anything whatsoever; and then he confutes the skeptics, who doubt everything and who claim that it is impossible to be certain of anything.

In Chapter Two, he proceeds to examine the two words *genus* and *species*. Among the Latins, he says, *genus* denoted the form, and *species* is what the scholastics call individual and what we ordinarily call image or appearance. And because all philosophical schools agree that the genera are infinite, therefore, he argues that the view of the ancient philosophers of Italy was that the genera were infinite not in their extension, but in their perfection, and that as such are found in God only, whereas species or singular things are images made according to these forms. Because truth and fact signify the same thing, it necessarily follows that the genera of things are not the universals of the Schools, but precisely the metaphysical forms; that is, ideas and models upon which the physical forms of individual things are elaborated. From this he deduces many consequences very useful to the study of the sciences.

1. The method of synthesis is better for the sciences than that of analysis.
2. Those arts that set before the mind the idea of what is to be done achieve their aim better than those that proceed rather by conjecture.
3. It is very dangerous to linger too long over generalities and there is no better method for arriving at the truth than knowing how to

harmonize the universality of the idea with all the circumstantial details that are encountered in any singular case.

The third chapter follows. Among the Latins the terms *causa* and *negotium* are synonyms, signifying productive activity. They called what is born of them "effect." Hence if the true and the made, or the effect, are the same thing, it follows that to prove anything whatever from causes would be to have made it. And because the matter or the elements of things are their causes, it follows that whoever gives to ill arranged and disposed elements that order and arrangement from which results that form of the thing which induces in it a specific nature, proves from causes. Such is the procedure of arithmetic and geometry.

Then, in the following chapter, he discusses subtly and at length claims about the essences or powers of things, about metaphysical points, about impulses to move and about motion itself. Anyone who wanted to expound it all would not be making a compendious extract from the book, but a new book from which this present volume would rather appear to be the extract.

In Chapter Five he takes note that the ancient Latins distinguished the terms *animus* (spirit) and *anima* (soul); the former was the principle of sensation, the latter the principle of life. But because air, which he proves to be the principle common to all motions, was called by the same people "soul," he argues that the ancient wise men of Italy considered the soul and spirit of animals as nothing but [a] particular motion of air which, when introduced into the heart through breathing and from there to the arteries and the veins, forces the blood to move. In this way, it insinuates itself from the arteries and veins into the canals of the nerves, and by agitating their juices it causes all those motions that are usually attributed to the sensitive faculties. From this he even deduces that, since among the Latins the term *brutum* meant nothing but "motionless object," it was their view that animals did not have, as we do, an internal principle of motion. They were on their own account motionless, save insofar as they become determined to move through the presence of external objects.

In Chapter Six, he examines the term *mind* and notices that among the Latins this term often signifies what we call "thought." He considers those Latin idioms that assert that "mind is given to men by the gods," or it is "transmitted" to them, and offers the hypothesis that it was the teaching of the first masters of Italian wisdom that God is the prime author and origin in our minds; not only of our every idea and thought, but also of all the acts of our will. Thereafter, he shows how this statement can be consistent with the infinite goodness of God and with the freedom of our choice.

Chapter Seven is wholly devoted to the examination of the powers of our soul on these principles. It deals with what powers there are, and with the mode of their operation. The author here considers the three well-known operations of our mind: perception, judgment, and reasoning. These are the concern of logic, which he divides into topics, criticism, and method. Thus, topics is the faculty or, better, the art of understanding; criticism, the faculty of judgment; and method, the faculty of reasoning. He subjects the geometric method to critical examination and finds it to be of no use for some arts and sciences, and quite harmful in some others. Finally, he favors the synthetic method over the analytic because he holds the method of composition to be a safer way to arrive at the truth than the method of analysis, inasmuch as the true is reached by making it.

Finally, in the last chapter, he deals with the meaning of the words *numen, fatum, casus,* and *fortuna.* Then he offers conjectures on what the beliefs of the ancient philosophers of Italy were about the divinity and about the order and execution of his eternal decrees and plans. To this chapter, the author adds the conclusion of all his work, which is nothing but a brief resumé of what we have expounded above with much less brevity.

So if we have left completely unmentioned a great many of the things that are so subtly dealt with in this book, that is no wonder, for its learned author crowds speculations without number into every page and even into every line and with such brevity that to touch on everything, even slightly, would be to write a review as large as the whole book. And that makes one think that, in putting together this booklet, the author meant to give us only an outline and a specimen of his metaphysics, not the metaphysics itself. For we have observed that many theses are asserted in it that seem to need proof. And it is to be hoped that one day we shall have it, when the author gives us the whole work completed in print.[3] But above all, we want to see the thesis that is the main foundation and distinctive novelty of the whole work proven. On what grounds does he conclude that in the Latin tongue *factum* and *verum, causa* and *negotium,* mean the same thing?

[3]That is to say, the complete system, including physics and ethics.

VICO'S FIRST RESPONSE

Honored Sir:[1]

With the authority you exercise over me, you advance three serious objections against the first book of my treatise on *The Most Ancient Wisdom of the Italians*, which contains my metaphysics.

1. You want to see the thesis that is the main foundation and distinctive novelty of the whole work proven: on what grounds do I conclude that in the Latin tongue *factum* and *verum, causa* and *negotium*, mean the same thing?
2. You believe that by writing this booklet I meant to give you only an outline and a specimen of my metaphysics, not the metaphysics itself.
3. You find in this work many things simply asserted that seem to need proof.

With my customary brevity, and without forgetting the respect I have for you, I answer:

1. Those phrases, which are the first principles of my metaphysics, have among the Latins the senses that I have assigned to them.

---

[1]Perhaps Bernardino Trevisano (1653–1720), "one of the greatest minds of the century," according to the eulogy made by Vincenzio Pasqualigo on the occasion of Trevisano's appointment to the chair of philosophy at the University of Venice. (See *Giornale de' letterati* 5 [1710]:355.) Trevisano was a sincere Cartesian, much versed in philosophical argumentation, who, as a philosophical reviewer of the *Giornale*, had opposed L. A. Muratori's *Della perfetta poesia*.

2. My metaphysics in that little book is complete.

3. Nothing in it lacks proof.[2]

I. That among the Latins the Words *Verum* and *Factum*, *Causa* and *Negotium*, Meant Two Things

As for the first two terms, Phaedria in Terence's *Eunuchus*[3] asks Dorus, "Did Chaerea take your clothing off?" and he answers, "It is done." The young master continues. "And did he put it on?" And likewise the eunuch answers, "Yes" (*Factum*). Both answers could be translated into Italian by *È vero* (It is true).

Cremes in the *Self-Tormentor*[4] scolds his son Clitipho, "How intemperately you acted at the party last night." And Syrus, who pretends to agree with the old man, says, "Done" (*Factum*).

It could be said that in the above examples one speaks of events. Hence, *factum* could just as well stand for such expressions of ours as "it happened," "it occurred," and the like. But we have a host of other examples in which one speaks of things and *factum* cannot be understood in any other way save as *verum*.

In an example from Plautus,[5] Pseudolus and Calliodorus by turn abuse the pimp Ballio, who boldly agrees that all charges brought against him are true.

PSEUDOLUS: Shameless.

BALLIO: Yes.

CALLIODORUS: Criminal.

[2]Nicolini argues that, although Vico is correct in his last two counterclaims, he is wrong in the first one. Fausto Nicolini, *Giambattista Vico: Opere* (Milan: Ricciardo Ricciardi, 1953), p. 310. According to Nicolini, Vico's appeal to the two comic poets is useless and etymologically erroneous. Although the etymology is farfetched, Vico's intentions seem clear and consistent with the goals of his metaphysics. The epistemological criterion of the *verum* and *factum* is shown to be valid (1) by analogy with divine knowledge, and (2) by appeal to the idiomatic uses of the comic poets Terence and Plautus. By analogy with divine knowledge, the criterion is analytical. By appeal to the idiomatic uses of the comic poets, the criterion is descriptive because it exemplifies how it was actually used by the common people in Plautus's and Terence's comedies. To his own satisfaction, Vico succeeded in proving the validity of his principle. God and the common people are the only evidence he needs.

[3]Terence, *Eunuchus*, 707–8, IV, 4, 39–40.

[4]Terence, *Self-Tormentor*, 567, III, 3, 4.

[5]*Pseudolus*, 360–61. Abbreviated version by Vico.

BALLIO: You tell the truth.
PSEUDOLUS: Whipping boy!
BALLIO: Why not!
CALLIODORUS: Crook!
BALLIO: Excellently done! (*Factum*)

(Which cannot be understood in any other fashion but "It is very true.")

As for the other two terms, it is as much vulgar Latin that *causa* and *negotium* have the same referent as it is that in our own vulgar speech *cosa* (thing) derives from the Latin *causa*. Therefore, the Latins express with the neuter gender what we call "thing," while we say *buona cosa* (good thing) for what the Latins call *bonum* (good), for which the grammarians substitute *negotium*. But because the language of the grammarians is different from that of the Latins, to rid ourselves of these difficulties we turn to the Latin writers and to the distinction made by Quintilian.[6]

The jurists who faithfully preserved pure Latin through the most decadent times understood *negotium* (business, activity) upon hearing the term *causa*. So John Kahl testifies in his *Lexicon*.[7] Hence, the primary difference between *pact* and *contract* which they teach their students is that contract obtains where there is business, which they explain as "loan," "establishment of the price of goods," or the oath of questioning and answering. Thus mortgages, selling, and stipulations are considered contracts. Contrariwise, pact does not entail "business" or "deed," but "the state of doing," like "promise of giving a loan," "of selling," "of stipulating." They call them "bare promises" or "bare pacts" because deprived of causes, of deed, and of fact.[8]

[6]Quintilian, *Institutio Oratoria*, III, 3, 4.

[7]Calvin, alias Kahl, *Magnum Lexicon Iuridicum* (Geneva, 1689). "Causa verbum generale est, quod comprehendit principium negotii, cum proponitus, et cum quis deliberet et proponit ut litiget." See also s.v. *negotium*. "Negotium 'inquit Quintilianus' est congregatio personarum, locorum, temporum, causarum. Negotium ad omnem causam pertinet quae Quintiliani definitio fere convenitu cum Ciceronis verbis. Id autem discriminis inter causam et negotium credit esse Quintiliani definitio fere convenitu cum Ciceronis verbis. Id autem discriminis inter causam et negotium credit esse Quintilian liber IV, quod causam negotium intelligamus." Actually, Quintilian discusses these words in Book III, Chapter 5, of *Institutio Oratoria*.

[8]See Adolph Berger, "Encyclopedic Dictionary of Roman Law," in *Transactions of the American Philosophical Society*, n.s., vol. 43, pt. 2 (1953), s.v. *nudum pactum*. For Vico's reference to *pacta nuda* and *pacta vestita*, see *NS*, 569, 1030, 1072.

However, someone could say that these are recondite terms, and our purpose was to treat the ancient Italian wisdom from the point of view of colloquial Latin: he shall be satisfied with the countless passages of the comic playwrights whose idiomatic expressions are the most colloquial. From these, I choose passages in Terence's *Andria*, where Pamphilius says that Cremes is happy that Pasibula is to remain his wife using these words: *De uxore, ita ut possedi nihil mutat Cremes* (Regarding my wife, Cremes has not changed anything, as I had her). And Cremes answers, *Causa optima est.* We would render Cremes' answer into Italian as *Il negozio, il partito è buonissimo* (The transaction is excellent)[9]

The most subtle distinction between these two idioms is that noticed by Quintilian, for whom *causa* means ὑπόθεσιν (hypothesis) and *negotium* περίστασιν (*peristasis*), which is to say that the former signifies "the fact," the latter, "the circumstance." This distinction does not make the word *causa* synonymous with *negotium*.

Unless I am mistaken, I have proven to a man who is not ashamed of himself, who deals with the academic world with that good faith by which anyone who writes and argues without footnotes and authoritative references is obligated. Now your doubting mind may rest in that confidence your own courtesy could have bestowed on me.

II. That Our Metaphysics Is Complete

A complete metaphysics is one in which being and truth, or to put it in one phrase, the True Being, is established. The study not only of first truth, but also of the unique Truth drives us to the origin and criterion of subordinate sciences. This unique Truth is to be affirmed against the dogmatists, if they posit it in something else, and against the skeptics, who will not admit any truth [as certain]. We are dealing here with the ideas, which filled the Platonic metaphysics, and the universals, which are the subject matter of Aristotelian metaphysics. And since the first cause is investigated in this science, it is there established what type of cause it is. Because eternal and changeless entities are treated, questions of essences and substances occupy the most important place. What the substance of body and of mind are is

[9]Terence, *Andria*, 949.

demonstrated, and what the substance above both of them is, which maintains and moves everything. This is the science that allots the subject matter proper to all other sciences. From it are derived the primary definitions in mathematics, the principles in physics, the ability to use one's reason well in logic, the final end of all goods, that we may be united with it in moral philosophy. These are all the lines that sketch the blueprint of a complete metaphysics in which, as the harmony of a design, it is required that its subject matter be treated concordantly with the Christian religion, since its author is a citizen of that community.[10] The origins of the vulgar Latin words have provided me with this blueprint. I have argued about it as follows.

First, I establish that the true is convertible with the made. I understand in this way the convertibility of the Good with Being taught in the Schools. Then I surmise that the unique Truth is in God because all that is made is contained in Him. For this very reason, God alone is True Being, and in comparison with Him, individual entities are not true beings, but dispositions of the True Being. And making the gentile wisdom play handmaid to that of Christianity, I prove that, because the philosophers of the heathen darkness considered the world to be eternal and God to operate on it always from outside, they made the true and the made absolutely interchangeable. But because we consider the world to have been created in time, we must introduce the distinction that, in God, the true is interchanged *ad intra* with that which is begotten, and *ad extra* with that which is made. God alone is true intelligence because He alone knows all and the divine wisdom is the most perfect word. For this wisdom represents everything and contains within itself the elements of everything; and containing them it disposes the forms or manner of things from infinity, and in disposing them it knows them, and in knowing them it makes them. This divine cognition is reason, of which man partakes. Hence, the Latins called man "the animal sharing in reason." And for his share of it, man has not the intelligence of the whole, but the thought of it, which is tantamount to saying that he does not comprehend infinity, yet he can go about gathering it.[11]

---

[10]Quite appropriately, Nicolini (*Vico: Opere*, p. 313) notices that, had Vico belonged to a different commonwealth, he would have treated the same topic differently.

[11]See Chapter One of this work. Notice that *intelligere* qualifies God's power and implies "to read thoroughly," whereas *cogitare* qualifies man's intellectual activity and implies "to put things together." Namely, God alone *intelligit*; man *legit*.

Having molded this criterion of truth, I lead all human sciences to this criterion and measure the degrees of their truth according to it. First, I prove that the mathematical sciences are the only ones that lead to human truth, because they alone proceed on the models of the divine science. By defining various terms, the mathematical sciences create their own elements. They extend these elements ad infinitum with their postulates. They have established certain eternal truths with their own axioms; and by disposing of the elements throughout this feigned infinity and from all this feigned eternity, these sciences create the truths they teach. Man contains within himself a fictitious world of lines and numbers, and he operates in it with his abstractions just as God operates with reality. By using the same method, I proceed to establish the origin and criterion of the other sciences and arts.

Thus, I don't confute the "analysis," as you report, by which Descartes arrives at his first truth.[12] Rather, I approve of it, and to such a degree that I notice how even Plautus's Sosia, induced by Mercury as if by an evil genius to doubt everything, took comfort in it too ("But I think, therefore, I am"). But I say that thinking is an indubitable sign of my existence; yet since it is not its cause, it does not lead me to a science of being.

Then I turn against the skeptics and lead them to where they are forced to concede that the comprehension of all the causes from which the effects result is possible. This comprehension of all causes I posit as the primary truth.

I go on to discuss genera, or modes or modifications or forms, and also species or copies or appearances (whichever one pleases to call them in either case). I prove that the modes, in which every particular thing is brought to actualize its being by its principles from the first moment when they were moved and from every place whence they were moved, are metaphysical forms. Therefore, the true mode of every individual entity goes back to God. Consequently, genera are infinite—not because they are universal, but because they are perfect. This is the short and true meaning of Plato's long and intricate *Parmenides*.[13] And this is the interpretation we must give to the famous

---

[12]Vico becomes unnecessarily touchy. The reviewer had simply said, "He begins first to confute Descartes, who sets up for his metaphysician the primary canon that he must not rid himself . . . of every prejudice, but even of anything whatsoever."

[13]Only in Proclus's commentary to the *Parmenides*.

Ladder of Ideas used by the Platonists to arrive at the most perfect and eternal ones. I corroborate this from their effects, by enumerating exactly the advantages that the ideas bring to human knowledge, and the evils that universals bring. I prove that the physical forms are derived from the metaphysical ones, and that, when compared, the metaphysical forms are found to be true and the physical forms to be false. The latter are appearances and copies, the former are real and complete. But because the imprints carry self-evidence with them, I discuss what they mean. Thus, when I consider a peculiar form of mine placed in my thought, I cannot at all doubt it. But when I enter more deeply into the metaphysical form, I find it to be false that I think, and the truth is that God thinks in me. Thus, I understand that in any individual entity there is God's imprint. I argue that the scholastics were very wise when they called genera "metaphysical matter," if the expression is taken in this sense: metaphysical form is that which is purified of every particular form, that is, it can receive all the particular forms easily and readily. In this way, I gather the form to which the sage ought to conform his mind.

I pursue my course to prove that the truly unique cause is the one that needs nothing else to produce its effect, being that which contains in itself the elements of the thing it produces and disposes them, and thus it forms and comprehends the mode of them, and by comprehending it sends forth the effect. Because this definition of causality was not established in metaphysics, many philosophers have fallen into a great many mistakes. For they have held that God works like a demiurge and that the things He creates cause other things and are not, rather, parts of the modes that the eternal mind of God comprehends. But this must not be overlooked. Since the first cause has not been properly understood, the mathematical sciences are generally regarded as contemplative sciences that do not argue from causes. Yet they alone among all the sciences are truly constructive and prove from causes, for of all the human sciences, only mathematics proceeds on the model of the divine science.

Thus far, I have molded the head of my metaphysics. Now the body follows, as I enter the vast field of essences, and by the light of geometrical truth kindled at the fount of all the light of human knowledge (I mean metaphysics), I make clear that essence consists in indivisible substance, which is nothing but an indefinite power and an effort of the universe to produce and sustain all of the particular things. For nothing cannot begin or end that which is, and to divide is, in a certain way, to make an ending. Thus, the essence of body is an indefinite power to keep body extended, and it equally underlies all extended things no matter how unequal they are. This very power to be extended is also an indefinite power of motion which equally underlies all motions, however unequal. In God, this power is eminently act. It follows that God, matter, and body correspond in perfect proportion to rest, conatus, and motion. God enjoys absolute rest because He is absolutely pure act; He is absolutely perfect. Matter is power and effort. Bodies move because they are constituted out of matter striving at every point and, therefore, at every instant, and they impede one another's efforts through the continuity of their parts. Such motion is nothing but inhibited effort, which, if it could express itself freely, would go to the infinite to come to rest and would thus return to God, from whom it issued. Hence, substance as the power to maintain extended matter was called by the Italian philosophers *punctum*, and as the power to sustain motion, *momentum*. They took point and moment to be the same thing, and that one thing to be indivisible. And in this manner I reclaim for Italian philosophy the points of Zeno and I purge them from the evil reputation given them by Aristotle (who was followed in this matter by Descartes). I make it clear that these points are something very different from what they have been understood to be until now. The physical body does not consist of geometrical points. Hence, the objection that "a point added to another point does not create extension" has been generally accepted. But just as the geometrical point, having been defined as an entity without parts, enables us to demonstrate that lines, otherwise incommensurable, can be divided into an equal number of points, so there is an indivisible substance in nature that equally underlies unequal extended solids. Thus, the geometrical point is a paradigm, or likeness, of the metaphysical power that sustains and contains extended matter and that was, therefore, called a "metaphysical point" by Zeno. Hence, we can reason about the essence of body only on this model and not otherwise, because we have no other science, save mathematics, that proceeds on the model of divine science.

The sequence leads me to discuss *momenta* and motions too, so far as they are the concern of metaphysics. I prove that extended things do not exert conatus, but are moved; for the points are the principles of motion, and these principles of motion are the *momenta*.

[I prove further] that there are no rectilinear motions in nature, but that [all] efforts are toward rectilinear motions. Imagining bodies moving in a straight line in the void is the work of a mind besotted with the erroneous ideal of imaginary spaces. Bodies not only could not move in a rectilinear fashion through the void, but they would not move; and indeed, they would not exist at all, because bodies subsist and exist insofar as the universe sustains them with its own plenum and contains them in its plenum.

[And I prove that] there is no rest in nature because effort is the life of nature, and conatus is not rest.

Finally, [I prove] that motions are not communicated. For motion is body in movement. So, if bodies were to communicate motion, it would be as if they were to penetrate each other. To feign that the body moved carries on with it completely, or in part, the motion of the body that moves it, is much more than feigning their attraction.

Having reasoned about "extended substance" and about "motion," I pass on to "thinking substance" and deal with the "soul," or life, with the "spirit," or sensation; and with the "air," or ether, which the Latins called *anima*. I prove that the air of the blood is the vehicle of life, and that of the nerves is the vehicle of sensation. I do not maintain, as you seem to think, that the motion of the nerves is due to the blood. Rather, the motion of the blood to the nerves is due to the heart, which is all one muscle and a reticulate affair variegated with a mass of small nerves.

I suggest that the opinion about the animal's soul was known and approved by the ancient Italian philosophers, who called what is immobile *brutum*.

I discuss the seat of the spirit (*animus*), that is, the place where it performs most of its functions; this I locate in the heart.

So having completed the doctrine of both substances, I go on to consider mind or thought. Here I cite Malebranche, who will have it that God creates ideas in us, which is the same as saying God thinks in us, and [yet] concedes the first truth of Descartes and admits as true the proposition that "I think." I discuss the freedom of human choice and the immutability of divine decrees and how they can be reconciled.

As appendices to these discussions, the faculties of the soul are treated. Since a faculty is an aptitude to work, I infer that our soul creates its own subject matter with each of its faculties as colors with sight, odors with smell, sound with hearing, and so on. I discuss memory and imagination and conclude that they are one and the same faculty.

Next I derive the specific faculty of knowledge from these established principles and declare it to be *ingenium*. For with this, a man can put together things that appear completely unrelated to those who have no stock of it. Hence, the mother wit of man is nature in the arts, just as the mother wit of God is nature in the universe.[14]

Having established this, I discuss the three operations belonging to the human mind, and I assign three arts for directing them: topics, criticism, and method. I call them "arts," and not "faculties," as you suggest, because the faculty is that which is guided, ruled, and made secure by the art. Here, while speaking about the method, I explain the advantages of the synthetic method over the analytic, because the former teaches us the way to create truth, the latter goes blindly in search of it.

Finally, I come to a halt in the contemplation of the supreme Creator. I show Him to be the "Deity" because with a nod or, better, with instant effects, He wills and with His creative act He speaks. So that the works of God are His words, which were called "fates"; they are called "chance" when things turn out contrary to our expectations. And because everything He does is good for the universe, they are called "fortune."

I show briefly how, from this metaphysics, geometry derives the fiction of the indivisible point that is drawn and arithmetic the fiction of the indivisible unit that is multiplied; and how mathematics bases the whole great mass of its demonstrations on the definition of these two names.

Likewise, mechanics has drawn from metaphysics the indivisible power of motion, *momentum* or conatus; and assuming it to be in individual bodies, mechanics erects upon it its machines.

Physics takes from metaphysics metaphysical points; that is, the indivisible powers of extension and of motion, and from points and *momenta*, as terms of mechanics or of machines, it proceeds through

---

[14]See *De Antiquissima Italorum Sapientia* (hereafter *DAIS*), Chapter Seven, Section IV, where this confusing statement is clearly expressed. Human *ingenium* is analogous to God's *ingenium*, although it operates differently and in different domains. God's wit creates nature; man's wit makes an artificial world.

the expedients of mechanics, that is to say of machines, to treat of bodies in motion, which is its subject matter.

Ethics derives from metaphysics the idea of the perfect mind of the sage: a mind that is unformed by any particular idea or mold and that, through contemplation and the practice of human living, kneads itself like dough and makes itself very soft, so to speak, in order to accept easily the imprints of things down to their very last detail. Hence arises the active indifference of the sage, his capacity to comprehend many and diverse matters, his readiness to act, his judgment of things on their merits, and finally, his word and deed so apt that, no matter how hard another may try, he cannot speak or act more appropriately—which is why the memorable sayings and doings of wise men are so much commended.

Through these same principles of metaphysics, the truth of mathematics is asserted and confirmed, and the reason men generally assent to mathematical demonstrations is brought out. For in mathematics men are the whole cause of the effects they produce, they comprehend the whole manner of their production, and they grasp the manner and make the truth in [the act of] knowing it. From these same principles, and from nowhere else, springs the reason men also assent to the physics that makes theoretical conclusions evident through experiments, which present us with phenomena similar to those nature itself provides. Thus, physics rests satisfied with the phenomena for which metaphysics knows the causes. And rational mechanics, fostered by the flower of human wit, seeks to work out for us that likeness of nature. But what matters more than anything else is the fact that it supports Christian theology, in which we profess a God completely devoid of body, in whom all the powers of individual things are contained, and in Him they are pure act, for He alone is infinite act and in every finite thing, however tiny, He shows His omnipotence. Hence, He is all in all, and all as He wills the least part of the whole.

This is the gist or, better still, the spirit of my metaphysics stated in a nutshell; there is no need for the gist to equal the mass of the book. From it, any learned man can readily form an adequate concept of how everything fits together in a system of metaphysics that is already complete. [This is what one ought to provide] and not an incoherent and confused review, which creates in others who have not read my little book the impression that my metaphysics is indeed only a sketch. Furthermore, the speculations without number which, you say yourself, are crowded into every line of every page ought to have kept you from coming to such a conclusion. [You should have seen] that where I have expended so much thought, I did not have it in mind to make an outline that, however vast, can be sketched with a few lines only, but that I really wanted to publish a fully finished work. Forgive me, but although I do not deserve it, you treat me like a man who wants to arouse the curiosity of wise men with magnificent headings and then welsh on their expectations. But whatever the reason may have been for that, I ought, and [intend], to take it in good spirit—especially from you, most esteemed sir—even the fact that because the little book was so small, it appeared to you to be only a blueprint. You should have remembered, however, that there are two classes of scholars useful to the republic of letters. The first class contains those who wish to be useful to young students, for whom it is necessary to explain the subject matter from the beginning, to present the views of others in detail, and to state all the arguments with precision, whether one is building on them or refuting them. Then one can advance something of theirs in the middle, make all the consequences explicit, and arrive at the ultimate corollaries. These are the voluminous scholars. And when one is reviewing them, one can and ought to pass over many things; that is, whatever belongs to others. There are others who don't want to burden the order of the learned with extra labor, or oblige them to read over again the multitude of things they have already read elsewhere, for the sake of some few things that are new here. These are the ones who publish little tiny books that are packed full of original things. I have tried to belong to this second class; it is for the learned to judge whether I have succeeded. But if not, then it is because the subject of my metaphysics is the metaphysical points, and you have treated them as worth little or nothing. Hence, in your review, you pass over them very dryly, saying only, "He discusses metaphysical points," and then you say not another word about them. Perhaps this is the reason my metaphysics has appeared sketchy to you. But the way I am talking now is the way that men, and not things, do the talking—and I don't enjoy that at all—so I shall pass on gladly to your third doubt.

III. None of the Claims Made Lacks Proof

You say that very many statements seem to you to be in need of proof. This criticism is much too vague. Serious scholars have never deigned to answer unless the criticisms made against them were specific and precise. In spite of this, out of the respect I must bear you, I will investigate and see if I can come upon one of the many [propositions you say need proof].

Perhaps one might be this: what contains the elements of things, and the ways in which they are made, and consequently, the things themselves does not have to be mind. In fact, a pagan philosopher could call it an infinite, self-moving body.

But to this there is an answer where I say that just as unity, the power of number, generates number although it is not itself a number, so the point, the power of extension, generates extension, though it is not itself extended. To that example, I add now that conatus, the power of motion, produces motion though it is not itself motion.

The same critic will reply that he has no idea save of extension and of motion, whereas he has an idea of his own thought prior to extension because thought is the particular motion that constitutes his being man. And, therefore, he cannot reason about the other things, upon any principles except those of extension and motion.

There is an answer to this also, where we pointed out that Aristotle is as much mistaken in treating physics metaphysically, in terms of potencies and infinite powers, as is Descartes, who treats metaphysics in terms of actions and finite forms. The reason for both of their mistakes is the same. Each of them applied a completely inappropriate criterion to his topic. But Zeno did not reduce one to the other. Rather, between them he interposed geometry—the only science that treats infinite and eternal finite[15] [things]—and he reasoned about them with its help. For essence is a cause of being (ratio essendi). Nothing can neither begin nor end that which is; consequently, it cannot divide that which is, since dividing is one way of making an ending. Hence, the essence of body consists in indivisibles. Body,

---

[15]The finite things of geometry are eternal objects because they are defined *ideals*, but because they are *ideals*, they are *infinite* in the sense of being perfect. Since there are no demonstrably perfect triangles in physical nature, the geometrical ideal is the limit of an infinite process of approximation.

however, can be divided; hence, the essence of the body is not body. What, then, is it? It is an indivisible power that contains, sustains, and maintains body and equally underlies unequal parts of the body. The essence is a substance, and one can only argue about substance according to the principles of the one human science, which is similar to the divine and which is, therefore, uniquely competent to demonstrate human truth.

As he seeks to reason about it [substance] in this way, the great Galileo is compelled by those most elegant demonstrations that he offers about it in the first of his *Dialogues concerning a New Science* to burst out with the following words: "These are the difficulties that arise from the discourse we produce with our finite intellect, about infinite [quantities] when we ascribe to them the same attributes that we ascribe to finite, and limited things—which is, I think, a mistake—because I consider that these attributes of being bigger, smaller, and equal do not apply to infinites, since we cannot say of them that one is bigger, smaller, or equal to another."[16]

And just a little before this he naively confesses that he loses himself "among the infinites and indivisibles." Galileo looked at physics with the eyes of a great geometrician, but not in the full light of metaphysics. Therefore, he considers the indivisible different from the infinite and speaks of more than one infinite. There are not several infinites, but just one, and it is equal to itself in all its finite parts; let them be as unequal as you please. The indivisible is one because the infinite is one, and the infinite is indivisible because there is no way in which it can be divided, since nothingness cannot divide it.

Here my critic will lie in ambush for me and answer that all that I have claimed is true enough in an infinite body, which is indivisible because there is no void within which it can be divided.

But this ambush, too, we foresaw. For no matter how we may abandon ourselves in the vast fantasy of an infinite body, still the body of the smallest grain of sand is not infinite, and yet it contains an infinite power of extension, in account of which you can go on dividing it ad infinitum. This is what I meant when I argued that Aristotle differs from Zeno about different things, but agrees with him about the same one: he speaks of the division of body, which is motion and

---

[16]*Discorsi e dimostrazioni matematiche intorno a due nuove scienze* (1638) in *Opere*, edizione nazionale, 8:77–78. Notice that Vico reduces *two* new sciences to *one*.

actuality, whereas Zeno speaks of powers whereby every tiny corpuscle corresponds to an infinite extension. If you actually divide a grain of sand, there will always remain something you can divide. But whoever says that for this reason the grain of sand is a body of infinite extension and magnitude is not thinking what he says, because a small extension is implicit in the notion of a grain of sand, and the whole universe stands in the way of any indefinite extension. This is what I reiterate in many places: that those who want to employ formed things as the standard of the formless ones are on the wrong track. But contrariwise, the right way to speak of things is to say that in the grain of sand we have something such that when one divides that tiny corpuscle, it yields and sustains an infinite extension and magnitude so that the mass of the universe is potentially and virtually—but not actually—contained in the grain of sand. I conclude that the energy of the universe, which is neither the extension of the small body nor the extension of the universe, sustains even the smallest corpuscle. This is the mind of God, which, pure of all matter, stirs up and moves the whole in motion.

But my critic will persist, declaring that there is more evidence of thought and extension than of any geometrical proof, and that, therefore, these ideas ought to be the criteria of all human knowledge.

To this again the answer has been given, where I argued that to know clearly and distinctly is a fault of the human understanding and not its virtue; and here I proved that physical forms are evident so long as they are not compared with metaphysical ones; and where I confirmed this too, that whenever I consider myself I am quite certain that "if I think, then I am there." But when I immerse myself in God as the one and only True Being, I truly know that I am not. Thus, when we consider extension and its three dimensions, we establish eternal truths in the world of abstractions. In fact, "we seek heaven itself out of our stupidity"[17] because only in God are there eternal truths. We regard it as an eternal truth that "the whole is greater than the parts." Yet when we go back to first principles, we find that the axiom is false and we accept, as demonstrated, the thesis that there is as much power of extension in the center of the circle as there is in the whole circumference because lines can be drawn from every point on the circumference which passes through the center. To conclude

[17]Horace, *Carmina*, 1, 3, 38.

then, in metaphysics the man who profits is the one who suffers the loss of himself in the meditation of this science.

Another place may perhaps be where, granted the infallibility of divine decrees, the freedom of human choice appears not to be proved. But I ought not to think it of your great wit, that in reading the passage where I prove that motions are not communicated, you did not easily notice a likeness to this situation; for about an incomprehensible mystery we cannot reason in any other way. And that, I am sure, is why you summed up so ably my argument about the motion of bodies and minds. Just as motion common to air becomes proper and real motion of fire, plant, and animal through the particular mechanism whereby each of these particular objects acquires its peculiar form, so the divine will becomes true and proper motion of our will through our mind, which is the particular form of each of us. So that every act of our will is both our own true and proper choice and, at the same time, the infallible decree of God.

The fact that the Latins considered brute beasts "immobile" seems to be at odds with this statement.

I could say, in answer, that the Latins called the brutes "immobile" because they regarded them as moved by air and not as moving autonomously. But according to the arguments we have just made, their being moved by air does not exclude their moving by themselves. However, I do never try to maintain any such view, which the most faithful interpreters of the mind of Descartes consider to be just a very pretty fable, only to be commended for the neatness of its weaving.

But certainly the statement that bodies do not strive will seem to you asserted and not proven. The common opinion of the Cartesians will have driven you to this, for they posit as the foundation stone of their physics the thesis that physical bodies strive to move away from the center.

But the striving of the universe is one, because it is the striving of the universe, and the single cycle is the indivisible center, which it is not proper to find within the universe. Within the lines of its direction, it sustains all the particular things at once and spins them, maintaining all the unequal weights with equal strength. This is the substance that strives to send things forth by the ways that best befit its supreme power (i.e., the shortest and rectilinear paths), and being hindered by the continuity of bodies, it moves them in a spin. Whenever and however it can express its activity, it forms diastole and systole, through which all things get their particular shapes. Hence, it is not a property of bodies to move from the center; rather, it is a property of the center to maintain everything with all its might. But the mechanists have feigned that there is this conatus in bodies, since no science makes a good start if it does not derive its axioms from metaphysics. Metaphysics is the science that imparts to all the others their proper subject matter, and since it cannot give them its own, it gives them certain images thereof. Thus, geometry takes the point from metaphysics and draws it; arithmetic takes the unit and multiplies it; mechanics takes conatus and ascribes it to bodies. But just as the drawn point is no longer a point, nor the multiplied unit the unit, so the conatus of bodies is no longer conatus. I cannot think of anything else, unless perhaps you are in doubt about how essence can be a metaphysical entity and existence a physical one. It is true, I confess, that I have not derived this statement from the principles of the Latin language; but it does, in fact, derive from those principles. For existence does not have any other sense save "to be there," "to have emerged," "to be above," as I could prove from a thousand passages of Latin writers. What has come out from some other entity has left its origin behind. Hence, to have come out is not a property of principles. Neither is "being above," for "to be above" indicates that something else stays underneath, whereas principles do not point to something else that is beyond themselves. But being is a property of principles because being cannot be born from nothing. Hence, the writers of very low Latin most wisely called what stays beneath "the substance," and in this we have reposed the true essence. Substance gets hold of essence just as the attributes appropriate existence. We proved that essence is metaphysical matter (i.e., power); its attributes are the existence and actualization of power.

Here I cannot help but notice that Descartes misuses language when he says, "I think; hence, I am." He should have said, "I think; therefore, I exist." Had he taken this word in the sense that its learned origin dictates, he would have made a shorter journey when he wishes to reach essence from his existence. "I think; therefore, I am here." That "here" should have immediately aroused the idea that "therefore, there is something that sustains me, which is substance." Substance carries with it the idea of sustaining, not that of being sustained. Therefore, it is on its own account; therefore, it is eternal and infinite ("therefore, my essence is God, who maintains my thoughts"). The ways of speaking, of which the wise men are the authors, are so pregnant with import that they can spare us long sequences of argumentation. And for the same reason, Descartes's [improper speech] must be noticed again where he wishes to deduce God's existence from his own. This way of expressing his pity is much out of place, because from the fact that I exist what follows is that God does not exist; but "He is." And from the principles of metaphysics, which we have rationally reached, my existence is found to be false when one has gone from that to God's. For my existence is not in God, as Malebranche claims, for the reason that the existence of created things is essence in God. God does not "exist here"; He simply "is." For He sustains, maintains, and includes all; everything issues from Him, and to Him everything returns.

This is the quest that, to satisfy you, I have made in search of all the many things that seem to you to be in need of proof. I cannot see any others. Please make me aware of them; but at the same time, please consider these three things.

First, I understand as a true cause what needs nothing else in order to produce its effect.

Second, the way in which each thing is formed must have repeated itself forever since the elements were first moved and in all regions of the universe alike.

Third, the power is the energy of the whole by which it sends forth and sustains every particular.

See whether all of your difficulties cannot be resolved by beginning either from one, or from all three, of these definitions. Then write me. With most devoted respect.

SECOND ARTICLE

Giornale de' letterati d'Italia,
volume VIII, Article X (1711):309–38

The learned Giambattista Vico has published a little book containing his metaphysics. In the fifth volume of our journal, we reviewed
Vico's study with many tokens of esteem as any dispassionate person, who will take the trouble to read all the six articles, can testify.
But to the scholarly gentleman himself it has seemed otherwise. He
holds himself to have been attacked and injured by our reviewer, and
he both puts a malicious interpretation on the praises that we
sincerely bestowed on him as his due and complains too bitterly
about some small criticisms that we offered in all modesty against his
views. That is the reason that has led him to write out his present
response against the collaborators of the journal. Influenced only by
the respect we profess for his person and in order that it may not look
as if we thought lightly both of that response and of its author, we
have decided that we should put together this present article by first
presenting Vico's complaints one by one and then modestly attaching
our own defenses.

He divides and reduces to three heads of doubt all that we appear
to him to have criticized in his metaphysics.

First, that we want above all to see the main foundation and distinctive novelty of the whole work proven: on what grounds does he
conclude that in the Latin tongue *factum* and *verum, causa* and *negotium,* mean the same thing.

Second, that in putting together this booklet, the author meant to give us only an outline and a specimen of his metaphysics, not the metaphysics itself.

Third, we have observed that many theses are asserted in it that seem to need proof.[1]

And to these criticisms he replies:

> First: Those phrases that are the first principles of my metaphysics have among the Latins the senses that I have assigned to them;
> second: My metaphysics in that little book is complete;
> third: Nothing in it lacks proof.[2]

However, if it is permissible for one to state one's own views freely in one's own defense, we declare that Signor Vico is in error. For indeed, it was not three objections, but only one, that was advanced against him by us; and it is the one that he adduces in the second place: to wit, that his booklet contains only the plan for a metaphysics rather than a complete metaphysics. The reason for this is what he makes into the third criticism—that we note here too many statements that seem to be in need of proof. Then what he calls the first criticism is nothing but a development or, rather, is just part of our reason for complaint. For we want *especially* to see it proven that in the ancient Latin language the sense of the idioms *factum* and *verum*, *causa* and *negotium*, were one and the same.

We insist, however, that "his booklet has deservedly appeared to us to be, rather than a metaphysics perfect and complete, a sketch of the plan for a metaphysics." And in order to prove this proposition more clearly, we shall add the following arguments:

> first, we find in it not a few things that are too briefly touched on and that he might well have dealt with rather more diffusely;
> second, there are some rather obscure things that ought to be more clearly expounded;
> third, there seem to be things that are simply asserted which, because they are either unknown to his readers or subject to dispute among philosophers, seem to require some sort of proof;
> fourth (and we insist that this is not a reason different from the third

[1]See above, p. 118.
[2]Ibid.

one, but only an appendix to it), it is the case that not everyone knows that the Latin phrases referred to, which are the primary and unique foundations of Signor Vico's metaphysics, have the meaning he attributed to them.

I

First, then, we affirm that in that booklet too many things are touched upon very briefly which needed to be set out at greater length. This the author does not deny, for he approved as true what we said only to praise him, "that he crowds speculations without number into every page and even into every line." And furthermore, he himself declares in his reply that he wrote his metaphysics not for the benefit of the young, who are still beginners in studies of this kind, but in order to appear among scholars who have already mastered the field, who do not want to be lumbered with thick volumes; and therefore, a short treatise suffices for them which is replete with those few things that are not found elsewhere. And we, too, are of the same opinion that when one writes for learned men, it is unjust to oblige them to waste their time in the dull and boring perusal of some of the big books that come out every day loaded with things said over and over by others, and adding little or nothing original. But it is our view that when someone writes in a scientific field with new principles and a new method, offering for the most part, as Signor Vico professes to do, things previously unheard of, then he is under an obligation to treat his subject exhaustively. Just as the author delights his reader with the novelty of his work, so too he will not confuse them by crowding too many things together. Especially since, as Quintilian counsels us, it is better sometimes to say too much, even if one becomes boring, than to run the risk of not saying what really needs to be said.[3]

II

But it was more necessary to avoid this kind of brevity in order not to fall into the kindred vice of obscurity. Here necessity compels us to

---

[3]Quintilian, *Institutio Oratoria*, IV, 2.

say what was left unsaid in the aforementioned review for fear of looking as if we aimed to be critics rather than reviewers. Vico complains of what we passed by so dryly with the comment "He discusses metaphysical points"[4] without another word about them. But it seemed to us that the phrase "metaphysical points" called for explanation and definition. Left by itself in its obscurity, it envelops the whole treatise in a darkness that is almost palpable. All the more so because, in our judgment, there is nothing more difficult to conceive than his indivisible powers of substance, through which substance itself is the principle of extension without being extended, and the principle of division without being divided. This talk of "virtue," "power," and "acts" is as unintelligible as the talk of "sympathies" and "antipathies," and of "hidden qualities," which he wants to see banished from all good philosophy.[5]

III

Third, let it be added that Vico's claim that the existence of metaphysical points was taught by Zeno and by the Stoics[6] is in need not only of explanation, but even more of proof, because we do not even find the expression among the ancients. Likewise [he has to justify his assertion] that when Zeno argues about points and extension, he did not mean parts into which the continuum or extension can be divided because it is extended, but he was thinking of the substance of body taken in its metaphysical conception according to which "substance consists in the indivisible" and "is not susceptible of more or less," very much following the language of the school. And furthermore, since any such notion of substance is so well suited for spiritual and thinking substances, then one might infer that these substances are also the principle of extension—which, however, is manifestly absurd.

Likewise, his statements on conatus and motion are no less in need of proof and explanation.[7] He claims that matter or corporeal substance is momentum, conatus, and force insofar as it is power to sustain motion. Now, if body is power of moving, then it is also

4See above, p. 123.
5*DAIS* Four, III.
6*DAIS* Four, II.
7*DAIS* Four, III, IV.

conatus; but conatus, according to what our author teaches, is motion itself, so even the power of motion is its own motion. But the power of motion or conatus is the principle of motion; hence the principle and that of which it is the principle coincide with each other. But let us try again. God is the principle of conatus ("God arouses conatus"); conatus is the principle of motion ("conatus is the beginning of motion").[8] Therefore, either God is distinct from the conatus of matter and of bodies—and in that case, the conatus is different from the motion of the bodies—or else, just as motion and conatus coincide, so God and conatus coincide. Both alternatives appear to be absurd, unless some explanation is offered to clarify obscurities of this kind and unless mind is assisted by some reasoning to understand what cannot be understood by itself. The assertion that "the genesis of things presupposes motion, motion presupposes conatus, and conatus God"[9] is in the same category. From it, we can infer either that the product, the motion, conatus, and God are entirely distinct things or that they are all the same thing. Furthermore, conatus is some mysterious thing lying between rest and motion ("Conatus is midway between rest and motion"). But conatus is motion itself; hence, motion also is some mysterious thing lying between rest and itself. Hence, whatever relation holds between conatus and motion also holds between rest and conatus. But conatus is motion itself. So rest is conatus itself. So, again, rest and motion will be one and the same thing.

Let us proceed to another difficulty. There are, he says, three operations of our mind;[10] perception, judgment, and reasoning or discourse. But because man often apprehends what is false, makes rash judgments without consideration, and misuses language, the three arts of topics, criticism, and method are given to help him. Topics directs the faculty of perception, criticism that of judgment, and method that of reasoning. From now on, to please Signor Vico, we too will call that which directs and gives rules the "art" and that which is directed and to which rules are given the "faculty." However, both in the Latin and in the Tuscan vocabulary, the term *faculty* itself signifies "art." Hence, when we called topics, criticism, and

8*DAIS* Four, vi.
9*DAIS* Four, iii.
10*DAIS* Seven, v.

method "faculties," we did not make a great mistake.[11] But without being too concerned about this purely linguistic question, we will proceed to consider what his doctrine is and look for its foundations, if it has any. To begin with, he assumes that we have perceptions that are false (and perhaps this is a mistake, since a great many philosophers teach that perceptions are essentially true, just as all sensations are). In the second place, we would like to understand how topics can be an art through which the faculty of perception or apprehension is directed or ruled. For according to the definition accepted till now, and according to Vico's own definition of it as the art of discovery, all of its rules have only pointed out those universally accepted commonplaces by which one can find and marshal reasons and arguments to prove whatever one wants. Nor have we ever, till now, come upon any topic that is able to give rules for the proper direction of the simple apprehensions of our minds.

Likewise, criticism is known to us as an art that teaches how works created either by our wit or by that of others can be evaluated. But we don't know yet how it can be an art that directs those second operations of our intellect which are commonly called judgments.

As far as method is concerned, we observe that it is called by the Cartesians "an art for the proper ordering and disposition of our thoughts in order that we may arrive at some science, or be able to teach it to others." Therefore, since different definitions, divisions, postulates, axioms, and demonstrations can lead us to the same science, method does not teach us how to define well, to divide well, to judge well, to discuss well, because these problems belong to the other parts of logic. It merely teaches how we ought to organize and arrange all these things properly so that the acquisition of the desired science may be easy and useful. Consequently, if one considers method to be an ordering and disposing of our thoughts, it may appear to be a new operation of our mind different from the first three. And if one considers it as an art of properly ordering and disposing those same thoughts, then it will appear to be not an art that directs the faculty of reasoning and discussion, but an art that directs the faculty of ordering and disposing. From this we conclude that if he wanted to introduce such a new logic into philosophy, he ought to have defined more clearly those terms of topics, criticism, and method, and he

[11]See above, p. 117.

should have established his newly defined doctrine better with his arguments.

We also have some misgivings about what he teaches in Chapter Five.[12] So different are those two Latin terms, *animus* and *anima*, that anima signifies that through which we live and animus that through which we feel. But the ancient Latins also called the air anima, and because air is the body that is most easily able to move, it alone is the principle of all the motions of the universe. Therefore, he surmises that the ancient Latins believed that the animus and anima in us were nothing but a motion of air, or were air that moves within us. Hence, what today is ordinarily called "vital spirits" is the same air that, introduced into the heart and arteries through breathing, there causes the motion of the blood and becomes the vehicle of life. Likewise, what is called "animal spirits" is air itself, which insinuates itself into the nerve canals and then becomes the cause of all of their motions and the motions of their juices. Hence, the author argues also that in speaking of immortality, the ancient Latins ascribed it only to spirits and not to the souls. The reason for this is that the motions of the soul depend on the mechanism of the body, which is corruptible, whereas those of the spirit are free and voluntary and proceed from our will. This is an evident proof that the spirit (*animus*) is immortal. Hence he concludes that the metaphysics of the ancient sages of Italy was very largely uniform with that of us Christians. First, because in that old metaphysics, too, man is differentiated from the beasts by the fact that he has free will and the beasts do not, and second, because the Latins taught, as our faith teaches us, that the spirit is immortal. However, it seems to us that what he asserts to have been the view of the ancients about the human spirit and its immortality needs some proof. For, in the first place, if spirit is nothing but air moving in the nerves, and if air is body, and every body is corruptible, how can we ever conclude that the spirit is not corrupt but immortal?

Second, if the ancient Italians judged the animus to be air and body, and if our faith teaches us that the animus is pure spirit, how can we argue that in this matter the ancient Italian metaphysics and modern Christian metaphysics are in accord?

Third, if heart, arteries, blood, nervous system, juice, and animal spirits are all found in the beasts, then they possess not only soul but also spirit. So where is the difference between men and animals?

[12]*DAIS* Five.

Fourth, if the nerves receive their motion from the animal spirits that constitute the essence of the spirit, and if the heart, arteries, and blood receive [their motion] from the nerves, and if their every motion is not voluntary, how could the ancient sages of Italy assert that all the motions of the spirit are voluntary and all derive from a will that is free?

Fifth, if the spirit receives its motion from a will that is free, is this will in man soul or spirit?

Sixth, if *anima* (soul) among the Latins denotes air, it is also true that this same word derives from the Greek word ἄγεμος, which also signifies wind or air in motion; so is it not evident that a doctrine of this kind about our souls was not peculiar to the ancient Italian philosophy but was brought into Italy by the Greeks?

Here we cannot help complaining of the injustice of Signor Vico, who wrongly accuses us in his reply of having either misunderstood or misquoted his doctrine of the soul. He says that we reported that he wrote that "the motion of the nerves is due to the blood." But we never even dreamed of saying that. Here are our exact words: ". . . he argues that the ancient wise men of Italy considered the soul and spirit of animals as nothing but [a] particular motion of air which, when introduced into the heart through breathing and from there to the arteries and the veins, forces the blood to move. In this way, it insinuates itself [but what? the same air; from there, that is, from the arteries and veins] from the arteries and veins into the canals of the nerves, and by agitating their juices it causes all those motions that are usually attributed to the sensitive faculties."[13] Here certainly we do not report him as saying that "the motion of the nerves is due to the blood," but that the same air that causes the motion of the blood in its vessels passes afterward into the nerve canals and moves their juices, etc. It certainly seems that Signor Vico here commits the injustice that the author of the *Art of Thinking*[14] claims Aristotle was accustomed to committing against certain philosophers to whom he wrongly attributed some big mistake, so as to go on to prove that he had valiantly confuted them.

We take this opportunity also to reply to another objection made against us by the author himself in the above response when he states, "Thus, I don't confute the 'analysis,' as you report, by which

[13]See above, p. 116.
[14]Antoine Arnauld.

Descartes arrives at his first truth. Rather, I approve of it, and to such a degree that I notice how even Plautus's Sosia, induced by Mercury as if by an evil genius to doubt everything, took comfort in it too ('But I think; therefore, I am'). But I say that thinking is an indubitable sign of my existence; yet since it is not its cause, it does not lead me to a science of being."[15]

But since the author, in his metaphysics, calls Descartes's demon tricky, and since both there and in his response he says that in Descartes's analysis *Cogito* is indeed "an indubitable sign" but not the cause of our being, and hence it does not give us the science of our being, we could rightly argue that he does not confute Descartes's analysis, but he blasphemes against it. That he approves it, yet reproves it.

What we have remarked about the human soul leads to another small doubt regarding what the author goes on to say about the soul of beasts. The beast, he says, was called by the ancient Italians *brutum*, that is, immobile, because the beast has no principle of motion in itself at all, but only under the stimulus of objects like a machine that begins to move when pushed. Hence, I argue as follows: the ancient Italians believed that animals were neither composed of matter nor were bodies, because the essence of matter and bodies is conatus, through which bodies strive to move, and this conatus is motion itself.

I could add many other propositions to these other things that are simply stated but not proved in that booklet, and that are mutually inconsistent, since some come from the Peripatetics, some from the Moderns, and yet others from somewhere in between. So it would have been all the more necessary to prove them, because he presents them in his metaphysics with a brand new method and argues his points upon brand new principles.

IV

Finally, we come to the most important point. We were quite correct in saying that we want to see the thesis that is the main foundation and distinctive novelty of the whole work proven. On what grounds

[15]See above, p. 123.

does he conclude that in the Latin tongue *factum* and *verum, causa* and *negotium*, mean the same thing (etc.)?[16] The evidence that he adduces does not at all justify the assertion that *verum* and *factum* mean the same thing. For the author himself considers the passages from Terence's *Eunuch* and the *Self-Tormentor* to be very insecure evidence for the defense. It remains only to examine the passage of Plautus in the *Pseudolus* when Ballio, the pimp, boldly confesses that the charges brought against him in turn by Calliodorus and Pseudolus are true:

PSEUDOLUS: Shameless!
BALLIO: Yes.
CALLIODORUS: Criminal!
BALLIO: You tell the truth.
PSEUDOLUS: Whipping boy!
BALLIO: Why not?
CALLIODORUS: Crook!
BALLIO: Excellently done!

"These last words," Vico adds, "cannot be understood by anyone except as meaning "it is very true." If this is so, then whenever someone says, for example, "God is the rewarder of men of good will," he will answer in good Latin, "Excellently done." But then if the pimp had answered to the first two insults, "Excellently done," he would have been speaking Latin just as well. Perhaps others might think differently. Plautus very properly makes him answer to the accusation *Furcifer!* with *Factum optime;* that is, "It was a thing well done that I was condemned to the torture of maleficent slaves and that I was dragged through all the streets and squares of the land with the fork on my shoulders. It was well done." Or, "It is true, very true, that I deserved that fork on my shoulders. It was well done." Still, we could, if we liked, quite properly say those words in our language *factum optime* for "it is very true." But either manner of speech would be incomplete by itself; and by supplying the one with the other, one would make the expression complete by saying, "It is very true that this is well done." The reason is that, just as Honoré Fabri[17] very

---

16See above, p. 118.

17Honoré Fabri (1607–1688), a French Jesuit who claimed he had discovered the circulation of the blood before the publication of Harvey's *De Motu Cordis* in 1628. A voluminous writer in many fields, he was involved in several polemics with Borelli, Descartes, and Mersenne. His most important works are the *Dialogi Physici* (1665) and

wittily says, any proposition, besides what it expressly affirms or denies, also implicitly asserts the truth of itself; that is, it asserts that it is true.[18] So that, for example, it is the same thing to say, "Faith without works is dead" and "It is true that faith without works is dead." Hence, we can deduce that in replies of this kind, any other verb can be translated "It is true." When, for example, someone is accused, "You have stolen such and such a thing" (*Id mihi furatus es*), and he answers in the same fashion, *Furatus sum*, we could say in the vulgar tongue, "It is true"; that is, "It is true that I have stolen it from you." No one would say that *furatus* and *verum est* are synonymous.

Again, we shall admit that *causa* and *negotium* sometimes mean the same thing, as Kahl in his *Lexicon*[19] teaches us; or, rather, as Quintilian taught before him.[20] In fact, that great master of Roman youth pointed out that among the Latins the three terms *quaestio, causa,* and *negotium* meant the same as *thesis, upothesis,* and *peristasis* among the Greeks. So that when the question was infinite and universal, they simply called it "question" or "thesis"; whenever it was finite and particularized by the context, they called it "cause" or "hypothesis." When a great number of circumstances, or perhaps all of them, concurred to particularize it, they called it *negotium* and *peristasis;* that is, circumstance.

But to tell the truth, we are not at all convinced. The controversy is whether the term *causa*, which we call in the vulgar tongue *cagione*, and which is specifically the efficient cause as it is considered not by the orator and jurist, but by the metaphysician and physicist, has the same meaning as this other term, *negotium*, which is "operation" or "denial of idleness," as the author of our Metaphysics states. We want to see some proof for this. For example, can the *causa* in that saying of Cicero, "The cause of the trees and branches is in the seeds,"[21] be replaced by *negotium?* Or can we use *negotium* in place of

---

the *Physics* (1669–71), both published at Lyons. See Lynn Thorndike, *A History of Magic and Experimental Science* (New York: Columbia University Press, 1958), 7:664ff. For the polemics with Borelli and its repercussion on the Academy of the Investigators, see Nicola Badaloni, *Introduzione a G. B. Vico*—(Milan: Feltrinelli, 1961) p. 99ff. The reference here is to the *Tractatus de Homine*, Book II, prop. 60.

[18]Here is a place where the distinction between the true *verum* and truth must be drawn and kept or else we cannot translate what the reviewer is saying. The criticism has also a very contemporary ring.

[19]See s.v. *causa*.

[20]Quintilian, *Institutio Oratoria*, III, 5, 7.

[21]Cicero, *Philippica*, II, 22.

causa in that verse of Virgil, "Happy the man who could recognize the causes of things"?[22]

Among the Latins, *intelligere* was the same as "to read perfectly and to know completely." *Cogitare* was the same as our "to think" and "to be gathering together."[23] Granting that God alone is able to read perfectly and to know completely whatever is, and that the human mind can only collect the outer edges of things and not even all of these, he draws the following conclusion: "Thinking is proper to the human mind, understanding to the Divine." But it seems to us that one might argue differently. For the verb *intelligo* is formed from the verb *lego*, as in *colligo* (to gather).[24] And truly among the ancient writers one finds *intellego*, not *intelligo*. So that some people interpret *intelligo* the same as *intuslego* (i.e., to gather internally and mentally); others read it as *interlego* (because the assimilation of *r* to *l* is very common) meaning "to go collecting from among many things those that seem to me the best and the truest." For the above reason, therefore, the verb *intelligo* appears more fitting to man than to God. And to tell the truth, the use of the verb *intelligo* is very common among the Latin writers of the classical period in reference to the thought and knowledge of human minds.

By the word *genus*, the Latins understand "form."[25] This needs to be proven. We do find the term *genus* used in the sense of "species," and sometimes in that of "form" or "way of talking or working," etc. But we have never yet found a place where it signifies what the philosophers call "form."

The Latins used the term *species* to signify what the philosophers call "individual."[26] This, too, is in need of proof. Cicero himself, although a pagan, does not reject the term *species*, but he decides that this other term, *form*, is better for denoting that determinate part of things into which a genus is divided.[27]

Animus signifies that through which man feels, and anima that by which man lives. The significance of these terms is such that Lucretius took this distinction from Epicurus.[28] We argue in the first place thus: if

---

[22]Virgil, *Georgics*, II, 490.
[23]*DAIS* One, I.
[24]Vossius, *Etymologicum linguae Latinae* (1662), s.v. *intelligo*.
[25]*DAIS* Two.
[26]Ibid.
[27]Cicero, *Topica*, 7.
[28]*DAIS* Five, I.

this is the case, then the philosophy that Vico develops about animus and anima was not the doctrine of the ancient philosophers of Italy, but passed later into Latium from Greece when Lucretius plucked it from the beautiful Garden of Epicurus, where it was born and came to flower, and transplanted it. Second, we firmly believe that among the Latins anima meant the instrument of life which we share with the animals, and that animus meant the instrument of thinking and knowing (called "mind" and "intellect"), which makes man different from animals.[29] As evidence, I cite *Animus est quo sapimus, anima qua vivimus*[30] (We know by means of the animus, we live by anima). Also, *Sapimus animo, fruimur anima*[31] (With the animus we know, with the anima we enjoy). Also, *Animus consilii est, anima vitae* (The animus belongs to deliberation, the anima to life).[32] Furthermore, the view of Titus Lucretius about the animus and anima emerges clearly from these verses: "Now I declare that animus and anima are held together and make a single nature of themselves. What we call animus and mind is the deliberative faculty, the head, as it were, which rules over the entire body. This resides in and cleaves to the center of the breast. . . . The rest of the *anima* appears to be spread over the entire body and is moved at the behest of the mind."[33]

Certainly, I do not deny that very often that charming Roman poet and philosopher attributed feelings and sensations to the animus. But who does not know that the terms *sentio* and *sensus* often have for the Latins the same sense as *intelligo, intellectio, judico, judicium*?

May we be allowed to emphasize here that we are not bringing up all these things because we want to contradict Vico's findings or impugn them as false, or at least improbable; we only mean to draw attention to them as needing some sort of explanation and proof. For if Signor G. B. Vico, whom we have always considered to be as courteous as he is learned, would deign to regard our review as worthy of some new reply, then our goal will have been reached.[34]

---

[29]*Thesaurus Linguae Latinae*, s.v. *animus-anima*.

[30]Nonius Marcellus, a Latin scholar of the fourth century A.D., well known for his proficiency in lexicography, grammar, and antiquities.

[31]Accius, Roman writer of tragedy and other literary works (ca. 170–86 B.C.). Cicero borrowed extensively from his plays and was fond of quoting him.

[32]*Servianorum in Vergilii Carmina Commentariorum* (Oxford, 1965).

[33]Lucretius, *De Rerum Natura*, Book III, 137–44.

[34]A double-edged compliment, since Vico's reply is certainly not courteous (as the original review was) and the reviewer has now made his learning look quite doubtful.

Because only when we unite together in one body, as it were, his first booklet on Metaphysics and the second one constituted by his response, with what we have said in the present article and what it seems good to him to reply to us now—only then with a book made up of all these parts together shall we have no longer the briefest outline of a metaphysics, but a complete one perfect in all its parts.

Finally, we beg that that erudite gentleman will, of his kindness, give us leave to express our own feeling on the problem—which is that if he wanted to investigate what the most ancient philosophy of Italy was, he should not have tried to trace it in the origin and meanings of Latin words. This path is very uncertain and beset with a thousand problems. He ought to have hunted it out by unearthing and disinterring as far as possible the oldest monuments of ancient Etruria, from which the Romans received the first laws respecting both civil government of their republic and the sacred rites of their religion. Or at least he ought to investigate what were the principles of the philosophy that Pythagoras brought from Ionia to Italy. Having put down its first roots in those parts where now Signor Vico makes his eloquence and learning shine so gloriously, in a very short time the so-called Italian philosophy spread throughout Latium itself.

We shall terminate this discussion by offering our apologies to that kind gentleman for not simply "resting in that confidence" [of which he spoke] not merely in respect of just one doubt, but in respect of all our doubts. It was almost a matter of duty, and not just of "our courtesy," to have that confidence in him about them. But with it, we also beg him to remember that nowadays we have learned this maxim: "It is very dangerous in philosophical questions to try to ground one's knowledge on the good name of anybody rather than on the force and evidence of the arguments."[35]

---

[35]Nullius addictus iurare in verba magistra. Horace, Epistle 14.

VICO'S SECOND RESPONSE

I consider myself very fortunate, indeed very honored, by the reply that you, most noble sirs, have written in the tenth article of the eighth volume of the *Giornale de' letterati d'Italia* to the Response that I published in defense of the metaphysics contained in the first book of my *The Most Ancient Wisdom of the Italians*. I am addressing my response to an anonymous learned gentleman in order to demonstrate that I only want to defend myself and not to start a polemic with you. For although there are many examples of it in France, Holland, and Germany, I did not want to be the first to offer one in Italy,[1] especially with you, who contribute so much to Italian letters. I am afraid that others would follow this example and start a quarrel if they were not satisfied with your reviews and comments. I did not know for certain which one of you gentlemen had written the review of my little book. But even if I had known, I would still have answered him incognito, out of respect for you and for him, because it is wrong to unmask someone who wants to remain concealed, not to speak of one who ought to, so as not to damage the freedom that must remain inviolate for the whole class of those who play the part of true historians and dispassionate judges of contemporary letters. And anyway, out of

---

[1]The polemics between Mersenne and Descartes, Arnauld and Malebranche, Leibniz and Clarke, Leibniz and Newton, are a few of the many European intellectual battles that characterize so well the intellectual ferment of the seventeenth and eighteenth centuries. For similar examples in Italy (which Vico prefers to pass over in silence), see M. Fisch, "Academy of the Investigators," in *Science, Medicine, and History*, ed. E. Ashworth (London: Underwood, 1953), pp. 521, 563. See also Nicola Badaloni, *Introduzione a G. B. Vico*. (Milan: Feltrinelli, 1961).

your generosity, you did not decide, as you reasonably might have, that the anonymous critic should himself refute my response privately; but your whole committee, like a university of scholars, has favored me with a reply in the open pages of your journal. Thus, you have made me worthy in a way to stand beside you as an equal, though I certainly am not, have never dared, and could never dare to lay claim to such a status.

I was astonished, however, that at the very beginning you write that I hold myself to have been attacked and injured by your reviewer and that I complain too bitterly about some small criticisms that you offered in all modesty against my views.[2] That it is so far from the truth that my nature is either so aggressive or so sensitive I cannot say, because when I read your review I was indeed stung by a slight pang of passion. But because the more self-love flatters you, the more it is your enemy, I did not want to listen to it all by myself and I went to Matteo Egizio,[3] whom I selected above all others because I knew him to be respected more than anyone else by your committee. I gave him the review to ponder and asked him what he would have done if the same thing had been written about one of his works. And he, being otherwise a man of very placid temper, answered that he would consider himself obliged to give reason for what he had written. Hence, I decided to defend myself, not from a sense of aggravation or injustice, but in order not to welsh on my obligations.

Moreover, to anyone who has read my answer the tone used therein shows anything but bitterness, since I have always felt that matter pertaining to the sciences ought to be treated in the most sedate manner of argumentation. It is a weighty argument, as I see it, that theses maintained with anger and grudge have no truth or very little; and I observe in active life that the powerful man does not make threats and the man who is in the right does not cause injury. Apart from mental labors, philosophical disputes offer the mind, at the very most, nothing but some pleasant relaxation from the hard travail of concentration, which goes to show that thinking minds are placid and tranquil, and not perturbed and excited.

Whenever one must reproach, let austerity take over, with which one can punish with dignity and not offend like a villain. In this way,

---

[2]See above, p. 136.
[3]Matteo Egizio (1674–1745), Vico's learned friend and one of the few scholars with whom Vico used to discuss his works. An archaeologist of some renown, Egizio became the first librarian of Charles of Bourbon's library.

philosophers, who debate on topics that are not subject to our desires, distinguish themselves from vulgar men, who defend their
views with anger and pleas for sympathy. This is said in general
defense of my way of doing things.

Now I can come to the problems. But first, let me beg your kind
indulgence if I do not follow the order of your answer. In the first
place, to follow the path of an adversary's writings without interrup-
tion seems to me typical of a quarrelsome person who wants to crush
his opponent more than to track down the truth, which cannot be
followed down just any road, but simply and solely along the avenue
the things themselves leave open. In the second place, you set me the
example yourselves, when you did not follow the order I observed in
my Response.

I see your reply as containing altogether four parts:

1. A criticism of the way I divided the censure with which you backed
   up the assertion that my book contains "only the outline of a metaphysics and not a fully complete exposition of metaphysics."
2. An overturning of the position I have contemplatively arrived at
   therein.
3. Your refutation of the origins that I propose for the idioms *verum* and
   factum, causa and *negotium,* and many others.
4. Your proposal as to how you would have wished me to conduct my
   attempt to trace the philosophy of the ancient Italians.

To me, it seems best to begin by replying to the parts you have
placed last: the conduct of my inquiry. Then I will present my defense
regarding the way I classified your censure. Next I will confirm the
origins of the words. Finally, I will establish the positions I have
contemplatively arrived at. For the first thing in this enterprise was
the plan of action; the work itself followed that, and the origins [of the
words] should take precedence because they gave occasion for my
contemplative meditation on the things.

I. The Method of the Work

Regarding my method, your honor says the following:

Finally, we beg that the erudite gentleman will, of his kindness give us
leave to express our own feeling on the problem—which is that if he

wanted to investigate what the most ancient philosophy of Italy was, he should not have tried to trace it in the origin and meanings of Latin words. This path is very uncertain and beset with a thousand problems. He ought to have hunted it out by unearthing and disinterring as far as possible the oldest monuments of ancient Etruria, from which the Romans received the first laws respecting both civil government of their republic and the sacred rites of their religion.

Or at least he ought to investigate what were the principles of the philosophy that Pythagoras brought from Ionia to Italy. Having put down its first roots in those parts where now Signor Vico makes his eloquence and learning shine so gloriously, in a very short time the so-called Italian philosophy spread throughout Latium itself.[4]

As for what you say about Roman ceremonies and Roman laws, I do not deny that these are most noble goals. But either undertaking would have been subject to equal, and perhaps to greater, uncertainties. For the secrecy of religion, which was always considered very important because it makes it more venerable, would have greatly obscured the first topic, since one would have to unveil things that are mysteries precisely because they are difficult to reveal. In my judgment, it would have been just as hard as tracking down religion in the ancient legends. For the founders of republics took their gods from the poets and proposed them to their peoples to fear and to revere in awe.[5] And everyone knows how hard the mythologists have toiled in this enterprise with but little success.[6]

The other investigation of Roman law would have been equally problematic. For there are but few royal laws that could have been borrowed by the Romans from the Etruscans; and we do not know with certainty which fragments of the laws the Twelve Tables they are, as distinct from those that were brought from Greece and filled ten of the tables.[7]

But if in the end I had to trace this philosophy from Ionia and the Pythagorean school, that would not be an investigation of the most ancient philosophy of Italy, but of a more recent Greek philosophy. Because I, from those few very scanty and very obscure records of its views that have reached us, do of course derive it from Pythagoras, but I do not make it come from Greece, for I consider it to be more

[4]See above, p. 149.
[5]Varro in Augustine's *De Civitate Dei*, VI, V.
[6]Most likely a reference to Bacon's *Wisdom of the Ancients*.
[7]The thesis espoused here is of course rejected in the *New Science*.

ancient than that of Greece itself.[8] Hence, it is in the proem to my work as a whole that I offered the bold conjecture that in Italy there was an alphabet much older than that of the Greeks,[9] because Etruscan architecture is simpler than the other four extant in Greece[10] and because their creations are at first very simple, but then little by little become more ornate and complicated. Hence, I am firmly of the opinion that [this philosophy came from Egypt] at the time when that mighty empire, which extended over almost all of the Orient and down through Africa, flourished.[11] We would not today have had any knowledge of it if Germanicus had not been taken with the project of going to see the antiquities of Egypt, and among them its very ancient columns carved with magnificent monuments in hieroglyphics. The reason [for its coming] was probably, nay quite certainly, that the Egyptians, having mastered the Mediterranean Sea completely, could easily settle colonies along its coasts. Thus, they brought into Etruria their philosophy. And here there arose then a sizable kingdom, which gave its name to all that part of our sea which washes Italy from Tuscany to Reggio. Their language also necessarily spread, and the people of Latium, being the closest, were most influenced by it. To this one should add what is absolutely certain: that the augural science came to Rome from Etruria.[12] The belief that Numa studied under Pythagoras is as completely fabulous as it is true that he was the founder of Roman religion.

Therefore, when I came upon a great number of Latin idioms pregnant with profound wisdom, the authors of which could not, as I had already shown, have been the Greeks, I believed that I had found a new and reliable method for tracking down the most ancient wisdom of Italy by studying the origins of these idioms.

[8]For the fantastic origin of the Pythagorean philosophy, see NS, 93–95.

[9]This thesis is also rejected in the New Science, where the primitive Latin alphabet is derived from very ancient Greek signs. Ancient opinion on this subject was not at one with itself. See A. Wilmann's De M. Terentii Varro Libris Grammaticis (Berlin, 1884), fragments 103–8, on the origin of the alphabet and the Latin language. Vico probably knew what was being discussed among grammarians, but followed only Tacitus, Annales, XI, 14.

[10]Actually, there are only three Greek orders of architecture: Ionic, Corinthian, and Doric. Vico seems to have included the Tuscan order by mistake, only to exclude it. See Vitruvius, De Architectura, Book IV.

[11]Vico's sentence is incomplete. What he seems to hold is that the Etruscan wisdom came from Egypt. For the reference to Germanicus, see Tacitus, Annales, II, 59–61.

[12]This thesis is also rejected in the New Science.

I was stimulated to this enterprise by the example of Plato's *Cratylus*, where he sought to investigate the ancient wisdom of the Greeks by the same method; and also by the authority of Varro, who, although he was so well versed in Greek and so well read as to have gained the title of "most learned Roman,"[13] seeks in his *Origin of the Latin Language* to offer any derivation for Latin words rather than a Greek one. Thus, for example, he would rather derive *pater* from *patefaciendo semine* than from πατήρ.

Now, on the basis of all that I have argued, I dare to claim that Pythagoras did not bring his doctrine from Ionia to Italy. Carrying doctrine around was the custom of the Sophists, who went around selling their vain and illusory knowledge abroad to make a profit from their art—a custom that provides the occasion and the setting for Plato's dialogue *Protagoras*. But philosophers used to leave their countries and remove to faraway lands from a desire to acquire new knowledge. Thus, just as it is reported that Plato went to Egypt, so Pythagoras came to Italy. Here he learned Italian philosophy, and having become very expert in it, it pleased him to settle in Magna Graecia at Croton, where he founded his school.

This was my view when I asserted in my proem that "etymologies bear witness to the fact that the better part of the Latin language was borrowed from the Ionians." That is, the origins of Greek words used by the inhabitants on the Ionian sea, where the Italian school thrived, could be used to trace the very ancient wisdom of Italy. So if we find a Latin idiom pregnant with philosophical (*sapiente*) meaning that originated from there, then it has to be assumed that such terms were taken from Etruria, first to Latium and then later to Magna Graecia.[14]

Thus, by the method of [language] origin I cast light on the Pythagorean doctrine that the world is made up of numbers, so obscure hitherto that it has no adherents today. Through this Pythagorean dogma I explain the belief of the most ancient philosophers of Italy about points, which Aristotle so radically misunderstood in his treatment of Zeno. The Latins identified "point" and "momentum," and

---

[13]Vico says, *Doctissimus et romanorum doctissimus;* for Varro, see *De Lingua Latina*, v, 65.

[14]The proem will not bear this construction, for it clearly asserts that the two nations, Ionians and Etruscans, were older than the Latins and are possible candidates as their teachers. Only sheer cussedness could have led Vico to develop the Egyptian hypothesis after he read the Tenth Article.

they understood the same indivisible thing under both designations. But properly speaking, momentum is something in motion. Pythagoras said that things are made up of numbers. Numbers reduce ultimately to unity. But the one and the point are indivisible, and yet they form what is divided. Unity forms number and the point forms the line and all this happens in the world of abstraction. Hence, in the true and real world there is something indivisible that produces all the things that give us divisible impressions. For by this same method, I had discovered the maxim of our very ancient philosophers: that man works in the world of abstractions in the same way that God works in the real world. Hence, the best way to understand the generation of things can be learned from geometry and arithmetic, which differ only in the type of quantities they treat and are the same in every other respect. So that the mathematicians demonstrate the same theorem using either lines or numbers, according to what comes to their mind or to what they consider more suitable.

Instead of being difficult and problematic as you think, this doctrine of mine may rather seem to others to be impossible, because the Romans began to enjoy humane letters very late, whereas this hypothetical learned language of mine ought to have made them very learned from the beginning. I foresaw this objection in the proem, and it was for this reason I said that the Romans "had taken these expressions from some learned nation and used them unaware of their meaning." For all that is ordinarily ascribed to the good fortune of the Romans I reduce to this wisdom, which enabled them to make good use of the fruits of the teaching of other communities while maintaining their own ignorance, and thereby conserving their aggressiveness. In these times, they established absolute supremacy in the world through the destruction of Carthage. They took from the Etruscans the most tragic religion that could ever be imagined, as Polybius says,[15] and what is of more direct concern to us, an art of battle order unique in the world. An author most expert in the military art considers that they were invincible in battle order. This skill can only have been the fruit of Etruscan mathematics. They derived their laws from the Spartans and the Athenians, two of the most illustrious peoples in the world (the latter for their learning, the former for their valor). After this, the empire and fame of the Etruscans

15Polybius, *Historiae*, 56, 6–12.

was quite extinguished, and for three hundred years after the Laws
[the Romans] had no intercourse with the Greeks, deeming that the
inviolable observance of their religion and their laws was sufficient by
itself to maintain good order. From this arose that absolute punc-
tiliousness of theirs about protocol. And thus, the Romans spoke the
language of philosophers without being philosophers.

The origins I am investigating are not those that concern the grammarians, who consider only the derivations of words, as others have
done hitherto for other purposes. The etymologies, which the grammarians draw largely from the Greek language of the inhabitants of
the Ionian coast, serve for me only as evidence that the ancient
Etruscan language was diffused among all the peoples of Italy, as well
as in Magna Graecia. They have no other use for me. I have tried to
figure out the reasons that the concepts of these wise men became
obscure and were lost to sight as their learned speech became current
and was employed by the vulgar.

This is the secret way by which I thought I could discover what the
wisdom of the most ancient philosophers of Italy was. And so taking
up one of your disputed cases, for example, *causa* in its properly
philosophical meaning signifies "thing which makes." The Romans
signified by this word what is also called *negotium*. I set myself to find
out how it happened that the word that signifies "what makes" acquired the meaning "what is made." I reflect on the fact that what is
derived from the cause is called by the Latins *effectus*, and *effectus* in its
sophisticated meaning denotes "what is completely made." I do not
see how there can be any relation between the two terms, and yet I
am certain that they are not used at random. Hence, we must necessarily infer that those first sages who assigned names to objects held
the opinion that *causa* was what contained in itself the effect, that it
was united with the effect as one thing and could produce it with all
the perfection. Causality of this kind is proper only to God. Thus,
among the philosophers what is divided into species is called genus,
and among the vulgar men it is called the mode or model. On the
other hand, species denotes appearance in vulgar speech, whereas
philosophically it is the "[proper] part of the genus" or the "individual." I consider that the most different things fall under the same
expression. Some reason for their relation must have intervened. Nowhere else do I find it, save in this, that the wise authors of the
language were of the opinion that there was one true [being], which

is divided into a plurality of apparent unities. So that these latter were appearances and images of that one true [being]. The one is the model; the many are works modeled on it. The one is true because it is original; the many are false because they are pictures (*ritratti*).

Amid all this, will not someone wonder why it never entered the mind of any Roman born and schooled in that language to think to retrace the origin of his language by the same path? To him, I answer that it never entered the minds of any of them to investigate the reasons for their customs and habits in a philosophical way. But is what a foreign philosopher, Plutarch, wrote about them therefore false?[16] Let us dispel this amazing notion. The Etruscan realm was destroyed hundreds of years before the Romans cultivated humane letters. The Latin language, being predominant in the times of the learned, had obscured the other minor languages of Italy. The religious reverence of Roman grandeur disdained even the refinements of Attica, as we have seen in Varro. As usually happens, their prosperity flattered them into thinking that all the goods they enjoyed were homemade and homegrown. So it is not fantastic, but a necessary result, that they did not reflect on what I have reflected on.

Now then, please do put together on one side of the balance all this: that the Egyptians were the most ancient philosophers of the pagan world; their empire spread out in colonies along the coasts of the Mediterranean. Consider the powerful realm of the Etruscans in Italy and the diffusion of languages in the wake of political power. Consider that Etruscan architecture is more ancient than Greek, their religion more tragic, and the military art that passed from them to the Romans more effective; consider that authors of wise language have always been accounted sages; and that a great number of Latin idioms do not show any reason for their advanced stage of development. Yet if they are derived from the origins that I infer, then they are full of profound learning. On the other scale put the secrecy of religion (which is not easily unveiled), the small number and the uncertainty of royal laws, and finally, the few and very obscure doctrines of Pythagoras. Judge then which of the two approaches is better advised.

---

[16]Plutarch, *De Fortuna Romanorum*, 316–17.

II. On the Division of the Criticism of My Metaphysics, Which Appeared in the Sixth Article of Volume V of the Journal, Which I Made in My First Response

You reprove the way I divided your criticism in my preceding response and suggest that your grounds of opposition to my metaphysics are not three, but only one; to be exact, the one that I consider second. What matters, you say, is that I have given an outline of metaphysics rather than a complete metaphysics. The third and the first criticism [in my division] are grounds for the second, not separate parts of your criticism, and that they form one whole critical judgment was the second. To establish your case more clearly, you add the following arguments:

first, we find in it not a few things that are too briefly touched on and that he might well have dealt with rather more diffusely;

second, there are some rather obscure things that ought to be more clearly expounded;

third, there seem to be things that are simply asserted which, because they are either unknown to his readers or subject to dispute among philosophers, seem to require some sort of proof;

fourth (and we insist that this is not a reason different from the third one, but only an appendix to it), it is the case that not everyone knows that the Latin phrases referred to, which are the primary and unique foundations of Signor Vico's metaphysics, have the meaning he attributed to them.[17]

First, I could offer one excuse for my stupidity in that, while I was quite intent on something else, I violated the rules of good division by including the whole argument among the parts into which it is divided. I could, I say, explain my stupidity to your satisfaction. But now you, at the very moment that you are castigating my mistake, proceed to divide the matters that you declared in your original criticism to be all in need of proof into "brief," "obscure," and "simply stated and not proved"; of which the last category is tantamount to "in need of proof." Under it you include even the arguments debated among philosophers, and the origins as well.

17See above, pp. 137–38.

But I candidly admit that, in the light of your Reply, in which you have come down to details and have, I should judge, dealt with every objection that you consider appropriate to set against me, I confess; I say that my division is at fault. Previously, however, because your criticisms were so vague, I could not divine that the expression "idea" was meant to signify a sketch lacking the final touches concerning the origins of words and the proof of the propositions offered. [I thought you called the treatment an "idea"] because not all of the questions that are customarily discussed in metaphysics are dealt with in my book, and in truth not all of them are, for only the main ones, to which the others are corollaries left for specialists in the field to pick up, are treated there. [So I thought] the controversy was on the issue of what are the main questions that ought to be treated in metaphysics; and it sounded to me as if someone were saying, "This building lacks its foundations, and because not all the parts of which it is composed have been erected, it looks more like a blueprint or a plan than a finished building; and in many parts that are already erected it lacks the finishing touches."

This was the reason, then, why I [first] divided that Response as I did. And in the second place, I set myself to outline the idea[18] of a metaphysics complete in its principal and necessary parts upon which ours was elaborated. But now, because you have made definite the vagueness of the word *idea*, I willingly agree that my division was faulty.

However, in the light of your explanation, I now owe you justification of my "brevity," my "obscurity," and my merely mentioning things that "are still disputed among philosophers." As for brevity, I consider it a virtue here rather than a vice. Because we are not dealing with physics here, for which a copious and exact natural history, a great mass of mechanical equipment, and the carrying out of thousands of rationally designed experiments are required. Nor are we dealing with geometry, where a supply of well-defined terms, of uncontested axioms,[19] and distinct postulates are needed so that we can go step by step directly through a long, uninterrupted chain of demonstrations. We are dealing with metaphysics, in which man has

---

[18]Vico says "an idea," which accords well with his view that only God can have *the* idea; but of course he is referring to the particular idea that *he* used as his ground plan.

[19]Vico probably meant *incontestable*, but he had the wit to say *uncontested*, which makes his theory of mathematics applicable to geometrics other than Euclidean.

to know and explain his mind, a very pure and simple object. In this respect, what is remarked every day comes very aptly to hand: more profitable for the Christian mind are the meditations that present few points (thereby, man can enter into himself and purify his soul) than all the eloquent and fully expressed sermons of the most fluent preachers. For this reason, it seems to me that Descartes was very wise to call meditations the studies in which he treats the primary questions so briefly that his metaphysics is contained in a few pages. Yet what you object to in my case is true of him: "he wrote with new principles and a new method, things for the most part unheard of." So the counsel of Quintilian "that often it is more advantageous to repeat statements than to pass dangerously over in silence what is necessary"[20] does not seem to be in your favor. For Quintilian is here discussing the exposition of facts to judges who know nothing about them; where he intends to discuss something with those that understand it, he follows the saying "A word to the wise is sufficient." Since "obscurity" springs from failing to define one's terms, I will purge myself of it (whenever you convict me for it).

Finally, for the things "that are only outlined and are still debated by philosophers," I leave them for the philosophers themselves to settle, because my purpose was to publish a little book completely filled with my own ideas and I would be well pleased to have them proved.

Let us take as an example *ingenium*, which was called by the Latins "memory." There is a fine case of this sort in the *Andria*,[21] where Davus, eager to arrange a great trick with Mysis, tells her, "Mysis, now I need your memory and cunning ready for this business."

What we call "imagination" and "to imagine" is called by the Latins "to remember" and "memory"; hence, *comminisci* and *commentum* mean "to devise," "to find out," and "device" or "invention"—as in that other passage of the *Andria*[22] which is worthy of note, where Corinus complains of Pamphilius's maliciousness and treachery: "Is it believable or within all memory that anyone should be so completely mad that he takes pleasure in disasters, evils, and gets his own advantages from the misfortunes of others?"

[20]Quintilian, *Institutia Oratoria*, IV, 2.
[21]Terence, *Andria*, 722–23.
[22]Ibid., 625–28.

Yet *ingenium* is the discovering of new things, and the fancy or the power of imagining is the mother of poetic inventions. Grammarians do not take account of this, but say many things that have but little truth about Memory (the goddess of the poets), to whom they have recourse in their greatest need. By imploring her help, they make the vulgar believe that what they narrate really happened, but the truth is that they pray to her for the sake of making new discoveries.

This is enough to show once more that these terms were used in a profound sense by the ancient Italian philosophers because they held that we do not have any cognition that does not come from God. Whether knowledge is made by way of the senses (as Aristotle and Epicurus maintain), or learning is nothing but remembering (as Socrates and Plato falsely held), or that our ideas are innate and born with us (as Descartes meditatively declares), or that God everywhere creates them for us (as Malebranche argues), this I leave undecided (though I am inclined to agree with Malebranche), because I did not want to discuss the concerns of others in my little book.

III. About the Origins

About the origins of words you clearly show that you are not satisfied with the passages I offer as evidence for the first two pairs of terms, and you raise doubts about some later ones. And to begin with, the passage of Plautus, where I gloss "well done" as "very true," does not convince you. You reply that to the insult "Crook!" Ballio answers Calliodorus "well done," that is, "it was done very well," meaning "done with perfect justification."

I doubt very much that good Latin will permit such a translation, because that opinion was usually expressed with the idiom *iure factum* (rightly done) and not with the idiom *bene factum*. In fact, we see that the idiom *bene factum* is employed whenever the fulfillment of a desire is reported. Hence, in a great many passages of the two comic poets, we find the news of happy events responded to by those who congratulate or are happy about it by "well done," "well done, I say," "May the Gods love me! That is well done," which in Italian would be *Io ne ho un gran gusto* (I am overtickled by it). Thus, that passage should read more or less as follows: to Calliodorus's insult "Crook!" Ballio answers, "What a great pleasure you have given me!"

So that, in this interpretation, the other one that you suggest—"It is very true that it is well done," and all the arguments you bring to confirm it from Onorato [Honoré] Fabri, an Aristotelian of good taste—does not tell in your favor. For all that would be in place if Ballio had answered, *Iure factum*, and in line with the list of his earlier answers, all denoting truth—*ita est, vera dicis, quippini*—the last one would assert, "It is true that this is absolutely true." Nothing more useless or more vain than this could be imagined.

You say that *causa* ought to mean *negotium*, not as used by the orator or the jurist, but as used by the metaphysician in the sense of cause and, specifically, that of "efficient cause." For instance, as it appears in Cicero,[23] "In the seeds there is the cause of the trees and of branches," and in Virgil,[24] "Happy is he who knows the causes of everything."

In the same way, you would have liked me to present cases where the term *genus* meant "form" as it is understood by the physicists, and the term *species* meant what the philosophers called "individual."

I believe I have satisfied both of these requirements in my discussion of "The Method of the Work." Because [if I had supplied] the sort of proof for the origins that you asked for, I would have derived the ancient wisdom of Italy from those Latin terms, and not from their origin; but my topic is those origins.[25]

Your most trenchant counterexample is that the word *anima* in the sense of air is derived from the Greek, where "air in motion" was called ἄνεμος; hence, I was wrong in considering the Italian philosophers the authors of it. But this problem is solved by the whole discussion of the conduct of the inquiry. For from the proof I have given, one can readily infer that the most ancient Egyptians, who sent a term into Italy with that meaning, sent it likewise on to Greece; both

---

[23]Cicero, *Philippica*, II, 22, 55.

[24]Virgil, *Georgics*, II, 490.

[25]Vico avoids a direct answer to the reviewer. He had observed that, both in Cicero and Virgil, *causa* is not interchangeable with *negotium*, that there is no example of synonymity between *genus* and *forma*, and that *species* in Cicero (Topic 7) means not individual, but that definite part of things in which genus is divided. See *Giambattista Vico: Opere*, ed. F. Nicolini (Milan: Ricciardi, 1953), p. 342.

of these nations used it without there being any mutual commerce of it between them.

But I must deny your other claim: that Lucretius brought the distinction of the terms *anima* and *animus*, along with the subtle nuance that by means of life we live, and by means of sense we perceive, from the Garden of Epicurus into Latium. In that connection, you quote his very charming verses and you infer from them that it is a foreign doctrine and not native to Italy.

When I discussed the charms of these two terms, I did say this: "The elegance of those two words, *animus* (spirit) and *anima* (soul), whereby *anima vivamus, animo sentiamus* (with the soul we live, with the spirit we feel), is so well known that Titus Lucretius laid claim to it, as if it had been conceived in Epicurus's Garden." However, the term *velut* (as if) indicates that something is not right. Lucretius could not have brought this term from Greece because the Greeks signified both *anima* and *animus* with the term ψυχή. When they discuss immortality, they use the same word, while the Latins say *animorum* and not *animarum*. Thus the *Phaedo*, which expressly treats *de immortalitate animorum*, is called περὶ ψυχῆς. Besides, Lucretius found this sophisticated distinction of terms in archaic philosophical beliefs that were current among Romans long before the introduction of the Epicurean philosophy.

As far as the verses of Lucretius are concerned, I should like to add this. You could have polished the bold trope with which you rounded off your opinion, "But who does not know that the terms *sentio* and *sensus* often have for the Latins the same sense as *intelligo, intellectio, judico, judicium?*"[26] by acknowledging that I too said in the margin of the paragraph *De Sensu*: "Latins called all activities of the mind sensation,"[27] and that I investigate the reasons for it.

Returning now to the origins, my claim that *intelligere* signifies "gathering completely" and "knowing openly" is attacked by you with the authority of the grammarians. Yet even following their etymology, my interpretation does not seem to be undermined. Inasmuch as the word *intelligere* does not come from *intuslegere*, which would mean "gather internally," whence you derive the absurd consequence that *"intelligo* appears more fitting to man than to God."[28]

---

[26]See above, p. 148.
[27]See *DAIS* Seven, II, Synopsis.
[28]See above, p. 147.

But it does come from *inter-lego*, which assimilates to *intelligo*. The preposition *inter* is to be taken not in the sense of interposition of "being in between," which would yield the meaning "to select from among the many things the better ones," or "those that are true," but with the meaning of "growth" and "perfection," which is illustrated by *interminari* (to threaten violently), *intermortuus* (quite dead), *interficere* (to finish someone off with blows), *interdicere* (to order openly). Some legal interpreters do not understand the last word and wander far from the truth about the origin of the term *interdictum*.

In order not to pass over what you call a verbal question, there remains finally in this section on origins the problem of whether topics, criticism, and method should be called arts and not faculties.

The difficulty that the Latins had in rendering the word ῥητοριχή in their language arises precisely from this source. They commonly identify the aids of rhetoric as nature, art, and exercise. For nature fosters it, art directs it, and exercise strengthens it. And among the Greeks ῥήτορες does not mean those who teach the art, but the "orators," who are certainly not to be esteemed as such unless they have acquired that capacity to speak well through which they can defend their causes extemporaneously with eloquence. So when I dealt in my little book with the subtle distinctions that have to be observed in the proper use of words, it was important to me not to make any confusion—especially when I expressly distinguished them. For serious consequences result as, for instance, when man with each faculty makes himself the object of just that faculty. This can supply the foundation of all one's reasoning, as Lord Herbert [of Cherbury] shows in his book *De Veritate* with a method not previously employed by anyone else; the main thesis of his metaphysics is that for each sensation a new faculty unfolds and manifests itself in us.[29]

I close this part of my argument with the very ending that I offered for this topic in my Response, and which you employed to bring your Reply to an end. Your courtesy could not rest on simple trust in what I asserted because today there is the well-known maxim "It is very dangerous in philosophical questions to try to ground one's knowledge on the good name of anybody rather than on the force and

---

[29]Lord Edward Herbert of Cherbury (1583–1648), *Tractatus de Veritate Prout Distinguitur a Revelatione, a Verisimili, a Possibili et a Falso* (Paris, 1624; London, 1633). This treatise was refuted by Gassendi. Nicolini, *Vico*, p. 344.

evidence of the arguments."[30] For I did not ask for your indulgence where I treated of things and of their causes (where the maxim is to be religiously observed), but where I argued of words and their origin, where usage and authority are master.

IV. On the Things Meditated

Let us consider, finally, your charges against the meditated results of my metaphysics. This point is more important than all the other three put together. For the dispute about the division of your censure that I made in my Response is a question of one man's judgment, which counts for little or nothing in the republic of letters. The two disputes about the conduct of the inquiry and the origins of the words can perhaps be considered contests of wit in which the most extravagant plights and the greatest paradoxes usually receive the greatest praises. But this question, which concerns the principles of human knowledge, this is indeed the one that needs and ought to be regarded as a high and very serious enterprise.

Before I begin, however, I cannot help but say how disappointed I am that you did not pay attention at all to what I urged on you at the end of my Response. Before you raised new difficulties, over and above the ones that I presented and resolved, you ought to have kept in mind those three definitions of "cause," "effort," and "mode" and considered whether the problem could be solved by having recourse to one or all of them.

Now you accuse me of involving myself in direct contradictions. At one and the same time "I reject Descartes's analysis," by which he tries to track down the first truth of his metaphysics, and yet "I approve it," and consequently, "I do not confute it," but "censure it." To set your mind at rest, it is enough to answer you with what I wrote in my little book.[31]

I do grant that his method is useful for discovering the certain and indubitable signs of my existence, but it is no good for discovering the

---

[30]See above, p. 149.
[31]*DAIS* One, IV.

cause of it.[32] In my Response, I defined *causa* as that which needs nothing extraneous to itself in order to produce its effects. The immediate corollary of this definition is that science consists in having knowledge of this sort of cause. Hence, the criterion for possessing the science of something is being able to put it into effect, and proving from causes is making what one proves. And this being [is] absolutely true because it is convertible with the made and its cognition is identical with its operations. This criterion is guaranteed for me by God's science, which is the source and standard of all truths. This criterion guarantees for me that the only human sciences are the mathematical ones, and that they prove from causes. Beyond that, it gives me the way of classifying the nonscientific disciplines that are either certain on the basis of indubitable signs or probable on the basis of good argument or truelike on the basis of powerful hypothesis.[33] Do you wish to teach me a scientific truth? Grant me the cause that is completely contained within me so that I intend a name at my will, and I establish an axiom regarding the relation that I set up between two or more ideas of things which are abstract and which are, consequently, both contained in me. Let us start from a feigned indivisible and stop at an imaginary infinite and you could tell me, "Make a demonstration of the assumed theorem," which is tantamount to "Make true what you want to know." And in knowing the truth that you have proposed, I shall make it; so that there will not remain for me any ground to doubt it because I myself have made it. The criterion of the "clear and distinct perception" does not assure me of scientific knowledge. As used in physics and ethics, it does not yield a truth that has the same force as the one it gives me in mathematics. The criterion of making what is known gives me the [logical] difference here: for in mathematics, I know truth by making it; in physics and the other sciences, the situation is different.

The Cartesians, however, claim that they know that whatever has three dimensions is a body as clearly and distinctly as they know that the whole is greater than the parts. I ask: how is it possible that a

[32]What is *certum* in Vico's metaphysics is not *clear*, but rather misleading; what is indubitable is not distinct, but is only a datum that needs to be set in the light of the true theory.
[33]The scale is evidently an ascending one and Cartesian self-certainty is at the lowest level.

science is born from this mathematical axiom upon which everyone agrees, whereas from the physical axiom a definition is derived which the Epicureans reject in order to defend their concept of void? To present this confutation is not to censure Descartes's analysis. Rather, it does justice to it. In fact, I approve of it so far as there is truth in it. I disapprove of it in respect of the truth whose place it wants to usurp.

You claim, furthermore, that you have found no word among the ancient authors that Zeno and the Stoics had taught my metaphysical points.

I have to confess that, when the significance of the two terms *punctum* and *momentum*[34] gave me occasion to meditate on the metaphysical points, I turned my mind to Zeno. For I have always considered that, just as relying entirely on authority is like walking blindly, so trusting one's own judgment entirely is like traveling without a guide. Thus, authority must make us think of investigating what could have led our authors—even the most profound ones—to think in one way or another. Like everyone else, I held Zeno in great esteem, especially in metaphysics.[35] On the other hand, I considered his view about the points according to Aristotle's report of it to be improbable: that body consists of geometrical points is tantamount to the claim that a real thing is composed of abstract things. So I set myself seriously to pondering what reasoning could ever make such a view probable. From Greece, I turned once more to Pythagoras in Italy, who held the world to be constituted of numbers, which are in a certain way even more abstract than lines. Then I considered the very great reputation for knowledge which these two founders of philosophical schools had. I put their authority and the meaning of the terms *punctum* and *momentum* together with what I have now to add: that the Latins said *vis* for what we call "quantity," and they expressed what we call "essence" by the words *vis* and *potestas*.[36] And finally, I added the common assumption of philosophers, who posit essences in an immutable and indivisible thing. All of these reflections culminated with what I had already figured out by the same method on the question of principles; that is, that man operates in the

[34]See *DAIS* Four, II.

[35]For the importance of what was called Zenonianism before and during Vico's time, see P. Bayle, *Dictionnaire historique et critique*, 3d ed. (Rotterdam, 1720), vol. IV.

[36]*DAIS* Four, I.

world of abstractions in the way that God does in the world of real things.[37]

As a consequence of all this, I deduced that the one and only hypothesis by which we can ever descend from metaphysics to physics is the mathematical [assumptions].[38] The geometrical point is a likeness of the metaphysical point, that is, of substance; substance is a thing that truly is, and is indivisible. It makes possible and sustains unequal extensions with equal force. For through Galileo's demonstrations and others equally wondrous, inequalities as great as you please disappear into identity when they are brought back to their indivisible principles; that is, to the points. Thus, essences of all things are particular, discrete, eternal, divine powers, which the Romans called "immortal gods"; taking these all together [in pure act], we intend and worship one almighty God. Had I wanted to follow authority alone, I would have accepted the distorted reports of Zeno's views offered by Aristotle. Had I wanted to follow my own judgment alone, I would have neglected it along with all the others. You are now asking for authority for the view that I ascribe to Zeno. I am giving you the view itself not altered by Aristotle, not improbable as it stands in the record, but rescued from the false opinions of others and corroborated by reason. And if in the end you don't want to accept this statement as Zeno's, I am sorry, but I must give it as my own. But I will offer it to you anyway, alone and not supported by great authorities.

You want more explanation and proof for the assertion that the points are not to be understood: "parts into which the continuum or extension can be divided because it is extended, but [he was thinking] of the substance of body taken in its metaphysical conception according to which 'substance consists in the indivisible' and 'is not susceptible of more or less,' very much following the language of the school."[39]

[37]DAIS One, I.

[38]Vico uses hypothesis in a sense closely related to, and perhaps derived from, that which we find in some Platonic dialogues, especially Republic VII. He switches violently from singular to plural in order to move from the metaphysical one to the mathematical many. His unique hypothesis is an infinity of points and numbers.

[39]Obviously Vico spent many hours meditating on Zeno's paradoxes as reported by Aristotle and wondering how Zeno could maintain his theory and, at the same time, be a disciple of Parmenides. All that he admits here is that it does not matter if one does not agree with his interpretation of Zeno. Truth does not need the support of authority.

It never entered my thoughts that the substance of body can be divided; I only thought of it as the principle into which extended substances, though unequal, can be divided and to which, with an equal journey, they return. This I strove to make clear with a long discussion in my little book.[40]

But this term *point* appears to you to be obscure and undefined.

I define it through the whole argument as an indivisible entity that equally underlies entities that are really extended unequally; and the geometrical point supplies us with a likeness. You would like a definition in terms of proper ideas, not likenesses, but metaphysics does not allow us to view its objects in any other way. So why is it obscure? Nay, rather it is on this account as clear as light. "This is the way a metaphysical truth is luminous, bounded by no limit and distinguished by no form; for it is the infinite principle of all forms. Physical facts are opaque, that is to say, they are formed and finite, and in them we see the light of the metaphysical truth."[41] The appropriate means for detecting the metaphysical light in physical entities is mathematics alone. Mathematics abstracts from formed and finite things, from extended body, the infinite, the shapeless, and the point. Mathematics fictively defines the point as that which is indivisible and has no extension, and from the point so defined it proceeds to make mathematical truths.

Let us put it in your own words: "Left by itself in its obscurity, it envelops the whole treatise in a darkness that is almost palpable."[42] Let us add this, however: this is true for some Cartesians who regard metaphysical things in the manner of physicists, in terms of finite acts and forms. That is, they do not believe there is any light save where it is reflected. This is the fault (*vizio*) diametrically opposed to that of the Aristotelians, who look at physical entities in the manner of metaphysicians (i.e., in terms of potencies and powers). Therefore, they believe things that are opaque are actually light. We strive to look at them in the right perspective; physical entities in terms of acts, meta-

---

It grieves him to admit even this, since he wants to defend the value of reverence for authority against the Cartesians. But Zeno, being a Greek, is not essential to his ancient (Egyptian) wisdom theory. He never backs away from that claim. The wealth of evidence about Zeno is an embarrassment to him, since he has to throw some out and he can't expect everyone to agree. Actually, his theory about the Eleatic deserves some consideration; it is a pity that he got Zeno of Citium mixed up in the question.

[40]*DAIS* Four, II.
[41]*DAIS* Three.
[42]See above, p. 139.

physical entities in terms of powers: "Aristotle did not see it because he introduced metaphysics directly into physics; and hence, he discusses physical questions in a metaphysical manner, appealing to powers and faculties. Descartes did not see it because he directly raised physics to the level of metaphysics and thought about metaphysical matters in a physical manner by appealing to actions and forms."[43] We have put geometry in the middle, which is the one and only hypothesis through which one can descend from metaphysics into physics.

However, you reply that the refined good taste of the century has banished those terms like "virtues," "powers," and "acts" and therefore considers them just as unintelligible as "sympathies," "antipathies," and "occult qualities."

This is truly a great objection, and is great because it is not an objection. When adversaries retreat to the tribunal of their own judgment by saying that they have no idea what I am talking about, then they become judges instead of adversaries. Let them first offer a better definition of substance; then they can say that the terms *powers* and *acts* are incomprehensible. They define substance as "something that is" or "that exists." However, I showed in my Response how ludicrous and self-contradictory such a definition is, because it confuses what is with what exists: that is, being with being there; it confuses what stays under and sustains with what stays over and rests on it; it confuses substance with attribute; and finally, it confuses essence with existence. Here is the source of such improper modes of speech as *ego sum* and *deus existit;* that is, "I am" and "God is there," whereas *God properly is* and I am properly in God. The Schoolmen use words very properly when they say, "God is a substance; through His essence, created things are substances through participation." Let them teach me, then, another metaphysical criterion, whereby everyone can uniformly agree on geometrical truths [as the best], since the criteria of clarity and distinction cannot establish this. For though they use the "clear and distinct" criteria in physics, the knowledge of natural phenomena [things] has not in any way become more scientific. Let them explain to me with what clear and distinct idea they conceive that the line consists of points without parts; and when they cannot confirm this indivisible power in real things, [why] are they uniformly led to accept the indivisible point,

---

[43]*DAIS* Four, II.

and not rather to define it as "the least divisible in the infinite"? But the point defined as indivisible yields those marvelous demonstrations: that when incommensurable magnitudes and motions are reduced to their principles (that is, to the points), all inequalities are equalized. Finally, I would have liked to have been instructed about that little grain of sand mentioned in my Response which, through division, yields and sustains an infinite extension and magnitude. I want to know whether this magnitude actually is, and whether the grain of sand is actually infinite, or whether this magnitude is infinite in substance and in power through which it answers to every magnitude whatever.

[Before you can throw out "powers" and "acts" as unintelligible] you would first have to rule these matters out of court and to show me that they are mere shadows; then it would have been reasonable to appeal to the "refined good taste of this century." But leaving our time aside, meaning rather the Cartesians of this age, I return to you; please allow me to tell you that your reply does not do me justice at all. I use the words *power* and *potency* just as the mechanists—to whom they are very familiar—use them. There is this difference: that they attribute power or potency to particular bodies, whereas I say that it is a proper attribute only of the universe as a whole. In my Response, I defined power as "the energy of the whole by which it sends forth and sustains every particular."[44] And here I was following the refined good taste of the time, for it seems to me that attributing conatus to bodies is just like attributing talent, appetite, and wish to senseless bodies. So I very explicitly said, "Thanks to the better physicists, the language of 'natural sympathies and antipathies' and of 'nature's secret designs,' called 'hidden qualities,' has already been expelled from the schools of physics. The word *conatus* survives as a holdover from metaphysical language. So in order that the language of physics may be perfected, conatus should be taken out of the schools of physics and restored to the metaphysicians."[45]

The Cartesians themselves, according to their own principles, should be able to understand why there is only one conatus in everything; one that is, therefore, always equal to itself in all unequal motions. They accept, just as the Aristotelians do, the division of

[44]See above, p. 135.
[45]*DAIS* Four, III.

matter into parts that are divisible unto infinity; and in this we agree with them too, because Aristotle disagrees with Zeno about different things, but agrees with him about the same one. He divides extension, the attribute, unto infinity, whereas Zeno considers substance, the essence, indivisible. "[So it seems] to me that Aristotle is contending with Zeno about something else, but that he agrees with him about this matter. For Aristotle is talking about act and Zeno about power."[46] Hence, they will accept the same type of division in motion. For given a scale from which equal weights hang, if you add to one pan a grain, I ask whether it is the whole or a part of it that makes the scale lose its equilibrium? Certainly, no one will say the whole grain because I will divide it, and even with a part of it, the scale will behave in the same way. I ask again if the whole, half, or a part of a half is involved, and I will ask the same question about the smaller parts, and the still smaller ones, and so on ad infinitum. Hence, the principle of the motion that we call disequilibrium has to be present in the universe; but now I add, the whole is a plenum. Hence, what is motion in discrete bodies is not motion in the universe, because the universe has nothing with which it could change its spatial relation, which is what they [the Cartesians] take to be the essence of motion. Therefore, it is a force that acts within itself. This inward energizing is an inward conversion, and it cannot belong to the body because each part of the body would have to rebel against itself.[47] The energy would be as great as the extent to which the parts of the body [its parts] replicated themselves. Hence, I say that conatus does not belong to any body, but to the universe in which the body is.[48]

This metaphysics avoids the terrible rock of the "communication of motion," which is more indefinite, obscure, and imperceptible (i.e., not "clear" and "distinct") than "occult qualities," "sympathies,"

---

[46]*DAIS* Four, II.
[47]Proclus, *Institutio Theologica*, xv.
[48]Vico has shown that conatus is the metaphysical principle of motion and as such should be returned from the domain of physical nature to that of metaphysics. In the *New Science* Vico returns conatus from the domain of metaphysics to that of human nature. See *NS*, 340, 381, 502–4, 689, 1098. The theory of conatus as a psychological and physical principle of motion was common to the theories of Hobbes, Spinoza, and Leibniz. For Hobbes, see *De Corpore*, 15, 16. For Spinoza, see *Ethics*, III prop. 9. For Leibniz, see esp. *Studies in Physics and the Nature of Body* (1671) in G. W. Leibniz, *Philosophical Papers and Letters*, trans. and ed. Leroy E. Loemker (Dordrecht: Reidel, 1970), pp. 139–42.

and "antipathies." "Occult qualities" are honest names for ignorance of causes. Sympathies and antipathies are fictions of poets who attribute will and feeling to insensible things. But "communication of motion," which implies things that are mutually quite contradictory, cannot even become the subject matter of a fairy tale, because it is impossible and unbelievable. For "communication" implies that something leaves the body when it cannot continue to exist without the body, and that it passes from one body to another though it is substantially nothing but body through and through. In a human being, for example, the hand that strikes a blow is in motion. The ball that appears at rest is in motion—since we have shown that nothing is at rest in nature. In motion are the air that surrounds the ball, the hand, the space that is between the hand; and the ball is in motion, too; so is the air in the neighboring space, the air next to that, and so on for the whole universe. The universe responds to the motion of the hand, because it is a plenum; and thus, the motion of each part becomes the energy of the whole. The energy of the whole is indefinite in each of its parts. Hence, the blow is nothing but the occasion for the energy of the universe, which was so weak in the ball that it appeared to stand still; but it manifests itself more at the blow, and by manifesting itself more, it offers us the appearance of [a] more sensible motion.

It is so far from true that my metaphysics is out of tune with the good taste of our times that today in mathematics and, consequently, in mechanics, they talk in terms of infinites that are greatest, smallest, greater, smaller, greater and greater, smaller and smaller, and of one infinite being infinitely greater or smaller than others. Such expressions surely distort the human understanding, because the infinite is incapable of any comparison or multiplication, unless the understanding is aided by a metaphysics by which it is established that in any extended part or finite act, in every motion or accomplished act, there subsists a virtue or power of extension and of motion which is always equal to itself; namely, an infinite power in all the extended and actual motions.

Hence, conatus is a property of the matter of bodies, of metaphysical matter, I say, or substance; but conatus is not a property of physical matter, which is that body to which motion properly belongs. I explained the difference between physical matter and metaphysical matter in this passage: "This is the difference between physical and metaphysical matter. Physical matter evolves the best form for itself, no matter how peculiar that form may be, since the way it evolved was the only possible way. Because all peculiar forms are imperfect, however, so metaphysical matter contains the best form in the kind itself or in the idea."[49] In fact, physical matter is that which is best fit to receive some particular form; metaphysical matter, to receive all forms together, because physical matter is the body, which has a boundary, whereas metaphysical matter is the substance of body, which cannot be defined. Thus, for example, not every kind of rain, air, and soil is adequate for the growth of a plant. Under different skies, different kinds of plants are produced which, if transplanted, do not grow in other places. Metaphysical matter, on the other hand, is equally ready to receive all forms because substance underlies them all equally, since the energy involved in expressing and maintaining them is equal in all. Hence, we can infer that although things are dealt with in terms of "body" and "motion" in physics, they should be dealt with in metaphysics in terms of "substance" and "conatus." And just as motion is nothing but body, so conatus is nothing but substance. In the light of all these considerations, you will, I hope, see that I have answered all of your objections about conatus. Because all of them depend on your first minor premise, "But endeavor, according to what our author teaches, is motion itself," this certainly does appear in need of proof.

I want to bring this dispute to a close with this reflection: the refined good taste of our century is quite content today if it sees the phenomena of physics proved by those of mechanics; namely, with experiments that give results similar to those of nature. It ought, therefore, to be content likewise if it sees physical causes proved through geometrical causes. For geometry operates in the realm of abstractions, just as metaphysics operates in the realm of realities. And let it accept substance defined in the one way possible, with the demonstrated attribute of the equality of its sustaining powers and energies. Thus, we understand how *Iupiter omnibus aequus* (Jupiter is fair to all). For the only scientific cognitions we can ever have are those concerning relations of magnitudes and of numbers. So that the

[49]*DAIS* Two.

primary idea that the philosophers have of God, from which they then deduce all of His divine attributes, is that of the infinite, which is a relation of magnitude.

But you say, "And furthermore, since any such notion of substance is so well suited for spiritual and thinking substances, then one might infer that these substances are also the principle of extension— which, however, is manifestly absurd."[50]

This argument is like the difficulties you raise about the immortality of the soul, where it appears that you press against me seven distinct charges.[51] Had they not been put to me by you, I should judge that they went deeper and penetrated to a region that, although I must guard and maintain it with my life and moral conduct, can only be injured by [verbal] defense. But let us deal with them.

In my terms, "substance in general" is what lies underneath and sustains things; though in itself indivisible, it is divided in the entities it sustains. This substance equally underlies unequal divided entities. Let us divide it into its kinds. Extended substance is what equally sustains unequal extensions; thinking substance is what equally sustains unequal thoughts. Just as one kind of extension is divided from the other, and not divided in the substance of the body, so too, a part of thinking (that is to say, a thought) is divided from another thought and is not divided in the substance of the soul. If I am not mistaken, I believe I have avoided any absurdity.

Now, let us proceed to the problems of the immortality of the soul. The ancients believed that "spirit" (*animo*) was the vehicle of sensation, and that it was the air insinuated into the nervous system. They believed that the "soul" (*anima*) is the vehicle of life, and that it was the air insinuated into the blood. However, I have never believed that pagan theology can here be of service to Christian theology. In my Response, I defined metaphysical form this way: "the way in which each thing is formed must have repeated itself forever since the elements were first moved and in all regions of the universe alike."[52] Elsewhere, I said that true knowledge is knowledge of form, "to know is to hold fast the genus or form by which a thing is made." Likewise, I showed the difference between human and divine truth:

[50]See above, p. 139.
[51]Actually, the arguments are six, reduced to three.
[52]See above, p. 135.

"Divine truth is a solid image like a statue; human truth is a monogram or a surface image like a painting." And the basis of this distinction is explained there too: "Thus, science is knowledge of the genus or mode by which a thing is made; and by this very knowledge the mind makes the thing, because in knowing it puts together the elements of that thing. As we said, God makes a solid thing because He comprehends all the elements, man a plane image because he comprehends the outside elements only." Hence, the human mind comes to be, as it were, a mirror of the divine mind: and, therefore, it thinks the infinite and eternal. Thus, the human mind is not bounded by the body and, consequently, not by time either, which is measured by bodies; and so, finally, it is immortal. If I had not stated those definitions of form and science, and that difference between human and divine truth, then there might be some place for your seven difficulties.

But if you don't mind my saying so, at this point you are wrong to accuse me of injustice because I said in my Response that the motion of blood is due to the nerves; whereas, you had reported the opposite. For the explanation that you now offer in your Reply is lacking in your review ("but what? the same air; from there, that is, from the arteries and veins").[53] Besides, when you say, "from there into the nerve canals," it seems that you deny that the motion of the air is first insinuated in the nervous system. One could reasonably believe that, because there are blood vessels and nerve vessels in the heart, the air does not enter the nerve vessels, by which the muscles of its ventricles, the major vehicle of the blood, are moved, but first enters the blood vessels. And you sugarcoated the accusation of malice by saying, "It certainly seems that Signor Vico here commits the injustice that the author of the Art of Thinking claims Aristotle was accustomed to committing against certain philosophers to whom he wrongly attributed some big mistake, so as to go on to prove that he had valiantly confuted them."[54] But all the same, I would rather enjoy my own small but honest intelligence than be compared in my malice with a great philosopher.

Your last objection is the one you bring against my treatment of topics, criticism, and method. First, you say that I assume the exis-

[53]See above, p. 143.
[54]Ibid.

tence of false perceptions, "and perhaps this is a mistake, since a great many philosophers teach that perceptions are essentially true, just as all sensations are."[55] But I never intended to call apprehensions false in themselves. For the senses perform their function faithfully even when they deceive; and every idea, however false, involves some reality, since the false, because it is nothingness, cannot be perceived. But I called them false insofar as they urge and impel the mind toward the precipice of false judgments.

You state that topics is the art of discovery: "all of its rules have only pointed out those universally accepted commonplaces by which one can find and marshal reasons and arguments to prove whatever one wants. Nor have we ever, till now, come upon any topic that is able to give rules for the proper direction of the simple apprehension of our minds."[56] I do, of course, define topics in that way. But "argument" in this art is not "the disposition of a proof," as it is ordinarily understood (and called *argumentatio* by the Latins). Rather, it is that third term that one finds in order to unify the two arguments of a proposed problem, which the Schoolmen called the "middle term." Thus, topics is the art that gives us the "middle term." But I say much more than this. It is the art by which truth is apprehended, because it is the art of seeing under all the topical heads whatever there is in the matter at issue, which will enable us to distinguish well and have an adequate concept of it. For judgments turn out to be false when concepts are either greater or less than the objects they propose to signify. And we cannot be certain about this, unless we have looked at the object from every angle from which a question can properly be raised. This is the approach that Herbert adopts in his *Search for Truth*. His book is nothing but topics transferred into the field of experimental physics.

You say, ". . . criticism is known to us as an art that teaches how works created either by our wit or by that of others can be evaluated. But we don't know yet how it can be an art that directs those second operations of our intellect which are commonly called judgments."[57]

An art is nothing but a mass of precepts or rules organized for some purpose. I would like to know what else are we to call the com-

---

[55]See above, p. 141.
[56]Ibid.
[57]Ibid.

prehension of all those rules, which are prescribed in logic about the criterion of truth, but criticism, if we want to talk properly? Certainly not by any other name, the man who knows Greek will reply. So true is it that this art of judging is an important part of logic that the Stoics, who were versed in it above all others, pompously called it dialectic. Cicero argues as follows:

> Since every careful method of arguing [This is logic.—Vico] has two parts: one is invention the other judgment; Aristotle, in my opinion, was the master of both. The Stoics on the other hand exercise themselves in the second part. For they pursued carefully the method of judgment with that science they called dialectic. [It is not surprising that the Stoics called it thusly because the vulgar language would name it criticism.— Vico] In fact, they completely forsook the art of invention called topics, although practically it was more effective and surely in natural order prior to the other. [Because first comes perception and then judgment.— Vico][58]

But you have perhaps taken the term *criticism* in the signification that grammarians and men of letter give it, but philosophers do not. That may have led you to say what you do.

For the method, you argue:

> As far as method is concerned, we observe that it is called by the Cartesians "an art for the proper ordering and disposition of our thoughts in order that we may arrive at some science, or be able to teach it to others." Therefore, since different definitions, divisions, postulates, axioms, and demonstrations can lead us to the same science, method does not teach us how to define well, to divide well, to judge well, to discuss well, because these problems belong to the other parts of logic. It merely teaches how we ought to organize and arrange all these things properly so that the acquisition of the desired science may be easy and useful.[59]

Hence, you conclude that ordering is an operation different from the first three; and given that it is an art, it is not an "art that direct the faculty of reasoning and discussion, but an art that directs the faculty of ordering and disposing."

By method, you may understand either of two things: first, analysis

---

[58]Cicero, *Topica*, 2, 6.
[59]See above, p. 141.

as the Cartesians seem to employ it. Here the common aspects of the thing proposed are first separated out, in order to see what is peculiar to it, and get to know its properties, and so define it well. The ancient Greeks made much use of this kind of division; as, for instance, Plato does in the *Sophist*, which is nothing but a continuous analysis through which Socrates sets himself to divide the concept of "art" so that he can remove all the other species in order to define sophistry. Definition and division, however, are activities of the second operation of our mind, and they are regulated by criticism, in which sharp-witted men excel, because its practitioners have to make divisions, whereas the operation of simple work of mere perception, which is regulated by topics, is the comparison of a thing with all the others that are connected or related to it. This is the other kind of method called synthesis, which is, in fact, a rediscovery. This is the method that Aristotle follows, for he scarcely ever defines a thing until he has looked to see what there is in it, either inside or outside. Topics discovers things and piles them up. Criticism divides the pile and removes some of it. Therefore the topical wits are more fertile, but less true; the critical ones are truer, but are sterile. Second, you may understand by method, making truth arise from truth. This is the well-known rule of the Schoolmen, and the use of it is the main fruit of their logic. They always deny the consequent and never change the middle term. This is the art of governing discourse.

But you understand by method that which offers definitions, postulates, axioms, and proofs.

Let us use language properly so that we can exchange ideas that are distinct. What you, along with the Cartesians, call method generally, is specifically geometrical method. But method must vary and multiply according to the variety and multiplicity of the topics at issue. In a court of law, the rhetorical method reigns; in fables, the poetic method; in history, the historical method; in geometry, the geometrical method; in dialectic, the dialectical method, which is the art of governing an argument. But if the geometrical method is the fourth operation of our mind, then either oratory, fable, and history must be ruled by the geometrical method or there is no operation of the mind to which their governance ought to be reduced. Or again, if the geometrical method deserves to be considered as the fourth operation of the mind, then (because it has no justifiable authority over the others mentioned) oratory would be fifth, poetry sixth, history seventh; architecture and the ordering of battle can claim their place, too; and above them all, there will be the governance by which the state itself is governed, because it commands all the others. But all of them are orderings of thought.

But now you will say that we ourselves are only dealing with the method that guides us to the acquisition of some science and not other modes of cognition. But perceptions, judgments, and nonscientific discourses also reduce to the three operations of our mind. Hence, either method—even the way you want it—is an operation of our mind to which scientific and unscientific [modes of cognition] are reduced; or else perceptions, judgments, and nonscientific discourses are not operations of our mind.

The geometrical method applies only to measures and numbers. All other topics are quite incapable of it. Such a method cannot be applied if terms are not first defined, axioms established, and the questions to be asked agreed on. But in physics it is not names that we have to define, but things. There is no thesis here that is not subject to debate, and we cannot put any questions to stubborn nature. So such verbal formulas as "by definition iv," "by postulate ii," "by axiom iii," and conclusions with the pompous abbreviation "QED" appear to me empty affectations. Such talk has none of the force of truth upon the mind, but leaves it possessed of all the freedom of opinion that it had before being exposed to these bombastic methods. The true geometric method works silently. Where it makes a lot of noise, that is a sign that it is not working properly. Just as in battle assaults, the frightened man shouts but does not strike, whereas the resolute one is silent and deals mortal blows. Hence, when someone claims proudly on behalf of a method that has no logically compulsive force, "This is an axiom"; "This is demonstrated," he seems to me to be like a painter who writes beneath shapeless images that could never be made out on their own, "This is a man"; "This is a satyr"; "This is a lion"; "This is something else."

Let us remind ourselves: by the same geometrical method, Proclus demonstrates the principles of Aristotle's physics and Descartes proves his own principles, which, though not directly contradictory, are certainly quite different. Yet they are both great geometricians of whom I cannot say they did not know how to use the method. Hence, we must conclude that things that are not lines or numbers will not support the method at all, and if it is transferred to them, it does not work any better than topics, which is appropriate for enabling both parties to a disputed question to prove their case. Hence, to say that "this is a demonstration as far as I am concerned" is to confess that it is not a demonstration at all, because if it had been one, it would have been so for both parties. And if, perchance, an adversary fails to recognize it (as Cicero rejects the sorites, which is completely similar to Descartes's method),[60] then we can refute him with these words: "If you have reached this conclusion through any initial concession by me, the fault is mine. But I have not granted that bodies strive, or that there is a rectilinear motion in nature, or that there is rest in nature, or that motion is communicated."[61] These are the main threads upon which you are weaving your physical web. However, on this line we are beginning to attend to the parts. Let us just take account of the whole.

Philosophers have had no function in the world except to make the nations among whom they flourished affluent, skillful, able, acute, and reflective, so that men became open-minded, quick, magnanimous, imaginative, and prudent in their active life. Mathematics, on the other hand, has promoted in men a sense of order and developed a sense of beauty, fitness, and consistency. When the community of letters was first established, philosophers contented themselves with probabilities and left it to the mathematicians to treat truth. While this scheme, of which we have evidence, was maintained in the world, Greece laid all the foundations of the sciences and the arts. Those most happy centuries fostered plenty of incomparable republics, enterprises, works, and great words and deeds. The human community civilized by the Greeks enjoyed all the comforts and pleasures of life, far above the level of the barbarians. The school of the Stoics arose, and in its ambition, it aimed to disrupt the established order and to replace mathematics with their pompous maxim: "The wise man has no mere opinions."[62] And the republic of the learned had nothing better to benefit by. Instead, a quite opposite order [of philosophers], the skeptics, arose who were completely useless to society. They found occasion for scandal in the Stoics, since they saw that the latter

---

[60]Cicero, *Academica*, II, 16, 49.

[61]In fact, against Descartes's law of motion, Vico conceives of a type of motion which is here called conatus or *natura in fieri*.

[62]Antoine Arnauld and Pierre Nicole, *La logique ou l'art de penser*, ed. Pierre Clair et François Girbal (Paris: Presses Universitaires de France, 1965) Pt. 1, chap. 1, p. 52.

were asserting doubtful propositions as true, so they set themselves to doubt everything. The republic of the learned was destroyed by the barbarians, and only after long centuries was it restored on the same basis, so that the domain of philosophers was the probable, whereas truth was the domain of the mathematicians. Almost all the arts and the disciplines of the just, the expedient, and the humanly pleasant were reestablished in their lost ancient splendor, and even in many areas rose perhaps higher than before.

Of late, the orders of learning have been overturned again and probability has usurped the place of truth. The word *demonstration* has been cheapened by applying it to every sort of reasoning, not merely to what is probable, but often to what is specious. This is just what has happened to titles; for instance, *Signore*, which Tiberius refused because it was too arrogant,[63] is today accorded to the basest of men, so that today we have lost the sense of its dignity. In like manner, the term *demonstration*, extended to include probable reasoning and sometimes what is plainly false, has profaned the veneration for truth. Now we can see the advances, but we do not reckon the great loss that accrues to it, not to speak of the much greater loss that will shortly accrue because our own good sense has been made the regulator of the truth. For now, the ancient philosophers are not read, or very seldom read. This will be costly because the mind is like a soil that though it may be fertile with mother wit, becomes barren in a short time if it is not fertilized with varied reading. And if at times an ancient philosopher is read, he is read in translation, because today, on the authority of Descartes, the study of languages is considered useless. For Descartes used to say, "To know Latin is to know no more than Cicero's servant girl"; and since the same thing is understood to apply to Greek, the cultivation of these two languages has suffered considerable losses, of which Dupin, French though he is, bitterly complains.[64] These two nations, one the wisest and the other the greatest in the world, can communicate their spirit to us only through the reading of their authors.

We think up new methods, yes, but we don't discover any new things; our discoveries are stolen from experimentalists and dressed up with the new methods. Method is a good thing to discover when

63Svetonius, *Tiberius*, 17. Tacitus, *Annales*, II, 87.
64Ludovico Dupin (1657–1719).

you can arrange the elements with it. This is only completely successful in mathematics; in physics, it is impossible. But what matters most is the introduction of a skepticism dressed up as truth, because from every particular problem a system is created, which means that there is no common ground on which there is agreement and on which particular things depend. This is the vice that Aristotle notices in narrow-minded men who derive general rules of life from every particular event. We are certainly in debt to Descartes, who wanted his own feeling to be the rule of truth, because for everything to rest on authority was a servitude too vile [to endure]. We are in his debt because he wanted order in thinking, because previously men were thinking in a much too disorderly way with all those *obicies secundo;* but that only his judgment must be employed and only the geometrical method—that is too much.

Now would be the time to go back to a middle ground between these extremes [of authority and private judgment]: to follow one's own judgment, but with some respect for authority; to employ some order, but only one that the facts will support; otherwise men will realize, too late however, that Descartes has done what those who become tyrants have always been wont to do. They came to power by proclaiming the cause of freedom. But once they are assured of power, they become worse tyrants than the original oppressors. In fact, Descartes has caused the reading of other philosophers to be neglected by claiming that, through the force of the natural light, any man can know as much as others ever knew. Young simpletons readily fall under his spell because the long labor of much reading is tiresome, and it is a great pleasure to the mind to learn so much so quickly. But Descartes himself, although he can dissimulate the fact with the greatest art in what he says, was versatile in every sort of philosophy; he was celebrated the world over as a mathematician, solitary in a very lonely life, and what matters most of all, he had a mind the likes of which not every century can produce. A man of such parts can follow his own judgment if he will, but others cannot. Let them read as much as Descartes read in Plato, Aristotle, Epicurus, Augustine, Bacon, and Galileo. Let them meditate as hard as Descartes did in those long retreats of his. Then the world will have philosophers of equal worth. But though there is a Descartes and a natural light, there will always be lesser men than he. Descartes will reign among them and gather the fruit of that plan of wicked politics, to destroy completely those men through whom one has reached the peak of power. And here I protest that if I have said all these things a bit too clearly and at some length, it was because you asked me to explain myself and you found fault with my brevity. For I never wanted to displease very learned Cartesians, with whom I have close ties of friendship. But because they are learned beyond Descartes, they ought to take it this way: that for the good of all the world, I propose them as an example to the young who want to become good philosophers.

Finally, let me conclude with a response that can be applied to all of your objections. For all of the objections that you have leveled against me were made on behalf of the young, who delight in such studies. You took their cause and personality upon yourselves in the way of orators who speak of "their case," whereas in truth it is their client's case. The difficulties they could raise and which you of all people could completely satisfy for them you have brought against me, so that the book I wrote in the first place for a learned audience like yourselves may now be used even by them. The following passage induces me, and their politeness flatters me into believing this: "We shall terminate this discussion by offering our apologies to that kind gentleman, for not simply 'resting in the confidence' [of which he spoke] not merely in respect of just one doubt, but in respect of all our doubts. It was almost a matter of duty, and not just of 'our courtesy,' to have that confidence in him about them. But with it, we also beg him to remember that nowadays we have learned this maxim: 'It is very dangerous in philosophical questions to try to ground one's knowledge on the good name of anybody rather than on the force and evidence of the arguments.'"

Hence, I ought to want, and I do want, the world to believe that in this [new] response I have not contended with you, but obeyed you. I remain the most humble and obedient servant of your illustrious lordships.

VICO'S FINAL STATEMENT

So that no one can interpret anything I say in my small book on metaphysics with malicious mind, I offer here a resumé of some doctrines, scattered through it, from which one can gather what I profess.

Created substances are different from the substance of God, not only with respect to their existence, but also with respect to essence. In Chapter Four, Section 1, of my metaphysics I say that essences are the powers of things; in the first response I say that essence is proper to substance; in the second response I maintain that essence is proper to God and existence to the created entities. And this is very well put in the Schools: "God is substance through essence and created entities through participation." So that God being substance in one way and creatures in another, and the cause of being or essence being proper to substance, it is established that created substances even with regard to essence are different and distinguishable from the substance of God.

EDITORIAL DECLARATION
OF THE GIORNALE
DE' LETTERATI D'ITALIA

This work is written with great scholarship. The author defends himself against the criticisms, some of which he even graciously admits to be true. To this we answer nothing, out of respect for the author and in order not to extend controversies ad infinitum.

BIBLIOGRAPHY

The literature on Vico's philosophy is substantial. What follows is a list of the essential, general bibliographies in Italian and English and a number of essays helpful for clarifying the philosophical import of the *De Antiquissima Italorum Sapientia*.

Battistini, Andrea. *Nuovo contributo alla bibliografia vichiana* (1971–80). Naples: Guida Edition, 1983.

Croce, Benedetto. *Bibliografia vichiana* (1911). Revised and enlarged by Fausto Nicolini. 2 vols. Naples: Ricciardi, 1947–48.

Donzelli, Maria. *Contributo alla bibliografia vichiana* (1948–70). Naples: Guida Edition, 1973.

Gianturco, Elio. *A Selective Bibliography of Vico Scholarship* (1948–68). Florence: Grafica Toscana, 1968.

Tagliacozzo, Giorgio, Donald Verene, Vanessa Rumble. *A Bibliography of Vico in English* (1884–1984). Bowling Green, Ohio: Philosophy Documentation Center, Bowling Green State University, 1985. This bibliography is an invaluable tool for students of Vico who wish to further their knowledge on Vico's historiography in English. Some of the following essays are selected from this bibliography.

Badaloni, Nicola. "Ideality and Factuality in Vico's Thought." In *Giambattista Vico: An International Symposium*, ed. Giorgio Tagliacozzo and Hayden White, pp. 391–400. Baltimore: Johns Hopkins University Press, 1969.

Barnouw, Jeffrey. "Vico and the Continuity of Science: The Relation of His Epistemology to Bacon and Hobbes." *Isis* 71 (1980):609–20.

Belaval, Yvon. "Vico and Anti-Cartesianism." In *Giambattista Vico: An International Symposium*, ed. Giorgio Tagliacozzo and Hayden White, pp. 77–91. Baltimore: Johns Hopkins University Press, 1969.

Berlin, Isaiah. "A Note on Vico's Concept of Knowledge." In *Giambattista Vico: An International Symposium*, ed. Giorgio Tagliacozzo and Hayden

White, pp. 371–77. Baltimore: Johns Hopkins University Press, 1969. Also published in the *New York Review of Books*, 24 April 1969, pp. 23–26.

Bhattacharya, Nikhil. "Knowledge 'Per Caussas': Vico's Theory of Natural Science." In *Vico: Past and Present*, ed. Giorgio Tagliacozzo, 1:182–96. Atlantic Highlands, N.J.: Humanities Press, 1981.

Cassirer, Ernst. "Descartes, Leibniz, and Vico." In *Symbol, Myth, and Culture: Essays and Lectures*, ed. Donald Phillip Verene, pp. 95–107. New Haven: Yale University Press, 1979.

Child, Arthur. *Making and Knowing in Hobbes, Vico, and Dewey*. Berkeley: University of California Press, 1953.

Corsano, Antonio. "Vico and Mathematics." In *Giambattista Vico: An International Symposium*, ed. Giorgio Tagliacozzo and Hayden White, pp. 425–37. Baltimore: Johns Hopkins University Press, 1969.

Costa, Gustavo. "Vico's Influence on Eighteenth-Century European Culture: A Footnote to Professor Nisbet's Paper." *Social Research* 43 (1976):637–39. Reprinted in *Vico and Contemporary Thought*, ed. Giorgio Tagliacozzo, Michael Mooney, and Donald Phillip Verene, 1:247–49. Atlantic Highlands, N.J.: Humanities Press, 1979.

Crease, Robert. "Vico and the 'Cogito.'" In *Vico: Past and Present*, ed. Giorgio Tagliacozzo, 1:171–81. Atlantic Highlands, N.J.: Humanities Press, 1981.

De Santillana, Giorgio. "Vico and Descartes." *Osiris* 9 (1950):565–80. Reprinted in *Reflections on Men and Ideas*, pp. 206–18. Cambridge, Mass.: MIT Press, 1968.

Feibleman, James. "Toward the Recovery of Giambattista Vico." *Social Science* 14 (1939):31–40.

Fisch, Max Harold. "Vico and Pragmatism." In *Giambattista Vico: An International Symposium*, ed. Giorgio Tagliacozzo and Hayden White, pp. 401–24. Baltimore: Johns Hopkins University Press, 1969.

Garin, Eugenio. "Vico and the Heritage of Renaissance Thought." In *Vico: Past and Present*, ed. Giorgio Tagliacozzo, 1:99–116. Atlantic Highlands, N.J.: Humanities Press, 1981.

Gianturco, Elio. "Suarez and Vico: A Note on the Origin of the Vichian Formula." *Harvard Theological Review* 27 (1934):207–10.

Morrison, James C. "Vico's Principle of *Verum* Is *Factum* and the Problem of Historicism." *Journal of the History of Ideas* 39 (1978):579–95.

Pompa, Leon. *Vico: A Study of the "New Science."* Cambridge: Cambridge University Press, 1975.

Rockmore, Tom. "Vico, Marx, and Anti-Cartesian Theory of Knowledge." In *Vico and Marx: Affinities and Contrasts*, ed. Giorgio Tagliacozzo, pp. 178–91. Atlantic Highlands, N.J.: Humanities Press, 1983.

Stone, Harold. "Vico and Doria: The Beginnings of Their Friendship." In *New Vico Studies*, ed. Giorgio Tagliacozzo and Donald Phillip Verene, 2:83–92. New York: Institute of Vico Studies, 1984.

Verene, Donald Phillip. *Vico's Science of Imagination*. Ithaca: Cornell University Press, 1981.

Zagorin, Perez. "Vico's Theory of Knowledge: A Critique." *Philosophical Quarterly* 34 (1984):15–30.

INDEX OF LATIN TERMS

GENERAL INDEX

Library of Congress Cataloging-in-Publication Data

Vico, Giambattista, 1668–1744.
  On the most ancient wisdom of the Italians.

  Translation of: De antiquissima Italorum sapientia.
  Bibliography: p.
  Includes indexes.
  1. Metaphysics—Early works to 1800.   2. Philosophy, Ancient—Early works to
  1800,   I. Palmer, L. M. (Lucia M.)   II. Giornale de' letterati d'Italia.   III.Title.
B3581.D42E5   1988   195   87-47865
ISBN 0-8014-1280-3 (alk. paper)
ISBN 0-8014-9511-3 (pbk.: alk. paper)